CW00833209

A FAITH ENCOURAGED

A DEVOTIONAL GUIDE TO
Being Orthodox on Purpose

Barnabas Powell

ANCIENT FAITH MINISTRIES
CHESTERTON, INDIANA

A Faith Encouraged: A Devotional Guide to Being Orthodox on Purpose
Copyright ©2016 by Charles D. Powell

Published by:
   Ancient Faith Publishing
   A Division of Ancient Faith Ministries
   P.O. Box 748
   Chesterton, IN 46304

Unless otherwise noted, Scripture quotations are taken from the New King James Version, © 1979, 1980, 1982 by Thomas Nelson, Inc. Used by permission.

ISBN: 978-1-944967-15-4

30 29 28 27 26 25 24 23 22 21   14 13 12 11 10 9 8 7 6 5 4 3

Dedicated to Connie, Kandace, Kristin, Alexandra, and Katherine—
my wife and girls, who have put up with so much in having
a husband and father in the ministry—
and to my best friend, Photios. May his memory be eternal!

Through the prayers of our holy fathers, Lord Jesus Christ, our God,
have mercy on us and save us. Amen.

Preface

*"Your word I have hidden in my heart,
That I might not sin against You."* (Psalm 119:11)

A few years ago, I thought I'd take on the discipline of daily writing. Reading and thinking about each daily scripture lesson was a way not only to prepare for weekly Sunday homilies, but to ensure that I had the scripture deeply embedded in my heart.

St. John Chrysostom said, "From this it is that countless evils have arisen—from ignorance of the Scriptures; from this it is that the plague of heresies has broken out; from this it is that there are negligent lives; from this there are labors without advantage. For as men deprived of this daylight would not walk aright, so they that look not to the gleaming of the Holy Scriptures must be frequently and constantly sinning, in that they are walking in the worst darkness" (from the Introduction of the *Homilies of St. John Chrysostom on the Epistle of St. Paul to the Romans*).

What began as my daily discipline shared only with our parish family has blossomed, by God's grace, into a wonderful opportunity to encourage many to read the scriptures daily and contemplate their insight into living a purposeful Orthodox Christian life.

One of my favorite sayings has confused some: "Orthodox on Purpose." Consider how easy it is to take for granted the physical blessings and freedoms in our lives, How easy it is to relegate our beliefs to Sundays only, living Monday through Friday with little to no connection to our Orthodox Faith.

Consider the pain and heartache of those parents who have watched grown children squander what they have been given: a good education, quality healthcare, a safe and loving home. Now imagine the eternal tragedy that could result if we take this gift of our holy Faith for granted. Do we really want to stand by and watch the next generation abandon the Faith for the temporary comforts afforded by mere materialism? They are waiting for us to demonstrate for them this everyday Faith.

What follows are daily reflections on Scripture and its applications:

fifty-two workweek devotionals meant to aid the reader in breaking out of a "Sunday only" notion of faith. I pray that each entry will fan the flame of love for God in your heart. Join me as we encourage one another in love and good works (see Heb. 10:24), living as Orthodox on purpose!

Monday: Luke 2:20–21, 40–52

The Law-Abiding Lawgiver

Do as I say, not as I do

I REMEMBER HEARING THIS AS A CHILD and thinking, "That's not very convincing. How can someone who refuses to follow his own advice have any credibility at all? After all, shouldn't a person have some unchanging convictions?"

Let's look at our reading today. We are given two scenes to teach us about priorities, faithfulness, and purposeful living. The first is when the Lord of glory, come in the flesh and made weak by His own will for our sake, obeyed the law of circumcision. As a helpless baby, the Incarnate Lord was raised in a faithful home. He was circumcised in the flesh so that He would be able finally to provide the "circumcision made without hands" (Col. 2:11) to each of us, in order to write His Law on our hearts.

The second scene in this passage reveals His purposeful living in superseding even the traditions of family when, in His twelfth year, He remained in His Father's house after His family went home. The Theotokos and St. Joseph were frantic with worry about His whereabouts, yet He challenged their convictions by confronting them with the reality of His purpose.

Then He returned with them to their home and "was subject," or obedient, to them (Luke 2:51). What a perfect picture of both the Lawgiver and His faithfulness, and the radical new vision of that law which will exceed all previous wisdom given. God in the flesh invites us to embrace both faithfulness and the new reality that God has come among us to dwell in us.

TODAY: What are your unchanging convictions? Your convictions will shape you and make you into the person you were created to be—or not.

Tuesday: John 3:1–15
You Must Be Born Again

"You must be born again" (John 3:7)

WHERE I'M FROM, that scripture is as well worn as John 3:16. But what does it mean?

Let's look at it in the full context of today's reading. First, notice that Jesus confronts Nikodemos with a command: "Do not marvel" (John 3:7). The reason for this is that the message Jesus gives to Nikodemos is not new. All through the Old Testament, God, the Prophets, and teachers were telling the people of God that one day He would write the Law on their hearts rather than on tablets of stone (see Jer. 31:33). The coming of the Messiah was promised to bring a fundamental change in the relationship between God and humanity. What amazed Jesus was that Nikodemos, a teacher of the Law, seemed to miss this.

Next, the Lord reveals that this being born again He is talking about is a spiritual rebirth. The Lord confronts Nikodemos with the reality of this amazing truth: God intends to bridge the gap that existed between the physical and the spiritual, thus healing this broken connection.

Finally, the Lord reveals that this healing of physical and spiritual would be akin to what Moses did in the desert with the serpent on the pole (see Numbers 21). When Moses lifted up the bronze serpent for all Israel to see, all who looked upon it would live. In the same way, the Son of Man will be "lifted up" (John 3:14) so that whoever believes in Him will live forever.

TODAY: Are you being born again? Is the divide between the spiritual and the physical being healed in your heart? All the tools you need to unite the two are given to you in the Lord's Church. All is ready for you.

Wednesday: Luke 3:15–18
Knowing Yourself

Know yourself

WITH THESE TWO WORDS, ancient philosophers and Christian theologians have wrestled with a fundamental reality: Most people spend a lot of time either hiding from themselves or narcissistically focused on themselves. Knowing who we really are is fundamental to being who we really are.

St. Basil, in his homily on attentiveness, concludes, "Be attentive to yourself, that you may be attentive to God." Unfortunately, our lives are packed with busyness, schedules, noise, meetings, and media—the list goes on. This distracted living causes most of the problems in our lives, our relationships, and our work.

The lack of authentic self-knowledge nags at our souls. We sense we should be able to know our own hearts—consciously or unconsciously, we attempt to resolve this fundamental confusion with all kinds of lesser remedies, without success.

Today's reading shows us that St. John the Baptist knew himself. He understood who he was, what he was called to accomplish, and where his life was supposed to go. His self-knowledge made him free to be who he was, and this freedom gave him peace.

But this freedom wasn't embraced without cost. In other words, our self-knowledge isn't going to be cheap or easy to come by.

TODAY: Let's embrace with sober joy the invitation from God to know ourselves as we truly are, free from false arrogance or false humility. If we fall into either of these delusions, we will never discover our true selves. All the tools we need to do this hard work are in abundant supply in a normal Orthodox life.

Thursday: Matthew 3:13–17

It Is Fitting

Oh, the shame!

I FAILED MY FIRST DRIVING TEST as a sixteen-year-old. One of society's last remaining rites of passage into the adult world and I failed.

Today, our Gospel reading describes a pivotal moment in the Lord's ministry on earth. To this day, that moment ripples through time, profoundly affecting the created world. Notice St. John's initial reluctance to baptize the Lord—the saint knew he was setting the stage for the Lord's ministry on earth, but now, standing before Him, is that very Lord asking to be baptized. Why?

The Lord answers, "to fulfill all righteousness" (Matt. 3:15).

Our sinless Lord certainly doesn't need to be baptized for repentance. Yet He also knows that creation needs Him to enter into it. Creation's original purpose—to display God's glory and love—needs to be restored. Water longs to be set free to do what its Creator intended it to do: to truly cleanse, truly refresh, and truly quench humanity's thirst.

No wonder the Church uses water so frequently in worship. No wonder the first sacramental encounter people have with the Orthodox faith is in the waters of baptism. No wonder we shower our faithful with holy water at the Feast of Theophany.

TODAY: When we see the Lord return water to its truest purpose, and we hear the Father speak from heaven, saying, "This is my beloved Son" (v. 17), let us embrace the victorious truth sung by all of us: "As many as have been baptized into Christ have put on Christ! Alleluia!" Let's share this water with our world.

Friday: John 1:29–34

The Spirit Descends and Remains

Turns out the communists were right

ONE OF THE FAMOUS AXIOMS OF MARXISM is that religion is the opiate of the people. Father John Romanides said that Orthodox Christianity is the cure for the sickness of religion.

In today's reading, St. John recognizes Christ as "the Lamb of God who takes away the sin of the world" (John 1:29). Notice he doesn't say "who takes away the sin of the world if you ask Him to." No. The Lord takes away the sin of the world. If you decide—out of your freedom—to keep your sin to yourself, that is your choice. But if you learn to embrace the One who takes sin away, you will be healed from these wounds of your soul.

St. John recognizes the Lord existed before him. Even though St. John was six months older than Christ in the flesh, he saw past this temporary date to the eternal existence of the Son of God before all time. The Lord has come to change us radically from living a merely religious life to living in a relationship that so acclimates us to His Presence that it becomes light to us rather than the fire experienced by those unprepared to live with Him.

TODAY: Is your faith preparing you to dwell in Christ's presence? Are you still gripped by the sickness of religion that reduces our faith to nothing more than a mere nostalgic repetition of old words? Or is this Orthodox faith doing what it has done for its people for centuries—transforming your life into a fit temple of the Holy Spirit? Anything less falls short of normal Orthodoxy.

Monday: John 3:22–33

He Must Increase

I was wrong

Don't you just hate it when you're wrong? Is there anything so frustrating or even embarrassing? Yet there is nothing more character building than being able to say these three honest words.

Admitting we're wrong is hard. This partly explains why our first mother and father in the Garden of Eden resorted to passing the blame in the beginning: "It was that woman You gave me." "The snake deceived me." Our fear drives so much of our brokenness and spiritual illness.

St. John the Baptist was famous. Of course he didn't really care about that, but he knew that when his task was completed, the Messiah would surpass him in every way. Look at the way he handles the question from those who were concerned that Jesus and His disciples were also baptizing folks. Instead of sulking and hiring a public relations firm to increase his market share, St. John says, "He must increase, but I *must* decrease" (John 3:30).

St. John knows himself, and he knows the Lord sufficiently well, and so he is at peace with the reality of the situation.

So it is with us, dear ones. As He increases in our lives, we decrease, but something wonderful happens when we are mature enough to embrace this: in losing ourselves, we find ourselves.

Today: Is Christ increasing in your life? It's an amazing truth of our Orthodox Faith that we gain our lives by losing them, and in dying we live. As the old monastic saying goes, "If you die before you die, then when you die you won't die."

Tuesday: Mark 1:9–15

The Spirit Drives Him into the Desert

Who is in the driver's seat?

THE CENTERS FOR DISEASE CONTROL reported some forty percent of babies born in 2012 were born to unwed women. This is a very real consequence resulting from our society's moral choices, and living in this world can be discouraging for Orthodox Christians.

We are always tempted to believe either that we live in the "best of times" or "the worst of times," as Charles Dickens put it in *The Tale of Two Cities*. We have this amazing ability to vacillate between elation and despondency, depending on our view of the world's current circumstances.

However, our Gospel reading for today gives us a peek into how best to see the world as it is without being overwhelmed by it. Indeed, this is not only possible, but it is the perspective on life that should always be held by the person of faith.

St. Mark conveys two important truths. The first is that awareness of our mission drives us, and the second is that God isn't shy when it comes to redeeming people He loves. This is no lackadaisical rescue attempt—it is serious. There will be another point in the Lord's ministry, right before His Crucifixion, when we will see this same conflict played out when He tells His Father, "Not My will, but Yours, be done" (Luke 22:42).

TODAY: What drives you? Is it the Spirit, or are you driving yourself? To be sure, the faithful Christian life is not easy. Yet the disciplines of daily prayer, regular worship, and putting God first will pay off; these will enable us to face every test well and accomplish our calling. Remember: it's neither the best of times nor the worst of times, but God's time. The Lord extends His rescue mission to everyone around us through our obedience.

Wednesday: John 10:39–42
He Escaped from Their Hands

Claustrophobia

I'M AFRAID OF CLOSED-IN PLACES. The first time I experienced this uneasy feeling was when I was a boy and we were playing hide and seek. I found the perfect hiding place in a small cupboard in the kitchen, and it must have been a good spot because no one could find me. Quickly, though, I had to abandon the great hiding place by jumping out of the cupboard in a cold sweat.

We humans have a desire to be free—we want to make sure we know where all the exits are in our lives. But this desire for freedom often gets warped due to our spiritual blindness and broken human will. We yearn to be free; but without repentance and healing, without gaining freedom through slavery to Christ, we will be chained to our passions.

Our Lord's Coming and His Baptism inaugurated a new reality for the world. This new reality was a threat to the *old* ways, the *old* religions, and the *old* power structures. Since the Incarnation, those structures have attempted to stifle and thwart Christ's power. But there is no turning back—God has become flesh.

He really is the One who baptizes with the Holy Spirit and makes us a habitation fit for God. The appearance of Christ meant the end of humanity's kindergarten age. It's freedom for grownups.

TODAY: Has your definition of freedom been transformed by the Faith? Does your relationship with God, your slavery to Him, set you free from the old desires to be your own boss and to have it your way? It's time to refresh your baptismal vows and constantly allow the freedom of Christ to make you who you are meant to be.

Thursday: Luke 20:1–8
By What Authority

"Wise as serpents and harmless as doves" (Matthew 10:16)

BEING SHREWD ISN'T NECESSARILY THE SAME as being wise. An evil man can be shrewd and calculating, but only a good man can be truly wise.

That doesn't mean that shrewdness is always evil—far from it. In Matthew 10:16, when our Lord told His disciples to be "wise as serpents and harmless as doves," He meant that shrewdness must always be governed by love. The moment it becomes self-serving, it will always become evil. Always.

In our Gospel reading today, we see the Lord Jesus deal with some fairly messy relationships. The religious leaders of Jesus' day felt He was a threat to their status quo. Of course, they were right about that. He was, and frankly still is, a threat to ossified leadership, when the powers that be forget the dynamics of love and reduce themselves to mere shrewdness.

As usual, the Lord is speaking truth, and because He speaks with such authority, the people listen to Him and follow His words. The religious leaders ask the Lord, "By what authority are you doing these things?" (Luke 20:2). Jesus, knowing their hearts, turns this around on them and questions their own understanding of the very nature of authority.

The Lord was so completely at peace with Himself, He felt no need to satisfy the self-serving challenges of the religious leaders. He responded to their shrewdness with peace, thus revealing who they really were and who He was.

TODAY: Inner spiritual discipline will create a clear sense of purpose and humility in your own heart. This internal work, diligently pursued, will serve you when you face the messy times in any relationship. Sounds like heaven, doesn't it? That's because it is.

Friday: Luke 12:32–40
Your Treasure Reveals Where Your Heart Is

Do you know where your heart is?

I've always been both inspired and disturbed by the Lord's words, "For where your treasure is, there your heart will be also" (Luke 12:34). This passage is an immediate reality check, regardless of my what circumstances are when I confront it.

That makes sense—the whole purpose of the phrase is to arrest us and cause us to take a quick inventory of our hearts. The answer to the question "Where is your heart?"—no matter how challenging, how discomforting, or how disappointing—is always "wherever your treasure is."

Look at our reading today. "Be like men" (v. 36). Yes, be like people who are anticipating, ready, focused—people who are truly awake. That's the kind of person I want to be, but how do we become like this?

First, we must have a healthy disregard for our possessions. Next, we must value eternal realities more than temporary ones. And finally, we must love our Lord above all others with eager anticipation and wakefulness for His presence. People who adopt these attitudes have their hearts in a place where true treasures exist.

In an age when the clothes make the man, when we confuse pleasure with love and peace with the absence of conflict, we desperately need men and women who will make a different choice and walk a different path: people whose hearts are in the right place.

Today: Where is your heart? Look at what you treasure most in your life. You can find that place by looking at where you spend most of your time, your talent, and, yes, your money. Find that spot, and you'll find your heart. Perhaps it's time to have a spiritual heart transplant.

Monday: Luke 12:32–40

Deceived

I was snookered!

H
E WAS SLICK, AND I WAS YOUNG. He was offering me a great deal. It was only a twelve-month contract. I was naive, and I signed. Turns out, it was too expensive; it was a lousy deal, and it was an annual contract that automatically renewed. It took me months to finally extricate myself from this "great deal."

Deception always hides the downside and exaggerates the benefits.

Look at today's lesson.

"It is your Father's good pleasure to give you the kingdom" (Luke 12:32). With this, the Lord Jesus reveals an amazing gift and a terrifying opportunity at the same time. The gift is plain—the Father wishes, and has *always* intended, to give you everything He has. His humility, generosity, and love are boundless. The lie told to Adam and Eve is the same, tired lie we fall prey to today: "God is not good." "God is holding back." These lies have one intention: to steal from you and wage war against God by destroying the objects of His love.

Here is the terrible part. God's love for you is so profound and complete that He will not violate your free participation or lack of participation in His life. You certainly can foolishly continue to be deceived if you wish, but you can never escape the reality of His continual love. In your freedom, if you reject His love, you will be forever tormented by your own foolishness. That's why they call it hell.

TODAY: Are you free from the subtle lies of the deceiver? All the spiritual medicine meant to heal every aspect of your life is here and available to you for the taking. All you have to do is exercise your will to embrace your Father's good pleasure, and all He has is yours. Your life is full of wonder and joy.

Tuesday: John 21:14–25

Do You Love Me?

Tradition

I'LL NEVER FORGET SEEING the classic musical *Fiddler on the Roof* for the first time. The songs "If I Were a Rich Man" and "Tradition" were particularly compelling. But one of the most moving moments was when the lead character, Tevye, who is confronted with the new way his daughters are finding husbands (choosing for themselves, the horror!), asks his wife of so many years, "Do you love me?" What follows is a deeply tender moment for a couple who has had few such times in their hard life.

Look at our reading. Three times the Lord confronts Peter with the same question, though He knows even better than Peter what is in his heart. But the Lord wants Peter to know just as deeply. Interestingly, Peter denied knowing the Lord three times, and now he is being asked three times if he loves the Lord. The depths of repentance are reached by the undoing of the three denials.

Each of us confronts our desire to be loved, but God isn't like us in that He doesn't *need* to be loved or valued. He is complete within Himself. He is Father, Son, and Holy Spirit, and He is affirmed and loved in an eternal communion of loving Persons. So, His call for us to love Him above all things and persons isn't for His benefit. It is exclusively and completely for our own benefit. God's call to love Him first is the most selfless invitation ever given to humanity, because the benefits of this loving relationship are all on one side—ours.

TODAY: Do you love Him? Your answer may come quickly, but the truth is always seen in your choices. If you want to do more than pay lip service to this all-important question, then I invite you to struggle with me in being Orthodox on purpose.

Wednesday: Matthew 22:2–14
Friend, How Did You Get In?

In my pajamas

I T'S NOT JUST MY RECURRING DREAM (nightmare, really), but it has been found to be a common dream for much of humanity. You know the one: I'm standing in a fancy party with either my pajamas on, or my pants off. I am not dressed for the occasion. Why are we humans so susceptible to this fear?

I'm convinced that part of the answer is based on the fact that we are made in God's image, and He is three Persons in communion. We were made to be in community.

In today's Gospel reading, our Lord told a parable to show us how foolish it is to ignore His invitation to the transformation that prepares us for His eternal feast. The enemy of our souls uses our fear of embarrassment to keep us enslaved to feelings of unworthiness. This fear has to be seen as the weapon it is if we are to learn to escape its power.

Next, the parable finds the master of the feast inviting everybody he can to the feast, when he discovers someone who is still not dressed for the occasion. Notice, the master of the feast calls him *friend*—God does not reject us or hate us. Even those who foolishly choose to remain apart from Him, He calls His friends. But He also refuses to pretend that the state of our hearts doesn't matter. If we are ever to overcome our fear of embarrassment, we have to make peace in our hearts with these two realities: First, God loves us and desires us to be with Him. Second, we must struggle daily to put on the beautiful "wedding garment" (Matt. 22:11) of our baptism in Christ.

TODAY: Are you afraid of being embarrassed? The remedy is to face the wonderful provisions God has given you in His Church to dress you properly for His eternal wedding feast. All you need to adorn your spiritual life with the beautiful wedding garment of love is found in the *ascesis*—or spiritual effort—of a purposeful Orthodox life.

Thursday: Luke 6:17–23
We Got Trouble

Trouble, I say . . . with a capital "T"!

I LOVE THE OLD MUSICAL *The Music Man.* One of my favorite scenes is when Harold Hill begins to spring his trap on the good folks of River City by pointing out they have an "evil" pool hall in their little town. The old con man stirs up folks' natural fears about what might happen in order to swindle them.

We live in a world where troubles come to us. Sometimes those troubles are fast and furious. Sometimes they just trickle into our lives with the soul-depressing regularity that threatens to sap our strength and resolve. Troubles come to all of us.

Look at our reading. The Lord rebukes some of His disciples for being upset about the woman who anointed His feet with costly ointment. They made the excuse that this was a waste, and the ointment should have been sold and the money given to the poor. They are missing the point.

The Lord reveals that actually people going through troubles are blessed. People who are poor, hungry, weeping, hated—all these folks are blessed and should rejoice. Perspective is what matters.

You see, our trials offer us an invitation to grasp that there will be a time when these difficulties will be nothing but a distant, irrelevant memory. The troubles in our lives are flimsy and temporary—we must refuse to allow suffering to make us less than we are. But this attitude hinges on our willingness to see our circumstances from an eternal perspective, thus avoiding the temptation to see things through the lens of anxiety.

TODAY: Are you facing troubles and difficult times? Go to the church, stand in the middle of that eternal place, and watch as your troubles find their proper perspective.

Friday: Luke 12:8–12
Unforgivable

Why is blasphemy unforgivable?

THE POPULARITY OF THE BBC SERIES *Downton Abbey* is a phenomenon. It's a bit surprising to me, since Americans seem to be enamored with the notion of egalitarianism, at least in our rhetoric. In Downton's world, however, violating one's lot in life can have lifetime repercussions. "He is marrying outside of his class? Unforgivable!"

In today's Gospel reading, our Lord Jesus talks about something unforgivable. The Lord declares that blasphemy against the Holy Spirit "will not be forgiven" (Luke 12:10).

Let's broaden our thinking here, for it is the Holy Spirit, we are promised, who will do the work of drawing people to Christ. The Holy Spirit is the voice that whispers in our souls that we are on the wrong path. The Holy Spirit will lead the Lord's Church into all truth. The ministry of the Holy Spirit is absolutely essential to our very lives as Orthodox Christians. St. Seraphim declares: "Acquire the Holy Spirit, and a thousand around you will find their salvation."

When a person denigrates the Holy Spirit, his or her heart is closed by choice to His leading. It isn't that the action makes God so angry that He won't forgive you—this person simply refuses the forgiveness offered and places himself in an unforgivable place. The isolation is always self-imposed. As C.S. Lewis put it, hell is locked from the inside.

TODAY: Are you open to the active and intimate presence of God in your life? In our Faith, the disciplines, prayers, and liturgies are all meant to increase your sensitivity and cooperation with the constant work of the Holy Spirit so that He can transform you into someone who is like Christ.

Monday: Matthew 10:32–33, 37–38; 19:27–30

Getting Back What You Gave Away

*If you love something, set it free. If it comes back to you,
it's yours forever. If it doesn't, it wasn't meant to be.*

ALTHOUGH I FIND THIS SENTIMENT to be a bit saccharine, there is an element here worth exploring—we really do need to hold our lives, loves, and possessions loosely. Gripping anything or anyone too tightly risks strangulation.

Of course, the emotion behind our grasping attitude is fear. This fear can enslave us to behavior that ends up destroying the very thing we insist we need. In my own life, my fear of loss has driven me to irrational and costly actions.

Fortunately, there's hope. As usual, the Lord Jesus gives us the direction we need for our own freedom and spiritual health.

If my life is going to be free from fear and grasping, I am going to have to cultivate a consistent mindset: God comes first. All other relationships will be out of balance until this relationship is set right. If I am ever going to stop smothering others, I am going to have to make God my first priority. Only then will I be healthy enough not to hold on too tightly.

By putting my relationship with God first, I am even set free from the expectations of others. They may even reject me, but I am not rejected. They may try to manipulate me, but I am free. First things are first in my heart, and all is in the proper place.

TODAY: Have you suffered loss of things or relationships? Welcome to the human race. Have you learned to prioritize your relationship with God first? There is no guarantee that others around you will always understand you. All that is blessed and beneficial will be returned to us—if not here, then certainly in eternity.

Tuesday: Mark 2:23–28; 3:1–5
Hey, That's Against the Rules!

Following rules or gaining wisdom?

THIS QUESTION IS CRITICAL to understanding our Orthodox Faith. When I was a police officer, I had to memorize the rules of the road so that I could enforce those rules. It was tempting to reduce that central purpose to mere enforcement of rules as an end in itself.

In today's Gospel reading, our Lord Jesus and His disciples show us the folly of reducing our relationship to God to mere rule-following. The event took place on the Sabbath, when work ceases according to the rules, but as the hungry disciples walked through a field, they picked some grain and ate it. The outwardly pious religious leaders were furious when the Lord refused to play by the normal religious rules. The Lord lovingly attempted to correct their confusion by making two very important distinctions.

The first was that the rules were made for man, not man for the rules. It is instructive in our Orthodox Tradition that we don't refer to the directions or the disciplines of the faith as *rules*, but as a body of teaching and as *wisdom*. The Lord clarifies that the Sabbath disciplines were meant to change our thinking and actions about our priorities, not to become straightjackets that prevent us from doing good. A wise man embraces wisdom and doesn't try to reduce his relationship with God or others to simply following the rules.

The second distinction is equal to the first. The Lord doesn't say wisdom is useless but reminds these Jewish leaders that even King David allowed a higher wisdom to prevail—when he and his men were hungry, they ate the sacred bread in the temple. The Lord also healed a man with a withered hand in the synagogue, demonstrating that the law of love transcends all rules.

TODAY: The Holy Spirit has manifested His love and wisdom in the lives of many saints and leaders. They teach us to value our relationships with God and one another above all rules.

Wednesday: Mark 12:13–17
Render to Caesar

Breathtaking!

NASA HAS RELEASED THE LARGEST PICTURE ever taken. It's made up of 411 snapshots from the Hubble telescope of our nearest neighbor, the Andromeda galaxy. The picture is 1.5 billion pixels and takes 4.3 gigabytes of disk space to load. The scene it depicts is even more incredible. It shows over one hundred million stars that are forty thousand light-years away from us.

The power of information invites us to understanding, and understanding fosters both patience and insight into the wonders of God's good creation. But the mere gathering of information is never enough—there must be a foundational reality that allows for the information to become useful. That foundational insight is revealed to us today in our Gospel reading.

The religious leaders of Jesus' day are trying to trip Him up so they can discredit Him. They start with flattery and then lay their philosophical trap. They ask if it is lawful to pay taxes to the occupying (and very unpopular) Roman government. He sees through their trickery and turns their question upside down. First, He asks them to bring Him a coin. "Whose face is on this coin?" He asks. They respond, "Caesar's." So He tells them, "Render to Caesar the things that are Caesar's, and to God the things that are God's" (Mark 12:17).

Do you have a clear picture as to what your priorities should be in your daily life—career, family, bills, and society—and how they relate to your devotion to God? Daily seeking to know God and His will must always be at the top of your priority list; it is foundational to everything else. It's not enough to have information *about* Him. We need to take time to *know* Him.

TODAY: Evaluate where your faith falls on your priority list. Practice frequent prayer, scripture reading, regular worship, and confession so that you will be ready for whatever life has to offer. This is the way of wisdom.

Thursday: John 10:9–16
I Am the Door

Of thresholds and doors

Aᴍᴇʀɪᴄᴀɴ ʙᴜꜱɪɴᴇꜱꜱᴍᴀɴ Jᴏꜱᴇᴘʜ B. Wɪʀᴛʜʟɪɴ said, "Those who stand at the threshold of life always waiting for the right time to change are like the man who stands at the bank of a river waiting for the water to pass so he can cross on dry land." Thresholds are places of movement and change.

In the popular children's movie *Frozen*, Anna stands at her sister Elsa's door asking, "Do you want to build a snowman?" (I have two small daughters, and this is the only music I am allowed to listen to.) This closed door invites curiosity and pain as Anna wonders why her sister is now so distant.

That's the nature of thresholds and doors. They mark transition, opportunity, danger, mystery, and growth. They mark for us movement from one purpose to another.

Jesus describes Himself as "the door" (John 10:9), marking the barrier between safety and the thief. The "good shepherd" lays down His life for the sheep (v. 11). The Lord is the threshold between the slavery of mere religion and the abundant life of the Holy Trinity. He also declares Himself fully invested in the care of the sheep, unlike the "hirelings" that are only there for the moment in their self-serving ways (v. 12).

The sheep know His voice, and this intimacy is akin to the intimacy between the Father and the Son. Jesus is offering humanity nothing less than a passage from isolation and fear to the intimate embrace of a Shepherd who will never leave nor forsake them. He is inviting us to step through this threshold into a new and living way, where we are embraced and empowered to become who we really are. And He is clear: We can only get there through Him.

Tᴏᴅᴀʏ: The exclusive message of Christ is troublesome for those who want to say there are many paths to God. But all the other paths are populated with hirelings who will abandon the sheep at the first sign of trouble. Not Christ. He is the Door.

Friday: Luke 6:17–23
What Do You Desire?

We loved the show

MY FRIENDS AND I *really* wanted tickets to this concert. Standing outside for hours, missing other events, and even getting a little hungry did not stop us from doing what we had to do to get those tickets.

It is amazing what we are willing to pay to get what we want. Westerners spend about seventeen billion dollars a year on pet food, and Americans spend eight billion dollars a year on cosmetics. We are consumed by what we desire.

Desire can be a gift of God to pull us toward Him. Yet if our desires are never molded and transformed, they become our masters, demanding more and more of our attention, time, and resources. We were made for something (i.e., Someone) more.

In today's reading, a huge crowd is seeking to touch Jesus. Why? Because power was coming from Him, healing all who touched Him, and these folks longed to be restored to wholeness. Their powerful desire, debilitating illnesses, and the presence of Jesus all came together, enabling them to open their eyes. Do you see something important here?

Only when our needs and desires are enlightened through Christ's presence and we move toward Him are we able to desire correctly and receive healing of our physical and spiritual illnesses. When our desires are turned inward or we seek fulfillment outside of Christ, we'll remain sick, unfulfilled, and enslaved.

Today: Are your desires taking you toward Christ or away from Him? Blessed Augustine was right when he declared, "Our hearts are restless until they can find rest in You." Why not embrace the wise discipline of a purposeful Orthodox life and enter into the Church—a school of wisdom—where your desires can be shaped by daily prayer, regular liturgies, and the consistent practice that trains all your hopes and desires to find their fulfillment in the only true Lover of our souls?

Monday: Mark 9:33–41

He's Not on Our Team!

I was always picked last

AS A BOY, I DREADED RECESS. I was a bookworm, not an athlete, so the team captains usually picked me last. (Of course, when report card time came, all the jocks wished they were more like me.)

We are wired to choose sides—we make tidy distinctions between people based on race, ideology, nationality, economics, or education. One of my first Sundays after entering the Orthodox Church, I was at coffee hour when a precious older lady came up to me and asked if I was Greek. When she found out I wasn't, her rejoinder was, "Don't you have your own church to go to?" She had never imagined that someone outside her culture would want to be Orthodox. We became fast friends.

It's easy to sort people into groups. Sometimes, this is accompanied by the darker spiritual sickness of prejudice. We are made in the image of God, who is a Trinity of love; we are made for communion, and prejudice violates God's intention for us all.

The disciples of the Lord came across a man casting out demons in the name of the Lord, and they stopped him because he wasn't part of their group. The Lord corrected them—He saw the beginnings of communion there. They shouldn't snuff that out.

Of course, our Lord isn't suggesting that this beginning of communion is the end of the journey—a kindergartener isn't the same as a wise teacher. Development still needs to occur, and we should never confuse the launching pad for the finish line.

TODAY: What fears of the other lurk in your heart that keep you from seeing all people as created in God's image? While we need discernment, we can never allow our fears, our prejudices, or our ignorance to keep us from communion with others.

Tuesday: Matthew 5:14–19
Why Are You Hiding?

Get out of the way!

MY DAUGHTER YELLED AT THE TRAFFIC as we drove to her dance class. She was frustrated at the number of cars in front of us—perhaps she was imitating someone else who does the same thing? This frustration is familiar to all of us. It flows from the common misconception that what I'm doing right now is more important than what anyone else is doing.

Here's something I *should* be frustrated about: When are my choices, attitudes, and actions keeping me from moving forward? And how do I learn how to get out of my own way so that my life can become what it was meant to become?

Look at our Gospel reading. Jesus doesn't say *make* your light shine, but *let* it shine (see Matt. 5:16). All I have to do is get out of the way so that the light can be seen. If I put the light where it belongs, on a lampstand, it can do what it was made to do. So, how do I let my light shine?

First, I must show myself to be a purposeful student of the wisdom preserved in the Tradition of the Church. This is a revelation of my own devotion, obedience, and depth of love for God. This can only happen if I humbly embrace the truth that God knows more about living well than I do.

Once I embrace this truth, the light will automatically shine from my life rather than being blocked by my selfish choices and behaviors. No wonder the Church has us read this passage on the day when we remember the three holy hierarchs of the Church: St. John Chrysostom, St. Basil the Great, and St. Gregory the Theologian. Each of these holy heroes let their light shine so brightly that we remember them to this day.

Today: Are you in your own way? Is your path dark because you are hiding your light? Perhaps it's time to humbly embrace the truth that God knows how to live better than we do. When we embrace His wisdom, the light already burning in our hearts will radiate to those around us.

Wednesday: Luke 2:22–40
A Light for Revelation

I saw the light, I saw the light. No more in darkness,
no more in night. . . . Praise the Lord, I saw the light!

THIS OLD GOSPEL SONG, which I remember fondly from my youth, expresses an ancient fear of people everywhere: we don't like the dark.

Darkness means we can't use one of our primary senses to avoid obstacles, reach our destination, and observe our surroundings. Darkness impedes our ability to move, communicate, and get our bearings. Darkness hides the world from us and us from the world.

Jesus said that people love darkness because their deeds are evil (John 3:19). No wonder there are some enterprises that prefer dark alleys. No wonder we seek out the concealment of darkness when we sin. A sure clue that we are on a wrong path is when we are hiding our actions.

Yet we were meant to live and thrive in the light. Darkness makes our lives small and sequestered. Light opens up our lives to the wide possibilities of all of God's good creation.

St. Simeon declared that he could finally "depart in peace" since he had seen the Lord's salvation, a "light to *bring* revelation" (Luke 2:29–32). This powerful phrase suggests the eternal kindness of God toward His creation. The light of revelation has dawned for those who lacked the blessings received by God's chosen people. Through Jesus, this light extends God's wisdom and love to every person in the world, Jew and Gentile alike. God's intentions and His love toward all are revealed. No wonder we pray the prayer of St. Simeon at every evening vespers—we bask in God's light while darkness falls.

TODAY: During every church season, the Faith delivered once for all to the saints invites us to step into the light of revelation and avoid tripping in the darkness. Let's bask in the light given to us freely by our God, who loves us more than we ourselves will ever love.

Thursday: Luke 2:25–38
This Child

One life can make a difference

I AM GRATEFUL TO GOD that a faithful pro-life witness has continued in this generation. This consistent message has caused the number of abortions to drop as that fateful Supreme Court decision drifts further into the past. Only eternity will reveal those we've lost to what Pope John Paul II called this "culture of death." Think of all the lives lost due to humanity's love affair with violence and power. What might those children have grown up to accomplish, discover, or cure? Only God knows, but society will pay the price of our shortsighted selfishness.

Isn't it often the spark in one heart or mind that lights the flame of freedom, growth, and discovery? Names of heroes march through my head, those whose lives made a difference in the lives of so many others. One life can change the world—one life *has*.

St. Simeon took Jesus in his arms and, in a powerful moment of revelation, saw what his aged eyes had longed to see his whole life—the Messiah. The Holy Spirit had told Simeon he wouldn't die until this moment, and here it is, the One promised from the very beginning. A serpent would brush His heel, but He would crush the serpent's head.

Then Simeon speaks: The Child will set in motion the rise and fall of many. He will be a "sign" spoken against. The thoughts of many hearts will be revealed (vv. 34–35). He is going to reveal the truth about all of us. Those whose hearts love darkness will hate Him, and those whose hearts long to love and be free will rejoice because of Him.

TODAY: What secret places are you hiding? Not from God, who knows all, but from yourself? Today our Lord Jesus invites you to come into the light. He will not condemn you. The medicine for your soul is here in His Church; bring all into His presence.

Friday: Mark 13:24–31
The Great and Powerful Oz

Off to see the wizard

I REMEMBER SEEING *The Wizard of Oz* for the first time on a color TV when I was a boy. I was mesmerized by the bright color, the head floating in the air, the smoke, and the fire.

We are losing ourselves to make-believe these days. A recent study suggested that an emphasis on fantasy is slowing down the maturity process, especially in boys.

Let's not fall into the trap of thinking the words in today's Gospel reading aren't real. The sun will be darkened, and the moon won't shine. Stars will fall from heaven, and even the powers of heaven will be shaken. It sounds terrifying. Why does the Lord use such language? If His hearers are going to really pay attention, He needs to establish the level of importance of His message. He does this by emphasizing that the coming of the Son of Man is going to disrupt the regular flow of nature and transform creation itself.

It won't catch by surprise those who are paying attention, however. Just as you can look at the change of seasons and know what season is coming next, those who are paying attention in the spiritual life will not be caught by surprise at the Second Coming.

The Lord's words invite self-examination. Do we know the Lord so well and spend so much time with Him that His presence, His plans, and His purpose are no surprise? So much wisdom is offered to us in the life of the Church in her seasons, hymns, and liturgies; all are meant to acquaint us with our Lord. Let's not be surprised at His coming, either at the end of our mortal lives, or at His return—let's live every day in expectation of both.

Today: Are you prepared no matter when the Lord will come for you? Are you embracing the sober, life-giving wisdom of Faith and participating in the life of the Church so the Lord's plans don't catch you by surprise? All you have to do is stop, wake up, and start embracing a purposeful Orthodox life.

Monday: Mark 13:31–37; 14:1–2
Caught Napping

Mr. Powell, can you tell me why the lymphatic system
is so important to our bodies?

WE WERE COMING UP on summer break. It was almost 3 p.m. in biology class, with the most boring teacher in the school. The teacher's voice was hypnotically droning on and on. Soon, I fell asleep—and got caught. Lymphatic system? What in the world was that? I was half dreaming of riding my minibike when I got home. Needless to say, I was assigned extra homework on the lymphatic system.

A sleeping spirit is an even more dangerous thing than a sleeping body. If we remain unaware of our spiritual needs and hunger, we are in danger of sleeping right through life.

The centrality of the spiritual discipline of *watchfulness* cannot be overemphasized. St. Paisios said, "When our soul lives carelessly without watching over its thoughts, it will consequently fill up with dirty and sly thoughts."

How can we cultivate attentiveness? We start by believing what our Lord declares to us today: that heaven and earth may pass away, but His words will never pass away. Our watchfulness begins with applying God's Word in our everyday lives. Remember, we must read the Scriptures with the Mind of Christ, preserved in His Church. This wakes up and feeds our spiritual selves, strengthening us through the exercise of faithful study. Then when the "master of the house" arrives (Mark 13:35), we will be ready to receive Him.

TODAY: Are you awake? Are you as focused on your spiritual life as you are on your career, family, income, and hobbies? Do you have a set time every day when you stop and feed your soul? Our stomachs growl when we are hungry. Can you hear the growling of your soul hungering to be fed with nourishing spiritual food? Determine that this Great Lent you will discipline your physical stomach so that your spiritual self can be fed with food that forever satisfies.

Tuesday: John 10:9–16
One Flock

Reason-endowed sheep

THIS IS WHAT ST. JOHN CHRYSOSTOM called the faithful. I was raised in the rural American South (where there are plentiful pigs, cows, and chickens, but few sheep), so I looked up what it is about sheep that caused this phrase to make sense for St. John's audience.

Turns out sheep are herd animals, most comfortable with other sheep. A sheep usually doesn't get in trouble unless it gets separated from the flock. Also, sheep are docile, mellow animals—who ever heard of attack sheep? Finally, sheep need a shepherd to keep them from wandering off and getting into trouble. Leaderless sheep rarely survive.

I used to wonder, "Why sheep? They seem so wimpy." I preferred the image of a lion, or an athlete. But, truth be told, it is the *humility* of sheep that allows them to live so peacefully in community. Unfortunately, we so often insist on our own way and our own importance—how very different from the attitude of our Lord Jesus, who as God, humbled Himself and became obedient to death on a cross. His very humility and selflessness became the source of our healing and new life.

God refuses to force you to humble yourself. Oh, He may allow your choices to place you in humbling situations, but even that can be resisted. Acquiring humility is up to us. If we are willing to be simple, reason-endowed sheep, we tap into heavenly resources that fuel spiritual growth. Conversely, our stubborn insistence on our rights will only guarantee that we will be enslaved by our anger, depression, and pride. How's that working out for us?

TODAY: Are you willing to be a simple sheep in Christ's flock? Look at the many invitations of faith offered in this life of community. Frequent liturgies, times of prayer, seasons of fasting and feasting, the lives of the saints, Holy Scripture, and Holy Tradition guide and instruct us. The Shepherd is leading His flock to paradise; He will give you the strength to be a humble reason-endowed sheep in the flock of Christ.

Wednesday: Mark 11:1–11
The Lord Has Need of It

We are uncomfortable with paradox

PARADOX IS A CONCEPT that in our post-Enlightenment secular age, we have a hard time grasping. A paradox always feels like a problem to be dissected, a riddle to be solved. Jesus taught us that to save our lives, we have to lose them. To be leaders, we must be slaves. Paradox.

I'm convinced the Creator built paradox into His creation precisely because of our need to overcome our prideful tendencies and our slavish rule-keeping.

We know this Lenten Gospel reading well. The world is turning against the Lord, and yet in this moment, He sends His disciples to town to prepare for His last supper and entry into Jerusalem. What chutzpah! The Lord needs a colt, and they are going to have to ask complete strangers for the animal: "And if anyone says to you, 'Why are you doing this?' say, 'The Lord has need of it,' and immediately he will send it here" (Mark 11:3).

What trust and confidence these disciples displayed as they obeyed Christ! What faith and trust the owners of the colt demonstrated! No fear or doubt, only trust and peace: "The Lord has need of it." Though the circumstances are dire, they rest in the knowledge that God is aware of what they need. And Jesus knew what His disciples were capable of—remember, His work in our lives is always aimed at increasing our faith and trust. Finally, though our trust and confidence in God may seem paradoxical at times, it isn't ever baseless. God's goodness and His love are evident everywhere, if we but have the eyes to see.

TODAY: Though the world is gripped by doubt, can you trust God in the paradox that is faith? Are you able to live confidently in God's purpose for your life, knowing His work is to make you who you are meant to be?

Thursday: John 15:17–27; 16:1–2

Killing for God

Imagine a mindset so meticulous, yet so ill

WHEN A MEMBER OF A TERRORIST GROUP was asked why the group was killing children as well as adults, the terrorist said it was to keep the children from taking revenge when they grew up. How could anyone condone such atrocities and do these acts in God's name? Such honor killings diabolically pervert the meaning of the word "honor."

We can delude ourselves into believing just about anything. God, in His mercy, has given us a spiritual path to protect us from our tendency toward delusion.

The idea of killing for God isn't new. Our Lord Jesus told His disciples there would come a day when His followers would be killed, and the murderers would be convinced they were doing God's will. Genocidal impulses aren't exclusive to any particular religion or ideology, either. In fact, the secular ideologies promoted by Nazis, communists, and secular humanists have all been used to justify exterminating millions of lives.

In the face of increasing hostility toward the Faith, the Lord—through His Holy Church— answers with the power of love. Not just any kind of love is on display, but love that originates in the community and flows to the world. This love will sustain us in a world where some view Christians as enemies that need to be exterminated.

The Church is the antidote for human delusion. Those ready to live in truth will love the Faith, while those who prefer the stupor of delusion will hate it. Our martyrs are a testament to both the world's hatred and the power of love. No wonder the enemy works against the Church; no wonder the Lord prayed for her oneness—it heals the world.

TODAY: Is the practice of your faith building love in your heart, or are others the object of your suspicion, even hatred? The faithful practice of the Orthodox life builds love and mercy in our hearts and draws us all closer together. Let's put aside all hatred and fear and live in the healing grace of Christ.

Friday: Matthew 10:1, 5–8

Free to Be Generous

I support our troops!

THIS IS A SURE WAY for any politician to gain applause, and rightly so—the brave men and women of our military perform a vital function in the preservation of our liberty. Freedom isn't free, and it never has been—it's always hard-won and must be diligently guarded.

What is true of our constitutional government is also true in our spiritual lives. Freedom from the slavery of our own undisciplined desires requires us to war against the inevitable entropy that causes us to drift toward selfishness.

One of the greatest enemies of our spiritual—and even political—freedom is greed. Without purposefully developing a spirit of generosity, we quickly become enslaved to selfishness.

In today's Gospel reading, our Lord instructed His disciples to start spreading spiritual freedom around to everyone. Notice, first He gave them the power to do this work, then told them to get to it. He concluded His instructions with a phrase that reveals the heart of the matter: "Freely you have received, freely give" (Matt. 10:8). The disciples were meant to do all their good while being thankful for what they'd been given. None of us can keep what we've been given if we don't give it away.

If I am ever going to be truly, spiritually free, I am going to have to abandon the hoarder's mentality. The price I must pay for my freedom is a willingness to be generous. Without this central principle in my life, I will remain a slave.

TODAY: Are you generous? I have witnessed even people with little financial means be generous with their time, their love, their patience, and their understanding. Generosity must certainly affect your pocketbook, but that is only because it has first transformed your heart and mind. Freely you have received, freely give.

Monday: Mark 15:1–15; 1 John 4:20–21; 5:1–21

Give Us Barabbas

Isn't it funny how much we already know?

WHEN TAKING COURSES on pastoral counseling and psychology, I was surprised to learn that most people already know what they should do in their lives. Yet, even though we know what we should do, we can't find the strength to do it. But the good news of the Faith "once for all delivered to the saints" (Jude 1:3) is that it empowers us to follow through so that we can break out of the cycle of not doing what we should be doing.

In our Gospel reading today, the priests brought Jesus to Pilate to have Him crucified. They made all kinds of accusations against Him to convince Pilate that He was a dangerous criminal. Pilate offered the crowd a choice between Jesus and Barabbas, and the crowd chose Barabbas at the urging of the religious leaders. Throughout the ordeal, Jesus never hurled insults or lashed out. Our Lord was free even in the midst of this terrible trial of justice and honor. He trusted His Father and prepared the night before through prayer—this moment didn't catch Him by surprise.

In our epistle reading, St. John contrasts the clear difference between those who claim to love God and those who actually do. Lovers of God follow through on their baptismal vows. They are stable and consistent in their practice of the faith. They keep themselves from idols, refusing to allow anyone or anything a higher place in their lives than God Himself. They stay alert to temptations, and are prepared for adversity. And yes, they love their enemies in imitation of our Lord.

TODAY: Do you have a consistent prayer life and devotional practice that is the foundation for stability? Get this main thing right, and you will find yourself automatically making the right choice in every situation.

Tuesday: Mark 15:20, 22, 25, 33–41
Judgment Comes to All

Don't judge me!

NOWADAYS, WE SEE EVERY DESIRE as a right and every pleasure as a perfectly normal expectation.

But this is a fantasy. No one can escape from the consequences of his or her actions. Even those who foolishly go through life believing they've gotten away with something will find out all too soon they haven't. We are all rushing toward the moment when the fruit of our faithfulness will be revealed, as we pray in the liturgy: "For a Christian end to my life, peaceful; free of shame and suffering; and for a good answer before the awesome judgment seat of Christ, let us pray to the Lord." Lord, have mercy!

At the end of our emotional retreat, excuses, justifications, denial, and lies to cover up, each of us will finally be judged. Yet not even our sins can make God angry—He loves us with an everlasting love.

We will be judged not according to our sins, but whether or not we responded in humility and repentance. May we be wise enough to understand the gift Christ offers us in giving us His life for our own. Remember the words of St. Isaac the Syrian: "This life is given to you for repentance; do not waste it on vain pursuits."

Prior to the Sunday of the Last Judgment, the Church reminds us of our Lord's Crucifixion. Here we see the extent God is willing to go for those whom He loves. This is what our lives will be measured against on that Last Day: "Greater love has no one than this, than to lay down one's life for his friends" (John 15:13).

This is the love that will judge us all. How will we measure up?

TODAY: We will stand at the Final Judgment without excuse. The fasts, services, prayers, homilies, traditions, and saintly examples are there to prepare us. Let's make these gifts our own.

Wednesday: Luke 19:29–40; 22:7–39
Seeing Further Gives Strength

They say hindsight is twenty-twenty

MOST PEOPLE WOULD JUMP into a time machine and go back to certain moments in their lives, if it would allow them to handle a situation differently. Yet, even with the benefit of life experience, we still catch ourselves considering choices similar to regretful ones we've made in the past. It's unnerving how easily we repeat what we know we shouldn't.

What drives this behavior? What we need is a way to stay ahead of our thoughtless choices. There is certainly no shortage of self-help resources that offer us a way out, but what if we could find an owner's manual for our lives and avoid all its pitfalls?

We can. Great Lent is the season of the Church year where our Faith invites us to make lasting changes in our lives. Beginning with Forgiveness Sunday, we are invited to adopt a laser-like focus on our spiritual health.

In today's Gospel reading, the Lord gives us the gift of the Holy Eucharist. Here He instituted the meal that Christian communities would celebrate from that point on. He gave us the key to Great Lent when He says, "Do this in remembrance of Me" (Luke 22:19). Union with Christ is our journey's goal. When we remember *why* the journey is worth the labor, we are set free from the impulsive choices that trap us into the slavery of shortsighted lives.

TODAY: Are you awake to the reality that your spiritual life is worth your best efforts? Are you clear on the goal of your life? Are you willing to humbly embrace and be embraced by the wisdom of spiritual labors to see clearly and remember well? You can be, especially with the abundant wealth of spiritual wisdom in the Church.

Thursday: Luke 20:46–47; 21:1–4
The Widow's Test

I will never forget his face

Someone I knew was absolutely amazed that his pastor had preached a sermon on tithing—giving ten percent of one's income to God and the Church. "Hey, Barnabas, my pastor said I should tithe. Is the ten percent gross or net?"

I replied, "Oh, dear brother, the news is even worse than that. In the face of how much Jesus has given for us, the Lord expects one hundred percent."

What is it about giving money to the Church that upsets folks? It probably has little to do with actual giving and even less to do with money itself. Giving in the Church causes controversy and attracts the attention of parishioners because this subject touches us in a fundamental way: right in the place where we fear for our survival. Our money, resources, time, and possessions make us feel secure.

Money and possessions should not only be recognized as tools to help us in life; they also serve as a spiritual diagnostic of our real loves and our deeply held values.

In today's reading, the rich gave from their abundance, but the widow came and gave everything she had, throwing herself at God's mercy for her survival. If you ask me, she chose the safest path. Temporary riches have a way of disappearing—just ask anyone who invests in the stock market.

The Lord looks at what you keep back for yourself as the barometer of your trust in Him. If we truly believe that we expect the resurrection of the dead and the life of the age to come, then that belief will be reflected in the way we invest our time, talents, and treasures.

Today: What do you keep back for yourself? God places greater value on devoted love and sacrificial giving than on the amount. The spiritual discipline of giving isn't about the amount but about the trust and confidence in one's heart.

Friday: Joel 2:12–26

Blow the Trumpet in Zion

*When was the last time you called the police
when you heard a car alarm go off? Right.*

TODAY, MOST ALARMS are ignored. When I was a police officer, our department instituted a fine for businesses calling us in for false alarms. It happened so often at some businesses that we simply began to ignore them.

What is true of alarms is also true in our lives. We have warnings about behaviors that leads to health problems, relationships that aren't good for us, even spiritual dangers. Yet we sleep through them.

During Lent, let's listen to the warnings and pay attention to the Church's wisdom. One of her main tools is the wake-up call of fasting and repentance. Fasting is tied closely to repentance—the repentant heart *wants* to choose God and be less self-focused. Deprive the stomach of every little thing it wants, and one begins to learn to discipline selfish desires.

It's easy to miss the warnings in my life, because my soul and mind are flooded with my own clamoring voice. The selfish part of me wants to drown out that still, small voice that warns me when I am going down a wrong path. I am only going to wake up to these loving warnings if I fight my spiritual deafness by listening to the wisdom of Christ calling me to another path.

TODAY: Are you planning how you and your family will keep a spiritually profitable Great Lent? Have you gone through the refrigerator and pantry to make sure Clean Monday is really clean? Don't let the beautiful alarm of Great Lent be ignored because you've heard it so often before. Step up to a purposeful Orthodox life by hearing the Church's call to approach these forty days with love and confidence.

Monday: Luke 23:1–31, 33, 44–56

Perverting the Nation

I had to choose whether to become a politician or a preacher

TWO GREAT INTERESTS kept me engaged from my earliest years: politics and religion. Though my traditional Southern upbringing discouraged mixing the two, I was passionately interested in both. In lively discussions about politics and religion, it never ceases to amaze me that many of us think we are qualified to speak about both of these topics.

This misconception can lead to a judgmental attitude—we think we know who's right and who's wrong, who's going to heaven and who's going to hell. Yet we are promised that where sin abounds, grace abounds much more (Rom. 5:20). No matter how corrupt society gets, that corruption will never overcome God's grace.

In today's reading, our Lord stands accused. His detractors feared that if they let Jesus' message be accepted, their whole way of life would be destroyed. To them, Jesus was a dangerous man. They were convinced the Lord's message was "perverting the nation" (Luke 23:2). In a way, this was true—the Lord's message disrupted the status quo. A person of forgiveness can change the whole world. Jesus' enemies, gripped by selfishness and ego, saw this transforming message as a threat.

My dearest, if you can forgive, you are both a light to those who long for change and a threat to those who reject it. All the debaters will be powerless to trap you.

TODAY: Do you need to forgive or be forgiven? The Church has the tools. Every service is meant to strengthen you to enter into this freedom. Will you have the courage to accept forgiveness and extend forgiveness? To the extent you do, you will be free.

Tuesday: Zechariah 8:19–23

The Fast Is a Feast

We love to throw a party!

WHEN I WAS A BOY, I was always excited about my birthday party. My mom was a hardworking lady, but she always found a way to mark this landmark. Nowadays, let's just say my birthdays aren't nearly as celebratory as when I was younger.

A wise man once told me that the reason for this is that we have forgotten how to truly celebrate. We work so hard at creating a party to make us happy that we've lost the ability to see a party as the end result of our joyous lives. The reason for this lack of joy is that we've forgotten how to fast.

God created His world with the rhythm of the changing seasons, sunrise and sunset, heartbeats, music, and so on. In a similar fashion, our times of celebration in the Church are always preceded by periods of fasting and preparation.

It isn't an accident that the center of the Orthodox Christian year is Pascha, the Resurrection of Jesus Christ. Everything that happens in the Orthodox Church calendar brings us to Pascha or helps us understand what Pascha has accomplished. Accordingly, the days leading up to Pascha are marked by focused preparation for the celebration. Without the Great Fast you will not truly have a great Feast.

Zechariah declares that God wants His people to see their fasting as "joy and gladness" (Zech. 8:19). The only way to be able to do that is to see beyond the difficult discipline to the end result, which is joy. To truly embrace the joy and gladness of the Resurrection of Christ, I need to keep the fast well.

TODAY: Are you really convinced that Pascha ensures the destruction of death and new life for the whole cosmos? If not, no wonder you don't fast during Lent. The work is too hard for too small a motivation. Have you missed the point of the fast by confusing it with mere rule-keeping?

Wednesday: Isaiah 1:11–17

Ugly, Empty Liturgy?

Vain repetition, that's all it is!

A FRIEND OF MINE was absolutely horrified by the shift from my Pentecostal roots to the Greek Orthodox Church. He saw all the ritual, recited prayers, and prescribed movements as nothing more than the empty traditions of men.

Indeed, there is nothing more ugly, unfaithful, and insulting than timeless liturgy and beautiful ritual practiced by empty hearts out of mere nostalgic habit. We are duty-bound to make sure we embrace the wisdom and meaning of the Divine Liturgy.

This is what we read from the Prophet Isaiah today—he leaves little doubt about keeping rituals without the love and faith that are meant to fill them.

It would be equally mistaken to assume the answer to this problem is to abandon the liturgy. There is no virtue in abandoning wisdom for folly. The more courageous path lies in recapturing the wisdom and intimacy and power and love that were always meant to undergird these beautiful and timeless acts of worship.

And that's why the Prophet goes on to extend an offer from God Himself to Israel and, by extension, to us today: "'Come now, and let us reason together,' says the Lord, 'although your sins are like crimson, I shall make them white like snow, and although they are as scarlet, I shall make them white like wool. If you are willing and obedient, you shall eat the good things of the land. But if you are unwilling and disobedient, you shall be devoured by the sword,' for the mouth of the Lord has spoken" (Is. 1:18–20 OSB).

TODAY: Let's fill up our religious practices with true focus and intimate love for God during the seasons of fasting. Let's keep practicing these ancient ways, but add to them fresh devotion that flows from a life of true repentance, humility, and love for God. The added services and extra prayers can fill us spiritually.

Thursday: Luke 7:17–30
A Reed Shaken by the Wind?

Their examples are remembered to this day

THE HISTORY OF THE CHURCH is filled with saints who, frankly, seem crazy. There is even a category of saints known as holy fools. Two such saints lived on opposite sides of a bridge in two towns. The towns were rivals, so in their love for the people, the saints decided to act out their folly. One saint crossed the bridge to the other side; the other saint berated him and physically forced him back to his own side. Then they switched roles and repeated the actions, and so the saints demonstrated the foolishness of the enmity and bitterness of the townspeople.

Other Orthodox saints sat on the tops of pillars so they could pray. In so doing, they were exposed to the elements and depended on the kindness of others to send up food. They preached from these pillars, encouraging people to a more faithful Christian life.

St. John the Baptist's extreme example was meant to shake the world. Our Lord Jesus said that "among those born of women there is not a greater prophet than John the Baptist." That's high praise, coming from the Son of God. Yet, our Lord continues, "he who is least in the kingdom of God is greater than he" (Luke 7:28). John's ministry was meant to conclude one era of prophets and make way for the new era of God in the flesh. A new community will arise, melding people of different languages and cultures into a new family that will be one as the Holy Trinity is one. Some would call this crazy. It calls for extreme examples of devotion and piety—those willing to be fools for Christ.

TODAY: The example of St. John the Baptist confronts us with our need for spiritual labor, the spiritual ascesis that makes the radical faithfulness of true communion with God and others possible. Can you move toward a daily commitment to being faithful to this message of new life, eternal peace, and joy?

Friday: Genesis 1:24—2:3
Very Good

Don't forget your "why"

IF YOU FORGET WHY you do what you do, you will soon stop doing what you do. Worse, you will also not be able to perpetuate what you do in the lives of those who follow you—your children, grandchildren, and extended family and friends.

So when we say we want our children to stay connected to the Faith—when we say we want our parishes to grow—but then fail to reinforce the why of our Faith, our chances of subsequent generations keeping the Faith are dim. As the old preacher once said, "God's got children, but He ain't got no grandchildren."

This is why our Faith prescribes the reading of Genesis during the first week of Great Lent. In Genesis, our Lord preserves for us the fundamental why of all faith, all devotion, all worship, and even all theology. If you want a powerful reason to be faithful, start at the beginning.

God made us in His image. This gift from our Creator is not revocable. This fundamental *why* of our existence means we were made first and foremost to be in relationship with our Creator and with everyone who is in relationship with our Creator—we were made for communion. Whatever hampers or destroys communion is an enemy of our fundamental *why*. By repentance and disciplined practice of the wisdom of the faith, we can restore fellowship with God and each other.

This path toward this cosmic goal sweeps aside all the lesser goals of this fallen world. When we make communion our number-one priority, we mature beyond the destructive motivations that destroy our lives. That's our fundamental *why*.

TODAY: We will never complete this spiritual journey without keeping our *why* in front of us at all times. We are called to overcome the tug of secondary visions to be able to embrace the very good vision and intention of our Creator for our lives. Start today!

Monday: Genesis 2:4–19
What's In a Name? Everything

"What's in a name? That which we call a rose
By any other name would smell as sweet."
—*William Shakespeare,* Romeo and Juliet

W OULD IT? Would a rose smell just as sweet with another name? Or does the name "rose" somehow capture and convey something essential to the nature of that flower?

New parents think hard about what they will name their babies. We name buildings, roads, towns, and stars. Why this impulse to name things?

God has built this desire into us. Naming things was our first God-given task.

Do you begin to see the power in that calling? You were made to be so discerning that you would know the essence of things. You were created with the ability to name what you see.

Indeed, people can be so changed by their encounters with God that their names change: Abram becomes Abraham, Cephas becomes Peter, Saul is renamed Paul. Converts to the Orthodox faith often take a new name.

But this principle is at work in other ways. A doctor must know the cause of a symptom to cure the patient. The counselor struggles to help her client diagnose mental illness. Our spiritual fathers work with us to name the root causes of our spiritual illnesses. The Church's spiritual disciplines restore in us the ability to see and name the essence of things.

TODAY: It is time we recognize our need to name that which impedes spiritual growth. What's in a name? Possibly everything. So, who are you? What's your name? Are you actively laboring to live up to the name you've been given?

Tuesday: Genesis 2:20—3:20
Who Told You That?

He is the enemy of the people!

Politicians love to demonize their opponents. In every election cycle, they decry the mudslinging and negativity and then promptly increase their media budgets to create more negative ads. They wouldn't spend the money on the negative ads if they didn't work.

This is not a new pattern of human behavior, dear ones. In today's passage, Moses recalls that the enemy of mankind enslaved humanity first by slandering the Father.

"God isn't really good or loving; He is withholding things from you," he hissed. "You shall not die by death. For God knows in the day you eat from it your eyes will be opened, and you will be like gods, knowing good and evil" (see Gen. 3:4–5 OSB). Calling the character of the Father into question is his favorite tactic.

The enemy always wins if he can get us to doubt God's goodness, His love, and His purposes for us. Adam and Eve only needed the patience to mature until they were able to handle the fruit of the knowledge of good and evil. Instead, the enemy lied, and humanity died.

Of course, we know that our loving Creator did not leave us there but rescued His creation, reversing the damage caused by the Fall. His wisdom is now preserved in His Church, and He offers us the same path offered to our first parents: the path of disciplined maturity, the path of fasting, the path of trust and love rather than mere rule-following, and the path of true repentance. This restores us to fellowship. Repentance is the only way to undo and overcome the lies of the evil one.

Today: We can follow the path successfully traversed by God's grace in the lives of the saints since the beginning: the path of repentance. We are moving toward Pascha. In the iconography, we see our Lord Jesus pulling Adam and Eve from the tombs. This is our destiny as well, if we will only reject the slander of our good God and embrace the growing-up path of disciplined lives.

Wednesday: Genesis 3:21—4:7

Why Are You Angry?

Father, I'm angry

A FRIEND RECENTLY CONFIDED in me about his anger. He confessed that most of it was directed at himself—he wasn't satisfied with his job, his wife, his children, or his relationship with God. I had to confess to him that I also had periods in my own life when I was angry in the same way.

We read in scripture, "'Be angry, and do not sin': do not let the sun go down on your wrath" (Eph. 4:26). Psychologists tell us that anger isn't a primary emotion but is related to a previous emotion or unfulfilled expectation. If our anger fuels us to positive change, it can be productive. If it's driven inward or explodes, then it becomes poison.

When we feel angry, we need to explore the reasons, or we will cause harm to ourselves and others.

In today's reading, God sends Adam and Eve out of the Garden. Lest we feel angry about this, we need to realize that He did so to protect them from eating from the Tree of Life and experiencing eternal separation from God. Our parents tried to cover themselves with leaves, but our loving Creator offered the first sacrifice so their nakedness could be covered.

In the case of Cain, his anger was rooted in his insistence on having his own way, and this led to the first murder recorded in Scripture. God tells Cain that sin is crouching at the door of his heart and that he must master it.

Our fasting efforts, increased prayers, frequent attendance at services— indeed, all our Lenten efforts—are aimed at helping us gain mastery over our souls. Are we angry with God because our life seems difficult? This Lent, let's run into His presence with confidence and joy, knowing that God truly loves us and desires only our salvation.

TODAY: As you fast and pray and give alms in your journey, are you willing to harness the power of anger to heal, or are you often mastered and enslaved by anger? It's time to master your desires.

Thursday: Genesis 4:8–15
Where Is Your Brother?

My brother's keeper

AH, THE JOYS OF SIBLING RIVALRY. Whenever my older daughter recites the activities of her day, my four-year-old immediately pipes up with the accusatory question, "What about me?" She simply cannot allow big sister to suck up all the attention.

Siblings simultaneously love and compete with each other, a testament to both the selfishness and selflessness that is our lot as human beings.

This shouldn't surprise us. We are made in the image of God, and He is the wellspring of love and freedom. The scripture declares to us, "God is love" (1 John 4:8). Perfect freedom and perfect love in God create amazing possibilities for His creation, especially because we know that we can become by grace what Christ is by nature.

We know the story of Cain and his brother Abel, the sons of Adam and Eve born after the Fall. The brothers grew up hearing stories of Mom and Dad in the Garden, and they learned from their parents about the intimate relationship with God that was lost when our first parents fell for the snake's lie.

God confronted Cain after Abel's murder, asking, "Where is Abel your brother?" And Cain lied to God, saying, "I do not know. Am I my brother's keeper?" (see Gen. 4:9). This statement reveals his heart.

Cain had no excuse for his jealousy against his brother, since he knew the kind of offering God required. He chose to ignore that wisdom and insist on his own way. This is always at the heart of our own weakness in practicing our faith well.

TODAY: You are always moving toward the consequences of your choices. The path of faith is filled with self-awareness and sober honesty. Inasmuch as you choose God's wisdom and this path, your freedom will bring life and joy, but to blame God is to follow the way of Cain. Determine to embrace a purposeful Orthodox way of life by energetically practicing the three great disciplines of the Fast: prayer, fasting, and almsgiving.

Friday: Isaiah 5:16–25
Woe to . . . Me?

We can get in real trouble when we fail to pay attention

T HE SCRIPTURES CONTAIN strong warnings concerning behaviors and attitudes that lead a person into spiritual slavery. The prophets begin these warnings with the word *woe*, meaning great sorrow or distress. We when see the word *woe*, we'd better pay attention.

In our Scripture reading today, the prophet Isaiah declares four woes to the people of God. The first is "Woe to those who draw sins to themselves as with a long rope and lawlessness as with the strap of a cow's yoke, who say, 'Let Him speedily hasten what He will do that we may see it, and let the counsel of the Holy One of Israel come, that we may know it!'" (Is. 5:18–19 OSB). The prophet warns against choosing arrogance rather than humility, against the foolish notion that we can command God or demand that He perform for us. Woe to those who disguise their doubt in acts of false piety.

The second woe is "Woe to those who call evil good and good evil, who put darkness for light and light for darkness, who put bitter for sweet and sweet for bitter!" (Is. 5:20 OSB). In our society, many commit acts that enslave them. No matter how "acceptable" society says the darkness is, it's still darkness.

The third woe is "Woe to those who are intelligent in their own eyes and expert in their own sight!" (Is. 5:21 OSB). We should flee the self-assurance that blinds us to our own folly. The ability to learn humbly, even from our enemies, makes life fuller and wiser.

Finally, "Woe to your strong ones who drink wine and the mighty ones who mix intoxicating drink, who justify the ungodly for a bribe and take away justice from the righteous man!" (Is. 5:22–23 OSB). A lack of sobriety in our lives leads us to sacrifice the well-being of others by allowing the guilty to go free for a bribe and taking advantage of the less fortunate by depriving them of justice and mercy. Addictions feed selfishness.

TODAY: Let the wise spiritual medicine of the Faith cure your soul of illness. Let's humbly listen to the woes and the wisdom of the Church.

Monday: Proverbs 6:3–12
God Hates Six Things—No, Seven

As God's creatures, we have no power over Him

OUR SINS CAN NEVER overpower or exhaust God. If that were possible, He would not be God. If you believe that God can't forgive you, you're worshipping an idol and not the God of the Church or the Scriptures. Dearest, that is delusion; you just aren't that powerful.

Our human pride and the "I'm the center of the universe" attitude can pollute our thoughts. Herein lies our greatest temptation and our biggest challenge as we become true lovers of God. The Orthodox way calls us to change, even when we are feeling bad about ourselves.

Our passage from Proverbs reveals that there are some things God hates, but it isn't people. Each item on the list articulates the way we abuse our God-given faculties. From our eyes to our tongues, from our hands to our hearts—all can be used for selfish ends. Why does God hate this?

These things destroy people whom God loves. He hates these things because of the destructive power they wield over His creation, which He sent His Son to redeem.

This is almost too wonderful for us to believe: God loves us more than we, ourselves, know how to love. Even at His angriest, He is kinder than men when they are most kind. You cannot outsin God's mercy, and that very truth is the motivation we need to use—and not abuse—God's good gifts. God hates our selfishness because it harms us.

TODAY: Are you gripped with the narcissistic lie that God can't forgive you? Are you trapped in behaviors that are self-destructive? God is too humble to be angered by petty human sins. He hates what hurts you, and He loves you more than you know. Let's embrace the God who hates what hurts people.

Tuesday: Genesis 5:32—6:8

Sinners in the Hands of an Angry God

Perspective changes everything

ISN'T IT INTERESTING that the wickedness of man begins in the *mind*, and then flows into the *behavior*? There is a lesson here in how to reverse that pattern, if we have ears to hear.

In this passage, consider how Moses reports God's feelings concerning His creation. Moses describes God as being "sorry" He had made man and says people had come to "grieve" God because of their wickedness (Gen. 6:6). Then God said He would destroy humanity because they were now their own worst enemies (6:7), which would ultimately result in the Flood.

Words are powerful things, dear ones. They are icons for ideas, concepts, and perspectives. We must remember that our perspective is always hindered by the limitations of time and space. This doesn't make our perspective wrong so much as incomplete and, usually, too small. When we read in the Scriptures that God was "angry" or "grieved" or "sorry," we can't understand this through the lens of our own experience of such emotions, as though the Lord were changeable and fickle. God's ways are not our ways, and His thoughts are higher than our thoughts (see Isaiah 55:8–9). Had God not brought the Flood on the earth to end the increasingly downward spiral of wickedness in humanity, He would have been guilty of allowing the perpetual sickness to continue growing. His sheer love required that He stop the cancer growing in the heart of His creation.

TODAY: Do you misinterpret God's loving correction as anger toward you? This flows from the immature notion that you have power over God's emotions and actions by your behavior. God is perfect freedom and love. Through the Church's spiritual disciplines, let's grow up in Christ and become like Him—God's ultimate plan for us all.

Wednesday: Matthew 20:1–16
Do You Really Want Fairness?

That's not fair!

Our daughter was quite upset over what she perceived to be a bigger piece of cake dished out to her sister. She would accept nothing less than absolute equality—fairness was absolutely necessary to communicate her worth and place in the family.

Today, fighting for fairness is a major preoccupation. To be sure, we are all created in the image of God, so to deny another person respect is tantamount to rejecting the image of God. But we need to ask whether we want fairness or righteousness.

In today's Gospel reading, our Lord confronts humanity's poor understanding of fairness. A vineyard owner hires workers for a day's wage. As the day progresses, he finds other idle men, whom he then sends into the vineyard to work the rest of the day. Finally, just before the day is done, the owner finds more workers and sends them into the vineyard to work.

When the workers line up for their pay, all receive the same amount regardless of hours worked. Indignant, the first workers demand to know why the owner is being so unfair. "Friend, I am doing you no wrong," the owner answers. "Did you not agree with me for a denarius? Take *what* is yours and go your way. I wish to give to this last man *the same* as to you. Is it not lawful for me to do what I wish my own things?" (Matt. 20:13–15).

A desire for fairness tainted by envy, selfishness, and pride will never produce harmony or justice. In fact, this demand for fairness is rarely satisfied—no matter what others do, it is never enough.

Today: Allow the Holy Spirit to enlarge your desire for righteousness, and dismiss the fantasy of fairness from your hearts. Strive for justice in the biblical sense of the word. Our hearts, our homes, and our communities will never become truly loving and peaceful while the tyranny of false fairness drives our desires and behaviors. We were made for so much more: mercy, grace, and righteousness. We were made for a purposeful Orthodoxy.

Thursday: Genesis 7:1–5

And Noah Obeyed

If it sounds too good to be true, it probably is

WHY ARE ADVERTISEMENTS that promise transformation so successful at parting people from their money? Because they pledge incredible results for little effort. Take this pill, follow these four easy steps, and all will be well.

How do we combat this desire to expect easy results from little effort? We begin by admitting we have to work hard for that which is most valuable to us. We will have to *strive* toward our goals if they are worthwhile. We are always one generation away from forgetting what makes a person, a society, and yes, even a Faith worth the effort.

In today's Scripture reading, we see the Lord about to provide a radical cure for a terrible human sickness. The Flood is coming, but God wants to redeem the situation, so He finds a faithful man, telling him to "enter the ark, you and all your family, for I have seen you righteous before Me in this generation" (Gen. 7:1 OSB). Faithfulness in one generation sets up the next generation to follow.

We must abandon the foolish notion that we only live for ourselves. If we are going to be the people who leave a strong faith for the next generation, we have to practice the Faith and resist taking the easy way of trusting culture or (small "t") traditions. The quick fix of new programs cannot instill in our children what can only be passed on through example and effort. As wonderful as sports tournaments, dance groups, and special recipes are (and they are wonderful), they are not strong enough to transmit Orthodoxy without the actual *practice* of faith lived out in sincere, faithful, and purposeful lives. We must be righteous in this generation if we want the next generation to be the same.

TODAY: We have all the spiritual tools required to be righteous in this generation. It is not easy—we will stumble, we will make mistakes. We will want to give up at times. Let's keep at it anyway. Let's forever reject the false notion that we can have cosmic achievements without cosmic effort and divine grace.

Friday: Genesis 7:6–9
So Literal

After all, the best fiction writers are Southerners!

WHEN I WAS A BOY, I was blessed with a vivid imagination and an active interior world. As a true son of the American South, storytelling was an integral part of my experience. Unfortunately, our society has exalted and deified the myth of scientific certainty, and we've lost the whimsy and feeling of being comfortable with mystery that our souls need.

To be sure, accuracy is important for engineering, finance, and other endeavors, but this precision doesn't tell the whole story.

In today's Scripture reading we read the timeless story of Noah and the ark. Some have endlessly wondered whether there was a real flood. Was the ark really big enough to hold all those animals? These questions miss the point.

We dare not reduce all people to mere fleshly machines and the world to mere utilitarian usefulness or, worse yet, personal desires and claimed rights. The clinical mentality of a society that no longer plumbs the depths of story and mystery forsakes communion with God. He transcends our rational abilities and always dwells in mystery.

Beneath the desire to scrub the world clean of transcendence lie the twin weaknesses of fear and pride. We genuinely fear that there is something or someone bigger than our own intellects, and our pride is threatened by the possibility of what exists beyond our reasoning.

If we abandon amazement and wonder, we descend into hell. The evil one would have humanity discard the image of our holy God. In worship, we engage in wonder, and wonder makes us open to Him.

TODAY: Protect your childlike ability to wonder and stand in amazement—be open to mystery. Today, let the power of the disciplines of the Faith open your heart to true adoration. Let's worship the Holy Trinity.

Monday: Proverbs 10:1–22
Wisdom! Let Us Attend!

He's a smart boy, but he ain't got no horse sense!

MY GRANDMOTHER WAS KNOWN to say this about a friend of my grandfather's. Horse sense? What did that mean? Years later, I understood—a person can be well educated, but still lack the ability to learn from life's experiences.

We simply don't learn from our past mistakes the way we should. Sometimes, we tell ourselves that *this* time is different. Ah, the joys of delusion! Remember, the layman's definition of insanity is doing the same thing over and over again, expecting different results.

Attaining wisdom isn't as easy as simply learning a lesson—we must become wakeful to the impact of our actions, attitudes, and choices. This is why we need the Book of Proverbs, where we find one wise admonition after another, all inviting us to wakefulness. Let's embrace these maxims and pass them on to our children:

He who has a slack hand becomes poor,

But the hand of the diligent makes rich (v. 4).

He who gathers in summer *is* a wise son;

He who sleeps in harvest *is* a son who causes shame (v. 5).

A fountain of life is in the hand of a righteous man,

but the mouth of an ungodly man will hide destruction (v. 12 OSB).

Hatred stirs up strife,

but love covers all who are not lovers of strife (v. 13 OSB).

These are insights that give us a head start to right living, if we will only heed them.

TODAY: Are you awake to wisdom? Can you see mistakes coming before you make them? Ask God to teach you the wisdom of Proverbs, so that you can develop some horse sense. Make an appointment with your spiritual father for confession. Entrust your deepest thoughts to someone who is wise in the Faith.

Tuesday: Isaiah 13:2–13
Raise a Signal! Cry Aloud!

You're the meanest daddy in the world!

M Y DAUGHTER ANNOUNCED that I was both unfair and unreasonable to expect her to clean up the mess she had made with the Play-Doh. The fact that I had insisted she accept responsibility for her mess meant I was cruel.

Don't we interpret the consequences of our actions the same way? Rather than accepting that the chickens have come home to roost, as the saying goes, we blame God for circumstances that in reality, we have created.

Isaiah was a well-born man with all the right connections in society, but he put all that at risk to follow his calling as a prophet of God. In today's passage, he warns the Israelites that God isn't going to ignore their spiritual apathy, their prideful actions and attitudes, and their mistreatment of each other. A day of reckoning is coming.

Let's face it, just like the Israelites', our self-centered pride makes us stubborn and hard of hearing. Sometimes our hearts are so cluttered with selfishness that we need a siren to wake us up.

God loved the nation of Israel so much that He used His loudest warning bell to tell them that the consequences of their choices were going to be harsh. They were going to reap what they had sown, and in their anger they were going to attribute all those consequences to God. If that fear of God's justice would wake them up, then so be it. Isaiah's message is for us, too: the great and terrible day of the Lord is not going to be something we enjoy if we don't relinquish our stubbornness and repent.

TODAY: We are called to mature past the childish attitude that sees God as the meanest daddy in the world. Freedom comes when we accept the wise and loving direction of a God who, rather than being angry with us, loves us too much to ignore our foolish choices. Only a spiritually mature person can enjoy real and deep communion with God. Let's accept the natural consequences of our actions with maturity.

Wednesday: Isaiah 14:24–32

Same as It Ever Was

Same stuff, different day

As a teen, I worked in a factory. A buddy of mine had worked there for many years, and his monotonous job was a series of movements that never changed. Our lives can often feel this way. How do we free ourselves from boredom but simultaneously achieve stability?

The answer lies in knowing our central purpose. When we settle on a purpose too small for what we were created for, we'll be bored and restless. We aim too low.

Our theology, far from espousing narcissism, is absolutely vital to expanding our understanding of our potential and our purpose.

God is speaking through Isaiah to tell the beleaguered people of Israel that He has not forgotten His promises to them. He also warns the surrounding nations that He isn't going to ignore their behavior either. The Lord declares, "As I said, so it shall come to pass. As I purposed, so it shall remain" (Is. 14:24 OSB). A right understanding of our significance begins with the proper vision of God. Is He a doting old grandfather figure, there to make us feel better? Is He a distant and angry deity? Our sense of purpose will never be clear if we don't know Him. We can't love a god who is easily offended or easily manipulated. In both of these scenarios, *we* are actually the center of the universe, and that god is too small. Isaiah reminds us that this God knows the end from the beginning, doesn't forget His promises and His plans, and has every intention of fulfilling both. This God doesn't need appeasement or flattery.

The key to knowing our purpose is an accurate vision of God and His purposes.

Today: The Church reminds us just how seriously God is in keeping His promises and loving us. He will accomplish His plan—will we be humble enough, wise enough, courageous enough to participate in His purposes?

Thursday: Isaiah 25:1–9
He Will Swallow Up Death Forever

Doesn't he look good? He looks almost alive.

WE LIVE IN such a death-denying culture that this is what we say when gazing at a corpse in funeral homes. We've sanitized death to avoid reminders of our own mortality. Our ancestors lived with death as a normal part of life in this world, but we are so divorced from the reality of death that even when faced with a corpse, we do our best to distract ourselves with pleasantries.

How different from the counsel of St. Athanasios, who wrote, "Recall your exodus every hour; keep death before your eyes on a daily basis. Remember before whom you must appear." Years ago, I realized that the fear of death drives most of my sinful behaviors and choices—I grasp for earthly happiness, or embellish the truth, all in an effort to drive away that fear. When I encountered Orthodoxy's emphasis on Christ's victory over death, it all made sense. If death has been defeated, then what do I need to run from?

God's intention was to slay death and set humanity free from this terrible fear. Yet freedom from death isn't guaranteed to be a wonderful thing. God sent Adam and Eve out of the Garden to prevent them from eating from the Tree of Life—in their fallen state, they would have lived forever separated from their Creator. Christ has come and trampled down death by death. The path to the Tree of Life is open to humanity again, and God has extended His victory over death to everyone. Now the task is to properly prepare to live forever.

No wonder the Fathers teach us to remember our own mortality. We pray "for a good defense before the awesome judgment seat of Christ." We need to approach eternity well prepared.

TODAY: Let's renew our sober preparations for eternal life. The Church provides numerous aids to help us prepare for the eternal life that is granted to us all. We are all going to live forever. But will we be able to enjoy it?

Friday: Genesis 9:18—10:1

Don't Drive Drunk

Under the influence

AS A POLICE OFFICER, I was assigned to the local DUI task force. This assignment offered a fulfilling opportunity to really make a difference. I learned that drunk driving isn't just alcohol-related—a driver is impaired any time an intoxicant is involved, including prescribed medications. In our spiritual lives, we're called to avoid intoxicants too. The virtue of sobriety in our Christian lives is key to gaining both spiritual healing and maturity.

Today's Scripture reading demonstrates this. In the story of Noah and his sons after the Flood, the Bible doesn't hide the darker side of our human nature. We read about the faithful patriarch planting a vineyard, harvesting and fermenting the grapes into wine, then drinking too much and passing out. His younger son observed his father in this drunken state and told his two older brothers, who covered Noah to hide his shame.

Dear one, this is the path of intoxication. And when our spiritual sobriety is impaired, the result can be anger, fear, resentment, lust, pride, and ignorance. We make destructive choices when we're under the influence, and then we compound the damage by proudly refusing to repent.

In Lent, we are called to pray the Prayer of St. Ephrem for God to help us overcome intoxicants like sloth, despondency, lust for power, and idle talk, which all contribute to enslave us to the passions. The prayer calls us to embrace instead the virtues of chastity, humility, patience, and love.

TODAY: Moving toward sobriety in our spiritual lives takes time, effort, and humility. Regular attendance at Liturgy and participation in the Sacraments encourage us in the path of sobriety. Are you going through your life impaired by intoxicants that cloud your judgment and undermine sobriety? Admit your need for God and flee to His Church.

Monday: Genesis 10:32—11:9

Nothing Will Be Impossible for Them

What drives us to fill every moment so we won't be bored?

THE BEST GENERALS know their adversary so well that they can anticipate his moves and then plan for a counter strategy. But most of us clutter our moments with as much noise as possible in an attempt to drown out any silence or awareness of our adversary. The need for constant stimulation speaks more to our restlessness than it does to any real concern for productivity. Why are so we afraid of silence?

In our Scripture reading today, we read the story of the tower of Babel. The Flood has passed. Noah's descendants are obeying God's commandment to multiply. Ambitious and skillful, they build a city with a tower that reaches the heavens. They still retain the spark of divinity and long to build, create, and achieve. Yet their broken relationship with God is an infection—even their best intentions are colored by a lack of love for their neighbors.

With love and foresight, God intervenes, confusing the common language, so that their tower of Babel project must be abandoned. This is reversed on the Day of Pentecost, when God heals mankind's deepest wound through Christ's Resurrection and the coming of the Holy Spirit.

It may be confusing to understand God's actions toward us. But if we desire to be united with Him more than we desire our happiness and comfort, then we'll trust His plans for our lives. Our faith enables us to view our circumstances with confidence in our Lord.

TODAY: God sees our beginnings and our endings. He asks us to trust His guidance. Today, make the choice to trust Him. Then build your faith so that saying yes not only becomes easier, but automatic.

Tuesday: Isaiah 29:13–23

What God Is as Great as Our God?

It's marvelous! It's wonderful!

IN EARLIER TIMES, these words would have conveyed something more than delight and pleasure: they could have also suggested dread and fear. Think of the horrible persecution of Christians in the Middle East, videos of beheadings and the like. Certainly we marvel at such cruelty, and we wonder at such barbarism.

We live in a delusional age. The human person has been diminished, and life has been reduced to a shallow expectation of happiness in which sadness has no real meaning. Our need for comfort comes at the expense of our spiritual maturity. Our suffering is devoid of purpose, and God gets the blame.

What if we recaptured the power of marvel and wonder so that joy could be possible even in the midst of suffering? Talk about living life to the fullest!

In today's Scripture reading, the prophet declares God's wisdom to God's people, insisting that they not empty marvel and wonder of their fullest meaning. His people said all the right things, but there was no true change of attitude.

We need to outgrow our narcissistic tendencies and develop humble hearts. Life is about more than comfort. Even negative events can enable us to develop into the men and women God meant us to be, and in the process, we will find that even tragedy is emptied of its power to destroy us. In sad times we can own up to the sadness, but know that God doesn't waste one tear. What power! What freedom! What a marvelous and wonderful path for a life!

TODAY: Every life has ups and downs. Yet no event, whether good or bad, should leave you less than what you are. Take each moment of life as it is and squeeze every bit of wisdom out of it. This is the gift of grace God extends to you today. Your willingness to embark on this wise path of life will bring you rich experiences of wonder and marvel. Truly, who is so great a god as our God?

Wednesday: Genesis 13:12–18
Lift up Your Eyes

It's a paradox!

THE CONCEPT OF SACRED SPACE is at the heart of all serious theology. Without sacred places, all space loses value. My recognition of the holiness of the altar area, a church building, a plot of ground, or a burial space is necessary to see the sacred in all of creation.

If you set aside a place in your home for the family altar, you create an atmosphere that will infuse your whole home. Yet this is only the case if you purposefully participate in keeping that spot holy.

In our Scripture lesson today, God promised the land of Israel for his people. At this sacred spot near the Oaks of Mamre, Abram and his wife extended hospitality to three angels, depicted later in the famed *Hospitality of Abraham* icon as the Holy Trinity. This sacred-space encounter changed human history and reinforced God's gracious revelation of Himself to His creation. Abram's response was to build an altar and worship, thus consecrating the place as sacred and holy.

Today, if something is holy we imagine it has mystical qualities, but *holy* simply means set apart for a specific use. If something is holy, it is used only for one, singular purpose and nothing else. A church building is holy because it is only used to worship God. A chalice is holy because it is used only to hold the precious Body and Blood of our Lord in the Eucharist. And you are holy when you reserve your life for God alone and live only for His purposes in your life. It is exclusive devotion that creates sacred space. Orthodox Christian churches are used for worship, and when we worship, we do so to redeem the whole world—one specific space is holy so that every place can become holy.

TODAY: Where are your holy spaces? Make a space holy in your home, your heart, and your community, and then keep it holy by single-minded devotion. Then all places in your life can become holy as well.

Thursday: Genesis 15:1–15

To Believe Is to Do

I meant well!

THERE'S A PREVAILING NOTION that granting mental assent is the same thing as believing. But does simply *saying* you think something is true mean you actually believe it? Often, we want our good intentions to be enough without actually getting our hands dirty in the hard work of ministry.

We need to face the gap between what we say with our mouths and do with our lives.

How do we escape this delusion? In our Scripture reading today, we read about Abram becoming a man of faith. We see him transformed into someone whose belief informs his action. In Genesis 15:1–15, God and Abram (his name will be changed to Abraham as a result of a transformation in his relationship with God) grow in their relationship—God confronts Abram with his true calling and offers him a vision of what his life can become. Does he dare to follow God no matter the cost?

Abram is honest in his response to God. Dear ones, this honesty is the first step in transforming what we say into how we live. Be honest enough to question God but brave enough to step out in faith. This approach will carry us through challenging circumstances. In fact, one without the other simply never rises to the level of true belief.

Abram's closeness with God will be proven over and over again as Abram becomes Abraham, the father of the faithful. "And Abram believed God, and He accounted it to him for righteousness" (Gen. 15:6 OSB). His actions proved that his heart was sincere. He trusted in God's promises, and God used him because of this active faith.

TODAY: Do your actions indicate true faith? Before you fall into discouragement, remember that God knows your heart better than you do. He wants you to be healed. To be free to be the person of faith you were created to be, you will need to choose the dual path of repentance and action—mental assent isn't enough.

Friday: Luke 1:24–38
She Said Yes

Here He comes!

Tʜᴇ Fᴇᴀsᴛ ᴏꜰ ᴛʜᴇ Aɴɴᴜɴᴄɪᴀᴛɪᴏɴ reminds us of a story we know well. God sends the angel Gabriel to a virgin engaged to a man named Joseph, and the angel tells this young lady that she is going to have a baby, "the Son of the Highest" (Luke 1:32).

The Jewish people had been looking for the Messiah for thousands of years. Every Jewish man knew the prophecy, and every Jewish woman wondered if she'd be the mother of the Messiah. Every Jewish generation hoped to be the generation that witnessed His coming. Here it was, and here she was.

The Church insists we remember this event with liturgies, prayers, hymns, and devotions for three reasons. First, we are reminded that God fulfills His promises. In the Garden of Eden, when our first parents fell for the lie of the serpent, God promised to put enmity between the serpent and the seed of the woman (see Genesis 3:15).

Next, God not only fulfills His promises, but He enlists one of our own to participate in humanity's salvation. You see, God loves us but refuses to force us. He invites and He calls us, but he never insists—He doesn't force Mary. He tells her His plans through Gabriel, and He waits for her response. God wants companions, not slaves or cowering servants. It's best for us if we love Him, not for His benefit but for ours. He knows we will never be able to stay with Him forever if we don't do so willingly.

Finally, He invites us through Mary's example to follow Him. Christ invites me to a family, where I find my mother and brothers and sisters. Our mother said yes, and we are called to do the same. If we do, the same thing that happened to her will happen to us, and the Holy Spirit will be formed within us.

Tᴏᴅᴀʏ: You are being asked to trust an amazing message: that God wants you to so be transformed that you actually participate in the very divine nature Himself. Just like Mary the Theotokos, you are called to say yes.

Monday: Genesis 18:20–33
Will You Destroy the Righteous with the Wicked?

When we pay it forward

THERE REALLY IS SOMETHING POWERFUL about standing up for others, even when it doesn't look like there is an immediate benefit. Scientists and sociologists tell us that we are strengthened by acts of selfless care. We even know that the doer of a good deed experiences a rush of endorphins that reinforce selfless behavior—a wonderful sense of joy fills us when we sacrificially give of our time and treasure. This increases when we become more generous.

Why is that? In today's Scripture reading, Abraham negotiated with God over the destruction of the cities of Sodom and Gomorrah. Abraham asked God to spare the cities if He could find righteous people in them. Abraham was particularly concerned about his nephew Lot and his family, who lived there. God revealed that He would judge these two cities for their sin but promised not to destroy the righteous with the wicked if He could find fifty righteous people. Ultimately, He could not find even ten, but through Abraham's pleading, Lot and his children were spared.

Why did God allow Himself to be persuaded through His servant Abraham?

It is because God knows the best way to encourage us in our spiritual growth is to call us to selfless behavior.

TODAY: Let us dare to selflessly love even those who cannot—or will not—return our love.

Tuesday: Genesis 22:1–18
God Will Provide a Lamb

But I don't understand!

I F I HAD A NICKEL for every time I've said or heard this, especially from my children, I'd be very wealthy.

Truthfully, I don't understand why people make many of the choices they make. Why can't folks see the seeds of self-destruction they plant in their lives and those of their family and friends? More to the point: I don't understand why I do the same things in my own life. And I really don't understand why God does what He does. Of course I don't—I am still in the middle of the journey toward faith, peace, and spiritual maturity.

On that path, we are blessed with the examples of the saints and the life of the Incarnate God Himself, who shows us the way. It's only when I lose sight of Him that I struggle.

In our Scripture reading today, God makes a dreadful request of His friend Abraham, commanding him to make a human sacrifice of his son, Isaac. Yes, the pagan gods in those days required human sacrifices, but Abraham believed the One true God was different. *And now this? Lord, I don't understand.*

Amazingly, when Isaac innocently asks his father, "Where is the sheep for a whole burnt offering?" Abraham's answer reverberates with faith: "God will provide for Himself the sheep for a whole burnt offering" (see Gen. 22:7, 8 OSB).

Abraham didn't understand, but he believed God would never break His promise. Regardless of the pain of the moment, Abraham trusted His provision. And as he was willing to offer up his only son, we remember that our God did just that for us.

TODAY: We needn't understand everything at all times. Let's trust God anyway. God has demonstrated to Abraham and throughout history that faith must be valued over mere understanding, and trust over our smug self-sufficiency. God has provided a Lamb for us as well, and today He reminds us, "This Lamb is worthy of your faith and trust."

Wednesday: Genesis 27:1–41
Jacob Lied

He's a liar!

WE WERE DISCUSSING a politician who had been caught in an inescapable lie, one that revealed a real character flaw. As we struggled with this disappointment, I remembered my mother saying, "Son, always put your best foot forward." She meant for me always to be the best of who I am. It's good advice, especially if you're a leader.

Our society is littered with the false claims of companies, politicians, and leaders. Sometimes innocent people reap the consequences resulting from believing in these lies. Yet in moments of deep humility, we have to confess that we too have victimized others in our own dishonesty.

In our Scripture reading today, we read the story Jacob, who deceived his father, the great Patriarch Isaac, into giving him the blessing of the firstborn son. By rights, this belonged to Jacob's twin, Esau, a mighty hunter and Isaac's favorite. Jacob, on the other hand, was a bookish philosopher and Rebekah's favorite. Isaac's eyesight was failing, and he knew he was going to die. Jacob and Rebekah hatched a plan to deceive the old man so Jacob could get the blessing that belonged to Esau, and it worked. The trick was discovered, and the brothers were estranged for years, meeting again after decades of separation.

In life, people tell lies about us, and we at times are less than totally honest about others. The wise person of faith will pay close attention to what these moments can teach him, remembering that even our sufferings at the hands of others are temporary. The Lord of the universe faced his lying murderers with these words: "Father, forgive them, for they do not know what they do" (Luke 23:34). Even as He lay in the tomb, the story wasn't over. In a moment, all injustice vanished in the flash of glory, love, and hope in His Resurrection. And so it will be for us, someday.

TODAY: We are all broken. Let's allow God's grace to heal us and makes us like Himself.

Thursday: Genesis 31:3–16
The God of Bethel

Here's the church, here's the steeple,
open the door, see all the people

THIS HAND TRICK was shown to me first by a Sunday School teacher wanting to illustrate how important it was to go to church. I loved the cleverness of this picture.

There is something powerful that happens when we worship together. Some say people aren't attending church as much as they use to—we aren't as religious as we used to be, we've grown out of the need for worship, or we even believe we can praise God just as well at home.

The Scriptures instruct us in the real meaning of church. We have spent some time with Jacob, and we know he has struggled with dishonesty and was likewise deceived by his father-in-law. Now it's time for him to courageously break with familiarity and discover God's purpose for him and his family. What makes the difference for Jacob now? Why is he ready at this moment to make this break?

God said, "I am the God who appeared to you at Bethel, where you anointed the pillar and made a vow to Me" (Gen. 31:13 OSB). God reminded Jacob of the time when, in a dream, He showed him a stairway to heaven where angels were ascending and descending. Jacob named that place Beth-El, which means "House of God." In this house of God, Jacob repented and began preparing to make a clean break with the past to become what he was meant to be.

Being in the house of God is indispensable—only there do we begin to understand who we are in relation to Him. There we confront and commune with our Maker and are given the insights and instruction that enable us to be all we can be.

TODAY: God wishes to meet you in His house. In His Church, we are provided with every means to break free of mediocrity and spiritual delusion. The temptation might be to see this as just another liturgy. Don't fall for it—go to the house of God.

Friday: Isaiah 58:1–11
Why Have We Fasted?

He was doing all the right things for all the wrong reasons

I'VE SEEN PEOPLE be very strict with their observance of a religious practice, then turn out to be really mean people, even disrespectful. What's going on here? If we follow all the rules, aren't we supposed to win the game? If all this spiritual effort is producing anger and disquiet, isn't this a sign of trouble?

Let's look at our Scripture reading this morning. What the Lord says to the people is surprising. Those who are strictly observing the law are asking, "How come God isn't answering our prayers? We're following all the rules. Where's the payoff?" God cuts right to the heart of the problem and tells them they are fasting for themselves and their selfish desires rather than out of a desire for repentance. In fact, these folks don't see themselves as spiritually sick at all. They are just following the rules to get a reward.

The Lord went on to describe what a real fast looks like: isn't the fast, He asks, meant to "loose every bond of wrongdoing; untie the knots of violent dealings; cancel the debts of the oppressed; and tear apart every unjust contract. Break your bread for the hungry, and bring the homeless poor into your house. If you see a naked man, clothe him, nor shall you disregard your offspring in your own household. Then your light shall break forth as the morning, and your healing shall spring forth quickly. Your righteousness shall go before you, and the glory of God shall cover you. Then you shall cry out, and God will hear you. While you are still speaking, He will say, 'Behold, I am here'" (Is. 58:6–9 OSB).

TODAY: Have your religious disciplines made you more tender to others or motivated you to give to those who cannot repay you? Honestly assess the reason for your spiritual labors, and understand that the reward is your own transformed life. With this perspective, you will discover a sense of purpose, peace, and joy, and everything will align. Let's do the right things for the right reasons.

Monday: Isaiah 65:8–16
Why Do You Hate Me?

To disagree with someone these days is to hate them

"YOU JUST WANT to deprive me of my freedom—if I want to touch the stove, I'm free to do so. You're just trying to control me."

"Buddy, all I said was the stove is hot. If you touch it, you'll get burned."

"Hey, that stove is hot. I just burned my hand. That's not fair, and you better do something to make me feel better or that will prove you really do hate me."

This is a pretty ridiculous conversation, isn't it? Yet I have repeatedly chosen immediate gratification with little regard for the consequences. I blame God for my troubles, and He reminds me, "I told you the stove was hot."

In our Scripture reading today, the Lord confronted people whose choices were not in their best interests. He recited the consequences to these people, then told them that all this was happening to them "because I called you, but you did not obey; I spoke, but you refused to listen. You did evil in My sight, and did not choose the things I willed" (Is. 65:12 OSB).

The good news is that it's never too late to begin to choose what God delights in—and, by the way, the reason God delights in certain choices is because they lead not to His happiness, but to yours.

TODAY: Repentance has little to do with regret and everything to do with a transformed way of thinking. We need to relinquish our childish notions of autonomy and use our freedom and strength to choose wisely. After all, telling someone the stove is hot isn't hate speech—it's encouraging him in a life of loving, purposeful Orthodoxy.

Tuesday: Genesis 49:33—50:26
God Will Visit You

The all-knowing God

G OD KNOWS EVERYTHING. He sees the end from the beginning. That's why St. John wrote in his Revelation that Christ is the "Lamb slain from the foundation of the world" (Rev. 13:8). As we approach Holy Week and the tragic days of the Lord's sacrifice on the Cross, we are reminded that God sees past the momentary terror of the dark days for His Son to the end of human history, the glory of the Resurrection and the Final Judgment.

Our Scripture reading reminds us of God's omniscience. Jacob's sons sold their younger brother Joseph into slavery because they were jealous of him. Years later, Joseph had risen to a position of power and authority, which enabled him to help his family when a famine struck the area. Joseph brought his family down to Egypt, where there was food. Now Joseph's brothers were at his mercy and were terrified.

Yet Joseph told them, "Do not be afraid, for I belong to God. But as for you, you meant evil against me; but God meant it for good, in order to bring it about as it is this day, to save many people alive. Now therefore, do not be afraid; I will provide for you and your households" (Gen. 50:19–21 OSB). Joseph had learned that God knew the beginning and the end of their family story.

TODAY: As we enter into Holy Week liturgically, we are invited by the Church to see past the moment of pain to the glories of the Resurrection. Our Lord saw beyond the momentary agony to the powerful glory and the wonderful redemption His work would produce. Let's not lose heart in the middle of our own challenges, being confident that the Lord of time knows our end from the beginning and has our best interest at heart. Let us approach the labors of these saving days with confidence and faith, and allow that reality to strengthen us for the spiritual labors of our lives. After all, He sees further than you, and He loves you.

Wednesday: Matthew 21:18–43
Taken Away

Have you never read?

I LOVE OLD black-and-white horror movies. They are brilliant at building tension and excitement before the big scare. But there are other scary things that don't thrill; they just terrify.

In today's Gospel reading, our Lord was preparing His disciples for the end of His ministry. Looking the religious leaders straight in the eye, He asked them, "What will [the owner] do to those vinedressers?" They all responded, "He will destroy those wicked men miserably" (Matt. 21:40–42). Little did these religious people realize that they had just judged themselves.

The Lord's clear teaching was that these Jewish people had received centuries of spiritual advantages, instruction, liturgy, wisdom, and prophets and preachers—they still rejected the Messiah.

Our Lord responded to them, "Have you never read in the Scriptures: 'The stone which the builders rejected / Has become the chief cornerstone. / This was the LORD's doing, / and it is marvelous in our eyes'? Therefore I say to you, the kingdom of God will be taken from you and given to a nation bearing the fruits of it" (Matt. 21:42, 43).

Indeed, the Gentiles changed the world by preaching the Gospel after the Jewish nation rejected Christ. If the Lord didn't stop the Kingdom from being removed from His own kinsmen, do we really think He will stop another unfaithful nation from losing the same message?

TODAY: Let us be people that produce fruit for the vineyard owner and give Him the harvest He rightly expects from those who claim with their mouths to love Him and His Church. To do less is to risk losing the Kingdom to those who will appreciate and cherish it. Live the faith or lose it. This is the solemn declaration of the Lord to us on this day.

Thursday: Matthew 22:15–46; 23:1–39
You Know Neither the Scriptures Nor the Power of God

What you don't know won't hurt you

I'VE FOUND THAT SOMETIMES what I don't know hurts me pretty badly. Even worse, sometimes when I think I know something, I haven't a clue.

In the Lord's final days of ministry, He attempted to dislodge the misplaced confidence of the local religious leaders in their own pride. Scripture allows us to eavesdrop on the Lord's straightforward teaching during the period where He cleansed the Temple of the moneychangers and warned His disciples that dark days were coming. It turns out ignorance really isn't bliss.

There's an old joke about the Sadducees—they didn't believe in the resurrection, so that's why they were *sad, you see.* The religious leaders who were members of the Sadducee group were usually the wealthiest and the most educated. They were the elite of their day and felt they were too sophisticated to believe in the miraculous. The Lord's plain teachings were a stumbling block, but they had to admit they had no answer for Him.

Prior to this, the Lord silenced the Pharisees, too. They were the second party in leadership among the Jews, and although they believed in the resurrection of the dead and miracles, they were also offended by the Lord's teachings, because He exposed their hypocrisy.

The arrogance of the religious leaders of Jesus' day blinded them to the truth. When confronted with God in the flesh, their vaunted religious knowledge was no help at all.

TODAY: We must be willing to be confronted by our ignorance. We are called by the intensity of our Holy Week worship to confront own distance from true devotion, love, and faith. If what we say we believe isn't producing a deeper spiritual life, we need to repent. If we silence that nagging voice in our hearts warning us of our poverty, we will only destroy ourselves, never Him. It's time to hear clearly that God is the God of the living, not of the dead. Are you alive in Christ?

75

Friday: Matthew 26:6–16
Costly Perfume

Kindness is contagious

B UT SO ARE INDIFFERENCE and judgment of others. We live in fear of not being right—if I don't defend truth, my whole world will come apart.

Actions motivated by fear are rarely helpful, and fear produces small souls and hearts. That's why the scripture reminds us that "perfect love casts out fear" (1 John 4:18).

Are we living by love or fear? Do our underlying motivations produce peace in our lives or chaos? Are we becoming more loving or more closed off and suspicious?

The disciples have been with the Lord from the beginning of His ministry. They have heard Him teach, seen His miracles, and watched Him interact with those around Him. Yet they are indignant about wasting perfume on Him. They try to dress up their smallness by saying the poor could have benefitted from the valuable oil, but in fact they are far more concerned that associating with the woman of ill repute will harm their reputations. And this is the last straw for Judas. This act of kindness from the Lord uncovers his own greed and fear. Judas goes to the enemies of the Lord to see what they will give him if he betrays the Lord, and they offer him the notorious thirty pieces of silver.

Christ revealed that this woman's act of lavish worship was precisely for His burial. His disciples were ignorant of the meaning of her act, being caught up in judging her. Yet she was preparing Christ's body by this act of devotion and love.

TODAY: The Church anoints the faithful for healing of body and soul. We need to remember the gift of this precious woman and embrace the invitation by Christ to be lavish with our love, our worship, and our devotion. Let's leave behind our suspicion, fear, and greed, and embrace with joy the spiritual healing offered to us in the Lord's Church. We will never love the poor properly while our love for Christ is small. The Faith invites us to reject false excuses and embrace the true healing of our hearts in Christ.

Monday: John 13:3–17

Unless I Wash Your Feet

I wish I'd known then what I know now

I CAN'T TELL YOU HOW MANY TIMES I've looked back on a significant moment in my own life and said that. Hindsight is twenty-twenty.

In the Church we have the benefit of hindsight when we view the saving life of our Lord Jesus. But the disciples weren't so fortunate, and they needed significant preparation to face what was ahead of them. The Lord's way of preparing them was surprising: He washed their feet.

Our lesson today focuses on this scene. The roads in those days were made of earth; only main thoroughfares were paved with stone. That meant that most people's feet were dirtied by travel, and it was common courtesy to offer guests a place to wash their feet when they visited your home. The slave at the bottom of the pecking order was assigned this task.

Yet Christ wrapped a towel around Himself and fetched a basin in order to wash the feet of His disciples. When impetuous Peter protested, Jesus replied, "If I do not wash you, you have no part with Me" (John 13:8).

This action of humility and love from Christ offers life-giving instruction. If the Incarnate God stoops to clean His disciples' feet, we must forever banish the notion that leadership means anything other than service.

TODAY: Let's embrace the hard work of learning to serve one another. All we need has been given to us in the prayers, the acts, and the liturgies of our life-giving Faith. All that remains is to muster the courage to imitate Christ's humility and paradoxically summon the strength to appear weak.

Tuesday: Matthew 27:62–66
Life Dies

The only answer to grief is to pass through it

GRIEF HAS A WAY of blinding us to everything around us. I remember a particularly dark chapter in my life when a wise friend warned me that this was no time to make important decisions. He knew that grief was robbing me of perspective and a sober head.

Our lives are littered with times of grief and darkness that always threaten to swallow us whole. We weep, and the tears make it hard to see anything but our pain and sorrow—not a wise time to make life decisions.

On Holy Friday, we journey with Jesus to the Cross and the tomb. All the prayers, the hymns, and our movements evoke powerful feelings that stay with us from year to year. We are at that moment when all of creation mourns the death of Life Himself.

Christ had promised to defeat death. Even the Lord's enemies knew that and hatched a plan to keep it from happening.

Yet when it happened, the disciples' grief drowned out remembrance of the Lord's promise that He would rise again. They dared not let their hearts hope for such a joy. Besides (so they reasoned), if the authorities killed their master, surely they would come for them next. Their grief overwhelmed their faith.

If left unchecked, grief and sorrow can smother faith and hope. But only if we let them. Even while mourning, we must hold two truths in tension: our pain of loss is great, but He has conquered death. No longer can grief swallow joy, since God has conquered our greatest enemy. In the words of St. Paul, "O Death, where *is* your sting? / O Hades, where *is* your victory?" (1 Cor. 15:55).

TODAY: Humanity's worst is no match for God. The difficulties and losses of our lives are ultimately swallowed up in His life. The grave has been emptied of its power to terrorize. Soon, we will sing, "Christ is risen from the dead, conquering death by death, and on those in the tombs bestowing life!" The way is open for all.

Wednesday: John 1:18–28

God Can Be Known

"Though You went down into the tomb, You destroyed Hades' power, and You rose the victor, Christ God."
—Kontakion of the Apodosis of Pascha

WHAT JOY! What happiness, what a celebration! Words fail. Death is conquered forever—the whole earth basks in the glow of the victory of Christ over death. There is no more fear, no more night. The Son has dawned, and there are no dead left in the grave.

It all sounds like so much wishful thinking in light of all our world's troubles and doubt. Even we who believe struggle to reconcile our theology with our everyday lives of struggle and pain.

In Bright Week, the doors of the iconostasis are left open all week. The floors of our parishes are still strewn with the rose petals and/or bay leaves of our celebration and will remain so all week long. No fasting. No more mourning. Christ is risen from the dead!

How do we keep our joy in the face of an oblivious world?

Our reading today calls us to remember the beginning of the Lord's ministry, which holds the seeds of the fully matured fruit of His life. In the Incarnation, God reminds us that He desires to be found. He is going to enlist St. John the Baptist as the Forerunner to clear the way for the Lord by calling all of us to repentance.

The whole world is groaning under the weight of fear and death, and the only remedy lies within the joyous celebration of His Resurrection. How will our world come to know God if we hide Him away as if He were some fragile deity who is weak and in need of protection? Why should we hide Him when He so obviously wants to be found?

TODAY: Let's keep the joy of the Resurrection by making sure there is not one corner of our world where He isn't seen. Let's be wise enough to be like St. John, pointing away from ourselves and drawing attention to Jesus Christ, the Risen Lord, the Head of the Body, the Image of the unseen God.

Thursday: Luke 24:12–35
He Was Known to Them

Now I recognize you!

Sometimes I am flooded with so many distractions—new voices, changing images—that familiar people and places recede. The overscheduling of our time, the cacophony of voices in media, and the proliferation of technology threaten to smother our memories and our focus. We have lost the ability to discern, to remember, to be quiet. As a result, we suffer.

The Fathers are constantly calling us to wakefulness and *anamnesis*, or reminiscence, the constant discipline of bringing God to mind in the midst of our hectic lives. This focused and developed discipline is necessary if we hope to navigate daily life with all its distractions and competing allegiances. We will be victims of our scattered lives without this vital, spiritual discipline.

Look at our lesson. Wouldn't you have loved to listen in on this discussion? Well, in a way we can, through the consistent teachings of the Church for centuries that enshrined for us the Lord's teachings to His disciples—they taught us what He taught them.

But notice these two disciples of Jesus are blinded by the cares of their lives. Here they are, walking along with the Lord Himself, yet their eyes "were kept from recognizing Him" (Luke 24:16 NIV). Why? Well, because like us, they were blinded by cares and concerns.

By the way, this story also demonstrates an important point about how His followers can always truly recognize Him: He becomes known to us in the breaking of the bread.

Today: Christ reveals Himself to us in the breaking of the bread of the Holy Eucharist. We will know Him in the faces of those who break bread with us. We will know Him in the powerful liturgies where our life comes into focus and we are awakened to His presence among us in the Eucharistic meal. We will know Him in our world as we see His face in the spiritually hungry souls all around us.

Friday: John 1:35–52
Where Are You Staying?

"Most men lead lives of quiet desperation and go to the grave with the song still in them." —Henry David Thoreau

How many people reach middle age and experience a crisis? Unless we live with purpose and clarity, we will struggle with identity issues in a destructive way.

In our Gospel reading we see our Lord Jesus asking the very question and providing the very answer that will be our path to purpose and peace with our own mortality. "What do you seek?" our Lord asks (John 1:38).

If I am to struggle in a healthy way with my purpose in life and my fear of mortality, I have to wrestle with that question. Notice Jesus doesn't ask them *whom* they seek; He asks them a much deeper question. *What* do you seek? Stripping away all our delusions, what do we really want? What is our purpose?

These disciples answered well, asking Jesus, "Where are You staying?" (v. 38). In other words, we won't find answers to the fundamental questions of purpose and meaning on our own. We have to come to a place of humility where we can admit that we must go where Christ is in order to find out about ourselves.

The Lord gives us the second half of our healthy and life-giving spiritual journey when He tells these inquirers, "Come and see" (v. 39). No answers. No philosophy. No high-minded, esoteric concepts. He only offers the path of following Him in trust and hope. When we are with Him, we'll know not only Him, but ourselves as well. I will find my life's purpose, peace, and strength when I follow Him who is Life Himself.

TODAY: What do you seek? Hear the words of the Faith that Christ is risen and know that we don't find peace by following a philosophy or an idea or religious practices, but through knowing Him. If I am ever to escape a life of quiet desperation, it will be by embracing my true purpose in life—by following Him who has destroyed death and granted the world eternal life.

Monday: John 3:1–15

The Spirit Blows Where It Wills

Ah, the beauties of springtime!

BUT OH, THE HAY FEVER! For those of us susceptible to allergies brought on by pollen, spring is the season we love and hate. It seems every bit of pollen finds its way to my nasal cavities with the slightest breeze.

Yet I love this time of year, with its gentle wind and the spring showers that clean the air and cool the day. Just watching the breeze blow through the tree branches in my backyard is enough to put life into perspective.

No wonder Jesus uses this illustration with Nicodemus to explain how the Holy Spirit operates in birthing us into the new life of Christ. This new life isn't announced by a dramatic sign in the sky but, rather, will appear like the wind; you can't see it, but you sure can tell where it's been.

As a religious Jewish leader, Nicodemus comes to the Lord under the cover of darkness, out of fear for his reputation. He stumbles over the Lord's teaching that we must be "born of water and the Spirit, . . . born again" (John 3:5–8). Jesus focuses on Nicodemus' confusion as He confronts his inability to understand this basic teaching of Christ. Since Nicodemus isn't in tune with the moving of the Spirit, he misunderstands Christ's explanation about spiritual birth.

We too miss things that should be obvious to us. Without spiritual eyes, we won't be able to recognize the breath of the Holy Spirit as He moves in our midst.

TODAY: Have you felt the blowing wind of the Spirit in your life, that gentle breeze of God's refreshing presence meant to wake you up? You can, but it's going to take your willingness to shut out distractions and noise. You are called to live out the new life of being born of water and the Spirit.

Tuesday: John 2:12–22
The Zeal of Faith

What would Jesus do?

MANY TIMES IN JESUS' MINISTRY, He surprises us. We confront a Lord who forcefully cleansed the temple of commercial interests. His actions that day showed the power of appropriate zeal in making an important point.

The Lord and His family were in the city to attend the Passover temple liturgies, and Jesus finds business enterprises operating in the court of the Gentiles, a part of the temple reserved for offering hospitality to strangers, which was enshrined in the teachings of the Law. Yet the faith had become so exclusive and ethnic that there was no room for the Gentile seekers anymore.

The Lord took great offense at this breach of hospitality and drove out the moneychangers, prompting his disciples to recall the scripture that declared, "Zeal for Your house has eaten Me up" (John 2:17; see also Ps. 68[69]:9).

During the preparation of the Eucharist, the priest pours hot water into the holy chalice with these words: "The zeal of faith, full of the Holy Spirit." It is precisely our zeal and our warm love and devotion to the Faith that enlivens and fills the Church. Cold faith never survives the vicissitudes of life and cultural assault.

Faith is *supposed* to be practiced by those who are hot with the joy of new life in Christ. That's normal Orthodoxy, the kind of faith that survives from generation to generation. That's the zeal that produces purposeful faith and active participation.

TODAY: Is your faith hot, or is it cooling off in some lesser corner in your life? The Fathers tell us that only coal that gets separated from the fire goes cold and dark. All we have to do to rekindle that warmth is to nudge the coal close to the heat of God's presence and watch as it begins to glow again with the warmth of faith. Why not allow the Spirit to warm your heart until you light up with a renewed devotion and zeal for the Lord's house?

Wednesday: John 2:1–11
They Have No Wine

Obedience isn't easy

Let's count the reasons: It uncovers our need for growth. It reveals that we are not self-sufficient. It shows us we need to grow and mature and be more honest. Left to ourselves, we are either too easy or too hard on ourselves. The discipline of obedience brings me to reality, where I can clearly see both my weaknesses and my strengths without the polluting influence of arrogance and pride or shame and despondency. Obedience sets me free to see myself as God sees me.

In our Gospel reading, the Lord and His mother are at a wedding celebration, and the host runs out of wine. The Lord's mother alerts Him to this serious social breach of etiquette that will bring shame on the host and a cloud over the entire wedding feast. Some may be surprised by the Lord's response to Mary: "Woman, what does your concern have to do with Me? My hour has not yet come" (John 2:4). Yet here Christ's statement reveals the power of intercession. Ask and you'll receive—acknowledge your need for help.

"Whatever He says to you, do *it*," Mary said to the servants (v. 5). She was trained in this path by her years in the temple—when confronted with the angel's announcement about bearing the Messiah, she said, "Let it be to me according to your word" (Luke 1:38). She had practiced obeying, and thus she responded with obedience quickly.

This story also demonstrates the joy of obedience, which rewarded the master of the feast with the finest of wines. As difficult as obedience may be, the end result is always deeper joy and clearer sight.

Today: The Orthodox Christian path makes no sense without the spiritual discipline of obedience. This virtue is best exercised through a regular prayer life, consistent participation in the liturgical life of the Church, and a willingness to trust the direction of a spiritual father. These normal Orthodox practices lead to spiritual strength, joy, and peace, no matter what life throws at you. Follow the advice of the Theotokos and do whatever He tells you to do.

Thursday: John 3:16–21

Men Loved Darkness

. . . because their deeds were evil

WE INSTINCTIVELY KNOW, whether we acknowledge it or not, that when we are sneaking around, we crave the cover of darkness for our acts. That's why we do what we do in the dark.

Look at our reading. Darkness and evil have no real life in themselves but are the absence of the good. Darkness is the evidence that light is missing, and evil is the evidence that righteousness is missing.

The passage declares, "This is the condemnation," or judgment (John 3:19). An interesting phrase, don't you think? God doesn't keep a tally book in which He records all good and evil deeds. No, the judgment of God is simply that He shines the light of His presence on our world. We either recoil and run or embrace the light.

Our Orthodox life and discipline boil down to this question: How can we come out of hiding and embrace the light? To acclimate us to the brightness of His Presence, we attend Divine Liturgy, fast on appointed days, keep a prayer rule, read the lives of the saints, venerate the Theotokos, and mark the feasts. When we let the light shine in our hearts even when it exposes the darkness in us, we can be healed.

After all, being in darkness conditions our eyes for darkness, and when the light is turned on, we squint until our eyes become used to the light. The effort is worth it, however, because we are all rushing headlong to an unavoidable appointment with Him who is Light Himself. We'd better get used to it, or when we get there, we'll hate the place.

TODAY: If you're like me, your life is a combination of light and darkness. We need to allow the Light to remake us into His likeness so that when we are in His bright presence forever, we will experience it as joy rather than torment. This life is given to you exactly for this work. Don't waste it on anything less. We are called to be "children of light" (Eph. 5:8) and of the day.

Friday: John 5:17–24
Codependency or Communion?

Hey, that's not the real thing!

WHEN I WAS A POLICE OFFICER, we were trained to spot counterfeit money by being familiar with every detail printed on real money.

The enemy of our souls has a counterfeit for everything in the spiritual life too, and we are warned to be discerning. This can be seen clearly in the counterfeit of true communion, which is codependency. Codependency is a counterfeit for real relationships lived out in the mutual love of self-denial, modeled for us by the Holy Trinity.

True communion stands in opposition to the counterfeit version in three ways. First, communion is focused on others. In this passage, Jesus tells the people that the Son does nothing on His own, but only what He sees the Father doing.

Second, true communion is experienced when selfless love is offered. The power of true communion is like a good marriage: while you focus on your spouse, he or she is wholly focused on you. We don't worry about getting our needs met, because that happens naturally as a result of our communion.

Finally, communion always leads to discernment. Jesus says the Father "will show Him [Jesus] greater works than these, that you may marvel," because true communion always leads to deeper insight, clearer vision, stronger purpose, and unlimited spiritual strength (John 5:20). In true communion there is clarity, while codependent relationships are always self-centered. True communion sets me free to love even my enemies.

Today: As we continue to press out the deeper implications of the Resurrection of Jesus, let's become so familiar with true communion that we can spot the sickness of codependency a mile away. Let's use our best energies to commune with the Holy Trinity through the rhythm of Orthodox life. Becoming Orthodox on purpose means we enable ourselves to truly enter into communion with God and others.

Monday: John 15:17–27; 16:1–2

When the Counselor Comes

In the world, but not of the world

GOD HAS CREATED US for mature and life-affirming communion with Him and each other. This kind of mutual love, knowledge, and understanding creates peace, safety, honesty, and even confrontation without shame or lack of dignity. All this is so because God made us in His image to be made into His likeness, and He knows Himself as Persons in communion.

In today's Gospel reading, our Lord Jesus gives His disciples good direction concerning how the world will treat them after He's ascended into heaven. In many ways, our world doesn't know God, so Christians are a people without a country. And the greatest consequence of this lack of knowing God is a profound confusion about communion versus unhealthy codependency. Without clarity, that confusion will ripple through every relationship we have, blinding us and reducing all our relationships to selfish ends. This is counterfeit communion, but thank God that our Counselor, the Holy Spirit, has been sent by the Lord to teach, lead, and shape us so that we recognize authentic communion.

Let's not, however, delude ourselves into thinking that authentic communion is usually easy, comfortable, or pleasant. Jesus promises that this world, divorced from Him as it is, is so dysfunctional that it will hate those who are living in communion, precisely because this healing and wholeness reveals the brokenness of this world.

TODAY: Make your relationship with God your top priority, as the indispensable first step in having a good relationship with your spouse, your children, your family, friends, and co-workers. The good news is that God has sent the Counselor to the new community of the Church to make all this possible in your life.

Tuesday: John 5:30–47; 6:1–2
The Proof of the Pudding is in the Eating

Times do change

I COME FROM A GENERATION that considered tattoos suspicious. A generation earlier, my grandfather, a lifelong police officer, even said that tattoos were degrading. Today we call it body art and consider it a form of expression to be celebrated. Some folks, wanting to have it both ways, choose a small tattoo, to be edgy and conservative all at once. Times change.

Tattoos remind me that we can't keep up a facade of our preferred image to the world all the time, whether it's as a trendy fashionista, a wealthy business professional, or a devoted parent. We're going to get tired and caught off guard—we're going to slip up, and another less polished side is going to be on display when we least expect it.

Jesus Christ wasn't like this. He lived His life so transparently that those around Him, who were working overtime to hide who they really were, felt uncomfortable. His authenticity presented a stark contrast to the fictional selves of those in His orbit. His words confronted those fictional people with their own duplicity in living. They expected a Messiah who would confirm them in their specialness, and here was the very Son of God revealing their true selves instead.

In His love for them and in His loving attempt to wake them up, our Lord boldly says, "But I know you, that you do not have the love of God in you" (John 5:42). How does He know? Because He sees the real selves of those around Him, and He knows the image they are trying so hard to project isn't really them. The distance between fiction and reality always measures the spiritual sickness in us all.

TODAY: Where are you wasting energy and talent trying to hide who you really are? The faith "once for all delivered to the saints" (Jude 1:3) is available today for you, if you'll only channel your energy into following the path of spiritual maturity. Why not exchange the facade of the image you wish to project for the image of God you are meant to become?

Wednesday: John 4:46–54

Signs and Wonders

Step right up, ladies and gentlemen, see the most amazing sights you could ever imagine!

WE ARE DRAWN TO SPECTACLE, to entertainment, to the newest thrill. Indeed, we were created to experience a sense of wonder, and as I teach my daughters, God alone is worthy of the adjective *awesome*. If we draw closer to Him to satisfy our human hunger for awe, we will be satisfied. If we feed this human hunger with cheap substitutes, we'll go away hungry.

I can hear my mother's voice now: "No, you can't have candy before dinner, you won't eat right if you do." What was true about tuna casserole versus candy is also true of the spiritual food we consume.

In today's lesson, it might seem that the Lord was turning a deaf ear to the father's concerns, but there is more going on here. The moments in our lives of deep pain offer us unique opportunities to hear vital truths. The crowd around Christ was waiting to see something miraculous and entertaining, something that would offer a beguiling substitute for true repentance.

We are obsessed with being entertained, and we risk surrounding ourselves with so much noise that His still voice is drowned out by worldly spectacles and tricks. Yet there is hope. Our deafness to His voice can be cured by the wonder and beauty of the Faith, preserved and practiced in our Orthodox Church. Beauty will save the world. Yet it must be divine beauty, which comes from God and sets us free from sin, death, and Satan, and places us on the path of union with Him.

TODAY: Is your worship content empty of substance, or does it help you partake of transcendent truths? Are you willing to forgo the cotton candy of selfish titillation and embrace the deeper beauty of true wonder, or will you come to that fearful judgment seat of Christ unprepared, having allowed true beauty to escape through your fingers? Let's realize just what is at stake.

Thursday: John 6:27–33
Giving Life to the World

You are what you eat

OUR BODIES WERE MEANT for healthy food, exercise, and rest. Today's frenetic pace creates costly consequences for us all.

A similar reality is at work in our spiritual lives. A well-rounded balance of spiritual food is necessary if we are to have healthy and happy souls. While it is truly tragic that you and I destroy our physical bodies with junk food, our destructive neglect of our spiritual food has eternal consequences.

In our reading, Jesus confronts the Jews, telling them: "This is the work of God, that you believe in Him whom He sent" (John 6:29). Our first and foremost work for God is that we believe in Him. Of course, that isn't enough for this crowd. They want to see some sign or proof, and so they remind the Lord of the manna God provided their forefathers in the desert. Jesus agrees that yes, God fed the children of Israel in the desert, but He is now sending the true Bread from heaven to feed His children with the nourishment that satisfies eternally.

Our lives are made for balance. The broken world is set on upsetting that balance and sending us off on a binge that will not satisfy. But Jesus comes and says to us, "Whoever eats My flesh and drinks My blood has eternal life, and I will raise him up at the last day. For My flesh is food indeed, and My blood is drink indeed. He who eats My flesh and drinks My blood abides in Me, and I in him. As the living Father sent Me, and I live because of the Father, so he who feeds on Me will live because of Me. This is the bread which came down from heaven—not as your fathers ate the manna, and are dead. He who eats this bread will live forever" (John 6:54–58).

TODAY: What are you feeding your soul? Is it empty calories or the healthy diet of the liturgy, the lives of the saints, the Holy Scriptures, and the wisdom of the Faith? Why not start eating a balanced spiritual diet that makes your soul healthy?

Friday: John 6:35–39
Not Gluten-Free

. *With faith and love, draw near*

IN ANCIENT SOCIETIES, bread was *life*. The Old Testament explains that God fed the Israelites bread from heaven called manna (which means "what is it?"). In the New Testament, Jesus makes it clear *He* is the Bread from heaven sent to satisfy our deepest hunger.

In today's lesson, the Jews demanded that the Lord give them a sign such as their forefathers saw in the wilderness, when God fed them manna from heaven. However, the Lord knew that signs and wonders can reveal faithless hearts as well as convince folks to change their ways. He also made it plain to them that He is the Bread the Father has sent, and this is the last food we humans will ever need.

To access this food, we have to have the humility to abandon the notion that we are self-sufficient. We need to confess not only our hunger, but admit our inability to actually satisfy this hunger on our own. We avoid admitting this, instead medicating this hunger in our souls with all kinds of lesser foods that leave us unsatisfied and looking for more. No wonder we struggle with desires we don't know how to satisfy.

We must come to the end of ourselves and confess our need for Christ, the Bread of Life. He alone will satisfy our deepest hunger. It isn't a mistake that the imagery of bread is used now instead of a bloody sacrifice, since violence, sin, and death have been defeated by Christ, the Lamb slain before the foundation of the world. His sacrifice means now all we need is to embrace Him and hear the invitation from His Church: "With the fear of God, and with faith and love, draw near."

TODAY: What lesser foods are you consuming, trying to satisfy your soul hunger? The Faith once for all delivered to the saints provides a spiritual banquet of wisdom, insight, and satisfying nourishment, all coming from Him who is the Bread of heaven. All you have to do is have the humility to come and see.

Monday: Luke 9:1–6
Power and Authority

Real authority flows from service, not power

R EAL AUTHORITY IS BASED ON LOVE, not force—it's given, never demanded. Real authority is like respect: if you have to ask for it, you don't deserve it.

If that's the case, why do we have so much trouble with authority and power? It comes down to the twin illnesses of fear and pride that feed on each other.

What is the proper way to understand—and exercise—authority? In today's Gospel reading, the Lord gave the disciples power to heal and authority to preach. Jesus is the source of true authority; the disciples can't act apart from His blessing. There is no room for them to gloat, since what they are sharing is a gift from God.

Look what they accomplish. They heal as Jesus healed. They preach the message that Jesus declares. They become by grace an extension of Him in the places they go. They carry no provisions with them so that it is clear that they are trusting God for their needs. They even release any claim on demands of respect and power by not staying where they aren't welcome.

The community Christ establishes is based on power to heal broken lives and to share that power for good. There is no real power to do evil, since to do evil is to become a slave. Authority in the Church comes from service, not force or demands. This authority flows through the servant from the Master, who is the only authority in the Body of Christ.

TODAY: The same Spirit that was given to the disciples is also shared with you and me by virtue of our common chrismation in His Church. Nothing has changed since the days of the disciples; the world is still filled with hurting, broken people longing to find someone they can trust to lead them. Will we heed the call?

Tuesday: John 6:48–54
Unless I Eat What?

Receive me today, O Son of God

CHILDREN SEEM TO GRASP deep ideas with a matter-of-fact joy that all too often is just not possible for grown-ups. Kids haven't yet been jaded by disappointment, pain, and fear.

No wonder Jesus commanded us to be childlike, though never childish. Being childlike allows us the ability to feel wonder and amazement without having childish, immature attitudes as well.

In our Christian belief that the Eucharist is the Body and Blood of Jesus, we are called to embrace the childlike wonder of trust coupled with the mature focus on the mystery of relational communion that is the hallmark of authentic Christianity. Even sincere Christians sometimes reject this message due to a fatal misunderstanding of Scripture and a lack of connection to the historical faith. But the consistent testimony of the centuries of Christian teaching is that the Eucharistic bread and the wine *are* the Body and Blood of Jesus Christ. If we ask how this is so, we've already approached this mystery from the wrong end.

Jesus doesn't endeavor to explain this. He simply repeats the message and doubles down on its importance: "Unless you eat the flesh of the Son of Man and drink his blood, you have no life in you" (John 6:53). No explanation will ever satisfy His critics, and conversely no explanation is necessary to those who love Him. The scoffers will scoff, and the faithful will embrace His offering.

It really comes down to our willingness to crucify our own opinions and reasoning. Our desire for control has to be confronted and tamed as we step out in faith. At the end of ourselves, we can become ourselves.

TODAY: Do you approach the Eucharist thoughtlessly or with intellectual arguments? This mystery is given to you for your salvation. It is both a way to confront our spiritual blindness and an opportunity to respond to Christ's invitation to faith.

Wednesday: John 6:56–69
This is a Hard Saying

If it were easy, everybody would do it

MOST OF THE TRULY worthwhile efforts in my life have been difficult. We have no problem embracing those pleasant events and easy efforts that reaffirm us and make us feel good, but the second something gets tough, we must resist the urge to flee.

When the Lord's followers heard His eucharistic claims, the Scripture says that many of them "went back and walked with him no more" (John 6:66). The message about His Body and His Blood was too hard to hear, and they dropped out. That happens today—the message of communion confronts us, since we are fond of easy relationships and afraid of vulnerability. Authentic communion challenges our isolated lifestyles, our desire for significance without effort, and our fear of being discovered. But this is exactly what we need if we are to truly act as the Church, the new community that revives and heals all other communities.

For most of human history, people lived in the same place their whole lives. They grew up together, knew one another, married each other, and died together in villages, towns, and cities. Today we are free to move from one place to another, and the disintegration of the nuclear family, extended family, and communities is becoming commonplace. We hunger for this closeness and a sense of true community, yet find fewer opportunities to build community together.

TODAY: When you hear the challenging message of the eucharistic life of the Church, does it sound so difficult that it makes you want to throw your hands up and quit? Are you willing to at least make a beginning to embrace this shared life? Isn't it time we Orthodox once again discover the power and the blessing of intentional community that is based on our understanding of the Eucharist? After all, we are called to be in communion with each other and with God.

94

Thursday: John 7:1–13
My Time Has Not Yet Come

Timing is everything

I CAN'T TELL YOU how many times I've tried to force something to happen before it was the right time, and how many times that action ruined everything. Discernment is a virtue that becomes absolutely necessary for a mature Christian life. Discernment sets me free to live life at the proper pace and to be patient with others, knowing they are fighting a hard battle.

In our reading, Jesus created such waves with His ministry that certain leaders of His people were already trying to kill Him, but His time hadn't come. Even His kinsmen tried to manipulate Him to do ministry at a time that was all wrong. The Lord confronts His family with some straightforward words about God's timing.

There is going to be a time for this focused confrontation with the darkness of the world, but not now. There is going to be a time to die, but not today. There will be a time for His very public ministry, but it isn't at this time. The Lord's discernment meant He knew exactly when was the most opportune time to act and speak and when not to. This freedom allowed Him to do His eternal work of love and salvation in the most effective manner.

TODAY: Do you know when it's the right time to speak and act? Are you asking God for a spirit of discernment so the wisdom of your timing will be a help to you rather than a burden you bear? Perhaps it's time to seek the wisdom that flows from both humility and patience.

Friday: John 7:14–30
Join Him in the Fire

All has been provided for us

MIDWAY BETWEEN Pascha and Pentecost, the Church begins to tie together the two feasts with the teachings of our Lord Jesus in the temple. Today the Church has us read and contemplate a passage from St. John's Gospel. Jesus is teaching in the temple, speaking plainly and openly about how people react to Him: some desire to have Him killed, and others are confused about the Lord's identity.

Why is it necessary to understand the true identity of Jesus Christ? Because this is directly connected to how I understand my identity. If I know Him, I will know myself. Since I am made in His image, I best know myself when I know Him.

This is why Pascha and Pentecost are tied together. The revelation of the Resurrection of Christ with His complete victory over death and the gift of the Spirit to all humanity are theological mirrors held before you and me to show us who we truly are. We are persons meant to be God's eternal companions, connected to and sharing in His eternal life, filled with and consumed by His Spirit. We are made to be the companions of the three Hebrew children in the fire. We now join them in the furnace of God's unquenchable love and walk around in the fire with that fourth man. This fire does not burn us but purifies us.

Set your thinking on things above and stretch your soul to accommodate more of His grace and presence. We were made for higher things. Let us today reflect on the Resurrection and anticipate Pentecost. There is no grace withheld that could assist us in being truly free. God has emptied Himself into His creation precisely for this work—to make you His able companion.

TODAY: Set some time aside to think about these things. Be grateful that your Creator loves you so much. Give yourself over to His abundant mercy to transfigure you, your thoughts, your actions, your entire life. Today, know Him and you will know yourself. Today, let's get ready for the fire of Pentecost.

Monday: John 8:12–20
Who's Your Daddy?

"All by myself, don't want to be all by myself anymore."
—Eric Carmen

THIS SONG TELLS THE STORY of a young man all alone as he is stood up at the altar on his wedding day. Recently, a friend told me that when she speaks on college campuses the crowd really pays close attention when she says the word *loneliness.*

In addition to loneliness, there is a twin fear that we experience—the fear of being discovered. We're afraid of being alone, and we're afraid of being known.

In today's Gospel reading, the Lord confronts the religious leaders of His day: "You know neither Me nor My Father. If you had known Me, you would have known My Father also" (John 8:19).

We fear being alone because we were created in the image of Him who knows Himself as Persons in communion. We were made to be known and to know others. As Metropolitan Zizioulas says in his wonderful book *Being as Communion*, we can only know ourselves in the face of another. Real communion, however, is hard work and often doesn't come naturally.

We fear being discovered and known because, like our first parents in the Garden of Eden when they ate and discovered they were naked, we fear that our weaknesses will cause others to reject us. Instead, we employ defense mechanisms to keep others at bay. We say within our hearts, *If they see me for who I really am, they will not love me.*

Like us, the religious leaders of the Lord's day spent most of their energy hiding from God and each other. Thus they failed to see Christ for who He is; if they had known the Father, they would have immediately recognized the family resemblance in Jesus.

TODAY: Do you fear being discovered for who you really are? The Orthodox Faith helps us face these baseless fears and enter into the freedom of relationship with God and one another.

Tuesday: John 19:25–28; 21:24–25
Woman, Behold Your Son

"Woman, behold your son!" (John 19:26)

BEING RAISED IN THE SEVENTIES, my brother and I witnessed norms that were being challenged and changed. Yet even with the turmoil of societal shifts, one constant in my life was my mom. We were raised by a dear mother who was aware of the challenges of her day and did a marvelous job in bringing us up. Both my brother and I could have become statistics as boys raised by a single mother, but Mom would have none of that—she insisted we behave as men of honor and respect, and in turn, I have done my best to honor her.

Today's Gospel reading reminds us that the Lord of Heaven made sure His mom was cared for, too.

The scene is familiar to many of us—the Lord observes that His mother is standing as witness to her Son's bravery, love, and strength as He hangs on the Cross for us all. In the midst of the pain, struggle, and shame of the Crucifixion, the women have not fled from Him. As Mary's only child, Christ knows she'll need to be taken care of after His death. He entrusts His mother into the care of St. John, and in doing so, He gives her to us all in this act of filial love.

Ultimately, our Faith isn't a club, a philosophical construct, or a nostalgic habit—it is a family, fused together by love for God and one another. We are presented with many opportunities to mess it up. Yet this is still the only way to shape the communal love of God within us humans who are so prone to mistakes, missteps, and misunderstandings. We always fail in our faith when we reduce it to mere ideas. It is meant to shape our hearts, our homes, and our communities.

TODAY: Is your faith shaping you into a family member or merely a good person? Does your faith affect how you choose to live with those around you? Does the care Christ showed His mother from the Cross say something to you about your church family? Let's courageously face the reality that when we live as purposeful Orthodox, we will treat others as family members.

Wednesday: John 8:42–51

A Samaritan and a Heretic

It's bedtime

S HE HAD HER EYES CLOSED and her fingers in her ears. She kept saying, "La, la, la, la, la, I can't hear you." I had uttered the ancient and hated words, "Sweetie, it's time for bed."

In today's Gospel reading, we encounter childish denial, but it came from those who knew better. The Lord confronted the Pharisees with an uncomfortable and unwelcome truth—that the dividing line between the righteous and unrighteous has nothing to do with bloodline, culture, or even education. These items can contribute to righteousness and holiness, but they are not guarantees. And holiness has little to do with this or that interpretation of Scripture, either, nor with a specific religious practice or understanding of history or politics.

No, the dividing line between those who are truly righteous and on the path to life and those who are nowhere near that path lies within each human heart.

Before we chastise these religious leaders, let's remember that the Pharisees were a group who insisted on the full tradition of the Jewish faith. They were sticklers for knowing and obeying the Scriptures. They insisted on honoring the traditions of their fathers and to keep all the faith traditions of the past. In other words, if we met some of the best of these men, we would be impressed by their piety.

Yet the Lord says to these very religious men, "If God were your Father, you would love Me, for I proceeded forth and came from God; nor have I come of Myself, but He sent Me. Why do you not understand My speech? Because you are not able to listen to My word" (John 8:42–43).

TODAY: All the practices of the Faith are meant to grow our love for God. Orthodoxy isn't immune to the dangers of self-righteousness. Let's be sure this spiritual medicine is healing—not condemning—us.

Thursday: John 8:51–59
You Can't Say That!

Outrageous!

O UR LORD JESUS makes a somewhat inflammatory comment in today's Gospel reading, so much so that we can understand why the people immediately took up stones to execute Him. The Lord wanted to provide these religious leaders a final chance to be cured of their spiritual blindness, and His statement created exactly the stir He intended. Rather than another parable, this was a clear declaration of His Divinity.

Jesus made two such claims in this passage. First, He said that the father of the Jewish nation, Abraham, actually rejoiced to see the day when Jesus would come to his people and redeem them. In other words, Jesus was saying He was greater than Abraham. That would have been hard enough for them to swallow, but the Lord doesn't stop there.

No, He draws in the second great figure in Jewish history, Moses, by quoting the very words God spoke to Moses when calling him to his prophetic task. In Exodus 3:13–15, Moses asks God to tell him His Name. In response, God says, "I AM the Existing One" and instructs Moses to tell Israel, "The Existing One sent me to you."

In other words, our Lord Jesus communicates the truth that will forever upset the status quo. Christ is God incarnate, the promised Messiah. God came among His people as one of them, but due to their blindness, His own received Him not (see John 1:11).

TODAY: What illness of soul blinds you to the Lord's presence in your world? What barriers do you have in your own heart and life that keep you from embracing the reality that God has loved you so much that He has taken on flesh, just like your flesh, and has done everything to enable you enjoy eternity in His presence? All the disciplines, liturgies, icons, candles, hymns, chanting, architecture, writings, Holy Scriptures, and saints' lives are given by a loving God to acclimate you to His everlasting presence. Let's embrace all these spiritual tools.

Friday: John 6:5–14
How Will We Feed Them All?

It's impossible!

THE SUNDAYS AFTER PASCHA confront us with people in impossible situations, and in our Gospel reading today, one such situation presented itself. Jesus asked His disciple Philip, "Where shall we buy bread, that these may eat?" (John 6:5). Philip named a huge amount of money, the equivalent of eight months' salary for an average worker of the day, and confessed the impossibility of being able to feed these people. Yet the problem wasn't the need but the disciples' lack of faith.

Andrew piped up, "There is a lad here who has five barley loaves and two small fish, but what are they among so many?"(v. 9). It turned out that was enough in the hands of Christ. The Lord took what was freely offered in faith, and He made it more than enough. Everyone was fed, and the disciples discovered they had more left over than they started with.

Oftentimes when faced with financial need in our homes and parish communities, we make excuses for our lack of resources, insisting that we aren't able to properly honor the dignity of the Faith we say we love and believe. Rather than giving generously, we hoard our money. Brothers and sisters, these things ought not to be.

At the sending of the Holy Spirit, God empowered each follower of Jesus to do the impossible—to become by grace what Christ is by nature. In a world of people enslaved to their passions, there's a longing for those who will dare to offer their resources to the Creator and a desire to see God meet our needs, totally and lovingly. It only requires courage and faith. We have everything we need to follow Christ, and yet we are cowed into mediocrity by our fear.

TODAY: What do you have to offer Christ? Does it look so paltry and small that you are ashamed? Your Creator is waiting for you to dare to trust that what you offer is always more than enough when you bring it to Him. The God who makes the impossible possible will do as He has always done when we choose to believe and love Him above our own doubts and fears.

Monday: John 9:39—10:9

A Thief and a Robber

Real men don't ask for directions

D O YOU LOOK FOR SHORTCUTS when you drive to new locations? Sometimes they work, and sometimes they don't. But when it comes to our spiritual growth, we should never take shortcuts.

Unfortunately, we don't always see the value in the measured, hard work of a faithful life. "Why can't I just go to God myself?" we say, or "Jesus and I have our own thing going." The end result is a spiritual life that's more about using God as a feel-better drug. In turn, this perpetuates our self-centeredness, a quality incompatible with mature Christian faith.

Most of our problems begin by justifying our weakness and insisting we're fine; we say we can see, but really we are blind. If given half a chance, we cut corners in the spiritual disciplines, don't we? "Do I really need to go to church so much?" "Is all this pageantry really necessary?" We use so many excuses and resist so much, rather than embracing the timeless wisdom that makes saints out of men and women.

Instead of "have it your way" religion, we need to embrace the only way through Jesus Christ. In obedience to the Church, we find wisdom and freedom. As we give the truth its rightful first place in our lives, the Holy Spirit will guard and guide our souls safely along. In the Church we won't find shortcuts but tools for our salvation.

TODAY: What shortcuts are you trying to take in your spiritual life? How are you trying to avoid the necessary difficulties that are meant to help you grow in your Christian walk? The Church invites us to a holy confrontation that leads to freedom, not condemnation or shame. Let's embrace this spiritual calling and allow God to form us into who we truly are.

Tuesday: John 10:17–28
My Sheep Hear My Voice

Prove it!

WE ALL STRUGGLE with the fear that began in the Garden. Eve, our first mother, was talking to that old serpent, and the serpent said to her, "Has God indeed said, 'You shall not eat from every tree of the garden'?" (Gen. 3:1). The enemy knew that if he could introduce doubt into the heart of our parents, he could perpetuate this stubborn fear through our race and delay or even enslave us to a poverty of soul that leads to death.

Since love for God casts out fear, it has been the enemy's expressed and first desire to introduce doubt by impugning the character of the Father since the beginning. This is certainly his first weapon of choice in my heart—when I doubt the goodness of God, the sickness grows in my life.

Is it any wonder that many alive during our Lord's life on earth couldn't believe that He was actually the Son of God, that God in the flesh was dwelling among them?

The Lord directly confronts this human tendency to see and yet refuse to believe. Listen to this exchange between Jesus and those who are standing around Him in the temple. They saw His works, they witnessed His miracles. They heard His preaching and teaching and still refused to believe. With all the proof they needed right in front of them, they still wanted more.

That's sometimes the way with folks who demand evidence of the Incarnation—no matter how much you give them, it's never enough if they don't want to believe in the first place.

TODAY: A heart filled with fear requires proof, and fear has always been a lousy motivator for spiritual health. Spiritual disciplines, meant to increase godly fear, can lead to deeper slavery if we ignore the wisdom of the Faith. The fear of God is experienced as awe, not terror. That nuanced understanding can set us free from the debilitating fear that leads us to doubt that God is truly good and loves us. Let's be free of fear and demands for evidence.

Wednesday: John 11:47–54
You Know Nothing At All

And you thought your dreams were strange

HAVE YOU EVER HEARD of the story of the donkey that saved a prophet by talking to him?

Balaam, an Old Testament prophet of sorts, was headed out on a mission to curse the Jews when his donkey sighted an angel barring the way with a drawn sword. The donkey refused to budge, but since Balaam didn't see the angel, he eventually beat the donkey for refusing to move. The animal finally spoke, saying, "What have I done to you, that you have struck me?" (Num. 22:28). The poor thing was, after all, trying to save both their lives.

Even beasts will do God's bidding.

In today's reading, the religious leaders are at a loss regarding how to deal with Jesus' popularity. They are afraid the Romans may perceive the Lord's renown as a political threat to their military rule. These leaders' fear is understandable—the Romans had a reputation for dealing swiftly with the first sign of disruption.

The chief priest intervened in the discussion with wisdom from God, telling the leaders that one man should die to save the nation. Sound familiar?

Believing he was solving a political problem, the chief priest ended up cooperating with God's will. Even those who oppose God and His Church can be used for good in God's plan. We can now rest, even in difficult times— "all things work together for good to those who love God, to those who are the called according to *His* purpose" (Rom. 8:28).

God uses even His enemies to serve His ultimate purposes.

TODAY: All who oppose the Faith aren't abandoned; all who hate us aren't enemies. We can treat "all that comes to us today with peace of soul and with firm conviction that God's will governs all," to borrow the words of Metropolitan Philaret of Moscow. Let us embrace the purposes of our Lord, who loves us and gave Himself for us, and let us rest in His story for our lives. Don't be so clueless that a donkey has to talk some sense into you.

Thursday: John 12:19–36
Untying the Knots of the Fall

Quitting's easy

WHAT IF YOU KNEW that your most cherished desire, the very heart of the reason for your existence, was only achievable by passing through great suffering? Would you still pursue your dream? Would the payoff be worth the price? Let's face it—few worthy goals are cheap. Most great visions require immense sacrifice and perseverance in the face of naysayers and false friends. Along the way, we also struggle against our own fears and doubts.

In our Gospel reading, our Lord Jesus is at another pivotal moment. He begins to see that His goal is in sight but recognizes there is a terrible price to be paid. Yet this moment only confirms the road He must take to remake the whole universe.

Our Lord is coming closer to His last week of ministry before the Cross and is with His disciples in Jerusalem. The Scriptures say, "Now there were certain Greeks among those who came up to worship at the feast. Then they came to Philip, who was from Bethsaida of Galilee, and asked him, saying, 'Sir, we wish to see Jesus.' Philip came and told Andrew, and in turn Andrew and Philip told Jesus. But Jesus answered them, saying, 'The hour has come that the Son of Man should be glorified. Most assuredly, I say to you, unless a grain of wheat falls into the ground and dies, it remains alone; but if it dies, it produces much grain'" (John 12:20–24).

Did you catch that? The Greeks have asked to see Jesus. Our Lord knows that if the Gentiles are coming to Him, the time when the whole world will finally have the opportunity to enter into communion with God is approaching. The barriers between Jew and Gentile are about to be removed forever, and the doors of paradise will be opened.

TODAY: Are you able to discern the moments in your own life that confirm you are on the right path? Is your insight into your faith so generous, so wide, so expansive that it makes room for the whole world? Don't miss a single opportunity for growth, and allow this purposeful journey to transform, inform, and reform your thinking, attitude, and behavior.

Friday: John 12:36–47
While the Light Shines

Now where is that flashlight?

STUMBLING AROUND IN THE DARK isn't just a problem for me when I'm looking for a midnight snack—it's a perfect metaphor for when I live apart from the light and wisdom of the Faith. That light is a shield to protect me from bad choices and missed opportunities, and when I choose not to walk in that glow, I stumble as a blind man.

Being lost in the dark is wholly unnecessary, because Christ the Light has come. It's not that He is hard to find—we often don't look for Him in the first place.

In today's lesson, the Light mentioned isn't a set of philosophical ideas or a list of rules and regulations. This Light isn't even a religion. It is a Person, and this Person has come to reconnect us to the Father so that our entire lives will be filled with clarity, purpose, and direction.

Philosophy didn't bring people to Christ. The religion of the day actually turned most of the religious leaders against Christ. Keeping all the rules didn't make the Pharisees follow the Lord. Some did follow, but their fear made them silent.

No, they needed to walk in the Light of Christ. It was that simple—and that difficult.

TODAY: The Light that strengthens and heals us is here. Christ calls us to Himself each liturgy when the priest beckons us "with faith and with love, [to] draw near." His Light is His life embraced, accepted, and faithfully practiced by those who are tired of stumbling. In turn, those people become lights themselves as they reflect His Light to all around them. Are you able to assist those who are stumbling by lovingly offering them the Light that makes you free? What could you possibly accomplish in life more significant than that? It's time to allow the Resurrection of Jesus to so permeate your daily life that you become a light for all around you.

Monday: Luke 24:36–53

He is Ascended!

When you forget your "why," you lose your way

W
E
E
K

21

ANY TRADITION SUFFICIENTLY REMOVED from its source can disintegrate until it becomes mere superstition. If this benign neglect continues unchecked and uncorrected, the life-giving truth behind the tradition will be lost. Let's guard our precious Orthodox Faith so that it doesn't get reduced to the counterfeit religion of nostalgia.

In today's Gospel reading, we encounter the Lord's Ascension into heaven to sit at the right hand of the Father. In this passage, the Lord affirmed His physical presence, opened the minds of His followers to understand the Scriptures, and told the disciples to wait in Jerusalem until they received the power to carry out His commands. Then the Lord led His disciples to the place of the Ascension and, blessing them, He rose into the sky.

Please notice: Our Lord ascended physically. This reminded His disciples and, by extension, all those faithful who would follow of the beauty and dignity of the human body. Jesus took His glorified, human body to join the other two members of the Holy Trinity—there is a Man in heaven. Since we are called the Body of Christ, our bodies will also be transformed by our intimate communion with Him who is glorified and transfigured. Jesus ascended, not for Himself, but to show us our destiny in Him.

In the liturgy, as the priest processes with the Body and Blood of Christ *through* the people in the Great Entrance, so our Lord processed in His Body *through* the sky to inaugurate the sharing of His life to the whole world. Triumph over death is accomplished.

TODAY: Will you join me in beating back the shallow sickness of thoughtless repetition that leads to a counterfeit of the original beauty of our worship? Will you allow the truths of our Faith to actually change your behavior, your choices, and your very life?

107

Tuesday: John 14:1–11
Let Not Your Heart Be Troubled

Why are you able to keep your joy even during bad times?

WE CAN SPEND OUR LIVES waiting for that perfect time when everything's humming along, but the longer we live, the more disillusioned we grow, since that moment never seems to come. To be sure, there are days when all goes well. But why is daily peace usually so far out of reach? And how often do unexpected challenges come out of nowhere to throw us off balance? We can begin to escape this pattern of elation and discouragement by recognizing that life will always be this way.

In our Gospel reading today, our Lord Jesus instructs us to keep our hearts untroubled by external circumstances. He is spending His last days with the apostles before His Crucifixion. He washes the disciples' feet and gives them advice on how to live once He is no longer with them. Three insights help to grant untroubled hearts:

1. The Lord promised His disciples that the Father's house is open to them as their final destination. Christ knew His disciples were about to face the most terrifying time of their lives. They would have to endure His Crucifixion in all its distress and horror. Jesus assured them they would always have a home with Him.

2. The Lord reminded His disciples that God's Word is trustworthy. Knowing Jesus meant they knew God as well. The disciples' intimacy with the Lord was also intimacy with Him who made all things.

3. The Lord assured His disciples that God was with them. He emphasized that He and the Father work hand in hand, in spite of the disciples' questions and concerns: "Lord, show us the Father," "Lord, we do not know where You are going" (John 14:8, 5). The disciples would never lack God's presence because of their communion with Jesus.

TODAY: We can be a source of strength, hope, and love to others around us, since Christ has gone ahead to prepare a place for us. Our faith guarantees us an eternal heavenly home.

Wednesday: Matthew 11:2–15
None Greater

Pawpaw was my hero

M Y GRANDFATHER was such an impressive figure to me that I thought of him as something other than a mere human. He was an Atlanta police officer who would bring his police car home and let me sit in the front seat and turn on the blue light. Plus, Pawpaw was a captivating storyteller— we loved listening to him recall his adventures on or off the job.

People always need heroes—those larger-than-life figures brave enough, faithful enough, strong enough, and wise enough to overcome great obstacles.

Jesus said of St. John the Baptist: "Assuredly, I say to you, among those born of women there has not risen one greater than John the Baptist" (Matt. 11:11). In today's reading, things were beginning to turn against the Lord in His earthly ministry, and the first sign of trouble was the arrest of St. John the Baptist. This event made John question whether Jesus was actually the One he had been waiting for, so Jesus sends word to him that all the promises of the coming of the Messiah are indeed being fulfilled.

Christ also told the crowd gathered around Him that John was no ordinary prophet but the one who had been sent to prepare the way for the Messiah. St. John's ministry would bless the whole world by preparing the way for the Messiah, as the prophecies had declared. He's a hero for the whole world.

Jesus adds a word to you and me in His final statement. He tells us that everyone who participates in the Kingdom of Christ is greater, because they live in the fullness of the Lord's finished work.

TODAY: As we recall that hero of the Faith, St. John, we are encouraged to see that even though we may doubt, our story isn't over. If we can embrace the Kingdom Christ has established in His Church, we will enjoy the blessings of that eternal Kingdom to shape us, mold us, and grow us into His likeness.

Thursday: John 16:2–13
When the Spirit Comes

Hold on a second, is this what I signed up for?

SOMETIMES WHAT'S BEST FOR US isn't apparent in the middle of our journey. Only later do we discover that an event, though difficult at the time, was actually the best thing for us.

In the afterglow of the Feast of the Ascension, we live in that necessary tension between promise and fulfillment. We need patience if we are to mature into faithful believers and followers of Christ.

In our Gospel reading today, our Lord Jesus reveals to His disciples and to us that there are times we need to hold on through difficulties rather than always looking for rescue. There will come a time, He says, when those who persecute and even kill His disciples will think they are doing God's will. Yet the Holy Spirit will comfort and guide us in times of tension and waiting. His three areas of ministry in the Church are:

1) The Holy Spirit will convince the world of sin, which is not by definition just the breaking of rules, but spiritual illness. The Spirit enables people to realize that their disconnection from God is causing spiritual sickness and that a cure is available.

2) The Holy Spirit is multiplying His presence throughout the world in the people of His Church.

3) The Holy Spirit will make it crystal clear in His Church that the kingdom of darkness can't hold a candle to the Kingdom of Christ. The defeat of death is total and irreversible, and this victory is extended to everyone, everywhere. The Spirit proclaims Christ's victory over death to every generation.

TODAY: You were sealed with the gift of the Holy Spirit at your chrismation, through the authority that Christ gives His Body the Church. You possess the potential to participate in this threefold ministry of the Holy Spirit in the world, and you are called to do so. If you are willing to view hardships as opportunities for growth, then your life will shine light on everyone around you.

Friday: John 16:15–23

A Little While?

No guts, no glory!

IT WAS SUPPOSED to be a surprise, and it sure was. You see, I told her I couldn't make it to her recital. Her little face fell, and she was disappointed. But, at the last minute, my plans got changed, and I was able to come. You should have seen her face. Talk about lighting up a room with a smile.

It's amazing how quickly we can go from sadness to joy when the circumstances change. Of course, it's equally amazing how quickly happiness turns to tears as well. All of life is filled with moments when we turn on a dime, and our emotions instantly change. Some people play it safe with life so they don't have to deal with radically shifting fortunes. Yet with all the planning and safe living we can muster, life will still throw us curve balls that end up changing everything.

All I have to do is think about that moment when I encountered the Orthodox Faith, and I can tell you, it radically altered my plans for my life.

In our Gospel reading today, we discover another group of people whose lives were radically changed. Jesus puts His upcoming momentary suffering in perspective for His disciples, using the phrase "a little while." This gives His followers a measure of peace and confidence in the face of their terrifying loss. The Lord even likens this time of heartache to the experience of a woman in labor during childbirth. At the bedside of my wife when our children were born, I watched as sorrow and even fear melted away the instant our baby was put in her arms. What an apt word picture our Lord creates, then, in order to help His disciples endure the temporary emotions of grief brought on by Christ's death. In "a little while," He promises, sorrow will be turned to everlasting joy (John 16:16).

TODAY: What painful or disappointing moment do you face today? What real or even imagined horror tempts you to despair? The perspective of enduring a little while will give you strength. When you pass through your trial, you can help comfort and encourage others. Today, perspective will set you free.

Monday: John 16:23–33

Ask Anything

All you have to do is rub that lamp

IN THE OLD STORY OF ALADDIN, as well as other stories where genies grant wishes, people are ruined when they received everything they want.

How can we ask God for what is best rather than what's comfortable or selfish? St. James hits the nail on the head when he writes, "Where do wars and fights *come* from among you? Do *they* not *come* from your *desires for* pleasure that war in your members? You lust and do not have. You murder and covet and cannot obtain. You fight and war. Yet you do not have because you do not ask. You ask and do not receive, because you ask amiss, that you may spend *it* on your pleasures" (James 4:1–3).

The key to successful asking can be found in this phrase: "Whatever you ask the Father in My name He will give you" (v. 23). Learning how to ask the Father in the name of the Son requires a mature perspective that presupposes love, humility, and courage. Praying in the Lord's name means that because you love Christ more than your own ego, you've gained discernment, and you don't ask selfishly. God cannot be reduced to some kind of cosmic sugar daddy—He grants what is best for us eternally.

If our requests are selfless and centered around what will further God's will and God's plan, that's another matter. This kind of spiritual maturity and authentic Christian character produced apostles who could be trusted with the message of the Faith.

TODAY: Are you willing to become that Orthodox Christian who can ask anything? If you are, the path to that place of spiritual maturity and peace and joy is through the wise disciplines of the Faith laid out for us for centuries. Let's resist the urge to treat God as our own personal genie.

Tuesday: John 17:18–26
I Want to Go

I want to go with you!

IT DOESN'T REALLY MATTER where I'm going; my daughters love to tag along. That makes sense, because daddies buy candy. There's comfort in the presence of one who is strong and has a sure sense of direction. With such a companion, we feel safe and focused. However, we also need to love and trust our companion, or we will be fearful and insecure when the direction they lead us isn't of our choosing. When my girls realize Daddy is taking them on a trip where they will have to be quiet or sit still, and there's no candy forthcoming, then the tears start.

In today's Gospel reading, the Lord Jesus is about to face His Crucifixion, burial, Resurrection, and Ascension into heaven. The disciples see only a glimpse of this plan—once they fully realize where the Lord's journey is taking them, they are going to scatter.

You see, the disciples are not ready to enter into the Lord's greatest desire for them to "be made perfect in one" (John 17:23). They are going to have to pass through the crucible of the Lord's death, the unbelievable joy of His Resurrection, the awe-inspiring vision of His Ascension, and the empowering presence of the Holy Spirit at Pentecost before they can ever enter into the fullness of the Lord's prayer for them.

If we are ever going to be where our Lord is and see Him in His glory, we are going to have to build up our trust, confidence, and love for Christ so that we can stick with the journey even in the most difficult moments. We will need to walk the same path as the first disciples. In fact, it's in the hard places of our lives that we gain insight into our own immaturity and fear.

TODAY: The bumps in the road of discipleship are wonderful opportunities for self-discovery. Do you have a good relationship with a spiritual father to enable you to make the most of these moments? We were made to follow the Lord Jesus into heaven and be with Him in His glory, but this means we have to say goodbye to childish wants and fears.

Wednesday: Matthew 18:10–20
Radical Communion

Love at first sight?

R EAL LOVE HAS LITTLE TO DO with romantic feelings or Hollywood's happy endings. Love is costly—knowing and loving God has been the most difficult and rewarding work I have ever done in my life.

In a culture guided by phrases like "love means never having to say you're sorry" and "love at first sight," deeper, truer love seems elusive. Yet a fairy-tale understanding of love ultimately wounds us and wounds our children. Eventually, some people conclude that there is no such thing as love—or God.

What is true love? First, if we live in real communion with God and others, we will consider the lost sheep worthy of our efforts to find them. This selfless attitude flies in the face of worldly advice on love and happiness.

Next, true love is honest. If your brother wounds you, don't be passive-aggressive or fake. When people are in communion, a wound in one member of the body is a wound for the whole body. We need to do everything in our power to protect this bond of love. Go to that person and risk transparency.

Finally, what if the other person won't reconcile? Honesty and true love require that we tell the truth about reality. If the other is hell-bent on division, then we have to tell the truth and point out that he or she has chosen to truly be other from us. Christ promises that where radical communion is practiced, He is in our midst, adding His strength and His love to ours.

TODAY: Is your commitment to communion and true love calling you to some hard work today? The Feast of Pentecost celebrates the coming of the Holy Spirit to the Lord's Church, and now we live in the empowered presence of the risen Lord in our midst. You have all the strength and motivation to become a person who loves well and is willing to pay the price to build communion with others. Now all that's left is the hard work of applying this wisdom to your life.

Thursday: Matthew 4:23–25; 5:1–13
Blessed Are

Lazarus, arise!

A DEAR FRIEND OF MINE recently visited the final resting place of Lazarus during his Holy Land pilgrimage. That got me to thinking about Lazarus, his miraculous healing, and what happened to him after Christ raised him from the dead.

It is amazing that in this materialistic age, people still yearn for physical healing. We want to be healed, but we want it to happen instantaneously, miraculously, and without cost or discomfort. We want salvation to be the same, too: instant, painless, and free. Yet both our physical and spiritual health is never that easy to obtain—it comes about through faithful, disciplined actions.

Today's Gospel reading contains some of the most amazing actions and teachings of Christ. Jesus has been involved in three areas of ministry: teaching, "preaching the gospel of the kingdom, and healing all kinds of sickness and all kinds of disease" (Matt. 4:23). Of course, His fame has spread like wildfire.

Let's remember, though, that every person the Lord healed physically eventually died, just like Lazarus. Each individual whose body received a miracle still faced the mortality of his or her physical body.

That's why the Lord went on to give us the spiritual healing treasures of these divine Beatitudes. He reveals to us that physical healing is one thing, but a true and eternal healing of our inner lives is the healing that lasts forever. If you become what He described in this wonderful list of virtues and faithfulness, you will gain not only an inner salvation, but even your physical body will be caught up in His eternal life at the resurrection of the dead. Now that's what I call being healed, forever.

TODAY: Why not abandon the narcissistic desire for easy healing in favor of eternal healing that addresses your soul's deepest wounds? If you allow the power of the Holy Spirit to transform your inner life, your outer life will be changed. This is the only path that truly leads to eternal healing.

Friday: Matthew 5:20–26
Doing the Hard Work of Communion

Looking out for number one?

TODAY, WE ARE EXPERIENCING an epidemic of loneliness. Of course, we all should be capable of caring for ourselves, but as with all other virtues, self-reliance can be twisted so that we live in isolation.

We need the grace of God to heal us and set us free from the delusion of our own self-sufficiency. In light of our life in Christ, with the gift of the Holy Spirit and His power given to us by the Church, with all the spiritual tools given to us in our precious and timeless Faith, how can we regularly apply the wisdom of the Faith to help us heal from this spiritual disease of radical autonomy?

Broken relationships directly affect our communion with God and one another. Left unattended, resentment, bitterness, fear, despondency, and anger infect all our other relationships, setting up a pattern of self-protection and defensiveness that reinforces the very loneliness we fear.

One of the remedies for this downward spiral into loneliness is honesty and transparency. Deal with misunderstandings and arguments as quickly as you can after a cooling-off period. The Apostle Paul admonished his readers, "Do not let the sun go down on your wrath" (Eph. 4:26). Keep short accounts, especially with those closest to you.

By doing this you invite the grace of God into all your relationships; the Holy Spirit can bring healing and humility, enabling you to approach the eucharistic chalice with integrity and peace. At each liturgy the priest turns to the faithful to ask for their forgiveness. Broken relationships poison communion, and forgiveness sets me free to receive Christ in peace.

TODAY: Are you willing to take up the spiritual weapons given to you through your Orthodox Faith to do the work to restore the broken relationships in your life? In so doing, your reception of the Lord's Body and Blood will heal you and set you free from loneliness.

Monday: John 10:1–9
A Stranger They Will Not Follow

I felt miserable

WHEN I WAS FIFTEEN, my best buddies talked me into sneaking into a movie theater without paying. We didn't get caught. We loved the movie—we laughed and congratulated ourselves for our stealth. Yet the whole time, I could hear my mother's voice in my head: "Young man, you carry your family name. That should make you think twice about doing things you know you shouldn't."

We are all tempted to take shortcuts from time to time. Trying to work smarter—not harder—is a good thing, sometimes. Yet when we cut corners because we are too lazy or sneaky to do things the right way, we shortchange our own growth and improvement in the process.

The Lord warns us about this in our Gospel reading. Trying to achieve union with God through shortcuts or false methods doesn't work, because there is one tried and true path that always works. We ignore this at our peril. This isn't because God is trying to be difficult or elusive, but because the enemy of our souls is good at diverting our attention from our true goal and destination. And often, the enemy of my soul turns out to be me.

This is why Orthodox Christianity doesn't allow for other paths to God. Our humble confession is that we don't know where other paths may lead, but we do know the timeless path of Orthodoxy leads to Christ and the healing of our souls.

TODAY: Do you find yourself choosing spiritual shortcuts over the proven path? God wants to be found, dear one. He wants you to become by grace what Christ is by nature. He knows that there are many times we'll be presented with wrong turns, so He lovingly calls us to refuse any path that will lead away from spiritual maturity. Enter by the Door. Don't try to sneak in another way.

Tuesday: Matthew 5:33–41

Do Not Swear

Let your yes be yes

THE GOSPEL OF JESUS CHRIST confounds and astounds us. His radical message stands in stark contrast to worldly philosophy and reasoning.

In today's Gospel reading, the Lord powerfully contrasted two phrases: "You have heard that it was said" and "But I say to you." Often in His ministry, the Lord would teach that the old ways weren't the best ways.

"Do not swear," He says (Matt. 5:34). Let your words be true. Isn't it amazing what lengths we go to in order to convince each other we are telling the truth? We even place our right hand on a sacred text when we testify in court. But Jesus declares that our communication should be so straightforward that a simple yes or no is sufficient.

In another admonition, the Lord says, "You have heard that it was said, 'An eye for an eye and a tooth for a tooth.' But I tell you not to resist an evil person. But whoever slaps you on your right cheek, turn the other to him also. If anyone wants to sue you and take away your tunic, let him have *your* cloak also. And whoever compels you to go one mile, go with him two" (vv. 38–41).

The Lord desires to set us free from the slavery of scorekeeping and unending revenge. He asks that we release all temporary desires to set things right for the better life of liberty from anger and grudges and hatred.

The world considers turning the other cheek an act of weakness. In truth, it is an acknowledgement that we have no idea what lies in our enemy's heart. Jesus asks that we show mercy and forgiveness to all men. Even if my enemy kills me, He adds, he only can kill my body; he can't rob me of eternal life.

TODAY: Are you free from fruitless scorekeeping and plans for revenge? Can you truly say your life is peaceful and simple? Discover the joy brought about by this very peace and simplicity within you.

Wednesday: Matthew 10:16–22
Sheep and Wolves

If you want a guarantee, buy a dishwasher

THIS WAS THE ADVICE of a wise man when I was discovering the Orthodox Christian faith. He was responding to my questions about assurance of salvation and calling out my tendency to view my relationship with God as a business agreement. My selfish desire was to be pampered by God rather than transformed.

Following Christ isn't usually easy or safe. Remaining faithful to Christ and His Gospel in the face of an increasingly hostile society requires the courage of our convictions.

In today's lesson, we hear of sheep among wolves. Our Lord sent His followers out into a turbulent world, counseling us to be "wise as serpents and harmless as doves" (Matt. 10:16). It takes wisdom to be faithful to the truth while also embracing the people for whom Christ died, even those who oppose His message.

Of course that means those of us who remain faithful have to abandon the notion of safety or acceptance from this modern age. And we have to face the fact that our fidelity to the Faith will bring us into conflict with the prevailing powers of today. Are you ready to face that reality?

The Good News is that the Lord promises us that the Holy Spirit will give us the right words to provide a witness to the timelessness of the wisdom of Christ. Ultimately, it isn't about convincing others. It is about enduring to the end. Those who do so will be saved.

TODAY: You have been sent out into this world by Christ to witness to His love and saving grace. You aren't promised you will be popular, and you aren't promised you'll be safe. What you are promised is that you'll have the words you need and that your faithfulness will provide you with His presence in this world and salvation in the next. The only guarantee you have is that you will be opposed, but God will not abandon you. Don't allow the madness of the modern world to cow you into silence or submission to the shifting sands of fickle philosophies.

Thursday: Matthew 7:15–21
Know Them by Their Fruits

Caveat emptor! *Buyer beware!*

COMPANIES IN THE UNITED STATES spend over two hundred billion dollars on advertising and marketing each year. And do you know why they do this? Because it works.

The power of telling a story in a compelling way is essential if you want to perpetuate your message. However, no amount of slick marketing will overcome the weaknesses of a product. Eventually the flaw is discovered when customers find that the product doesn't deliver what was promised.

In our Gospel reading, our Lord Jesus warns us about false prophets. Jesus tells us that we will be able to distinguish the wolves from the sheep by their fruits (Matt. 7:16).

Today, wolves in sheep's clothing are everywhere. The best way to avoid spiritual delusion is to do as the Lord declares: Be aware. Be a student of the truth.

The ability to distinguish truth from falsehood needs to be cultivated. We need to continue in a diligent life of prayer and participation in divine services. Reading the lives of the saints helps us too, as exposing ourselves to the good fruit of their lives will equip us with the ability to spot the bad fruit a mile away. Our faithfulness then becomes the good fruit that nourishes those around us.

TODAY: Are you able to spot the false promises in the multitude of messages bombarding your life? Have you so internalized the words of timeless prayer, examples of the saints, and the power of Orthodox liturgy, so that you can recognize falsehood and help others who are also being bombarded with these false messages? Your diligence in prayer, faithful presence in liturgy, and study of Scripture and the biographies of the saints will strengthen your immunity to the deceptive teaching and beliefs of our present day.

Friday: Matthew 7:21–23
Intimacy with God

It's all about relationship

WHEN WE WORK TO LEARN, to grow, and to deepen authentic relationships, we are paid immeasurable spiritual and emotional dividends. No wonder our Orthodox Faith always emphasizes the importance of relationships in our growth as Christians.

An authentic relationship with Christ always has clear and unmistakable tells. Knowing about God through the acquisition of information certainly is helpful, but when we truly know God with any intimacy, it will impact our actions and priorities. This is the difference between simply knowing about Him, and actually knowing Him. You know this difference: it is like reading about being in love versus actually being in love, to the point that you can finish each other's sentences. This kind of knowing takes intimacy, time, effort, and desire.

How do we come to not just know about Him but to know Him? Intimacy with God is no different than building intimacy with another person. You have to invest yourself. You must first truly desire this kind of relationship with Him, and that desire builds as you come to know Him. After desire comes investment—an investment of priorities, time, and sacrifice. You have to so prioritize this intimate relationship so that it gets your best efforts, your time, and your focus. Just like any relationship, you have to work at it.

Our Orthodox Faith has been building this type of salvific intimacy with God for centuries. What have we learned? We've learned that a daily prayer rule works. We've learned that fasting keeps our desire for God pure and focused. And we've learned that generosity through almsgiving breaks the back of that destroyer of intimacy and closeness, our own self-sufficiency.

TODAY: Do you know God in this way? All the wisdom of the Faith is meant to foster this kind of intimate relationship with God—the liturgy, the prayers, the hymns, the candles, the incense, the vestments, the movements, the rhythm of the year, the disciplines, the Scriptures, the theology. We want to know God so well that the family resemblance is unmistakable.

Monday: Matthew 5:14–19
Diluted Medicine

"You are the light of the world" (Matthew 5:14)

IT GOES WITHOUT SAYING that diluted medicine isn't as effective in curing disease as the full-strength version. I know this from personal experience—I tried watering down my medication once when I couldn't afford a new prescription. So much for that experiment.

Diluted medicines don't heal our physical diseases, so why do we suppose that diluted spiritual medicine can heal our inner lives?

In today's lesson, Jesus doesn't say we should *try* to be the light of the world, or *attempt to be* a city that can't be hidden. He simply declares that His true followers *will be* these things.

You see, your fidelity to the Faith and your active participation in the life of the Faith makes you the light of the world. And this purposeful Orthodoxy provides spiritual medicine for others at full potency, rather than presenting people with a diluted version that doesn't have the strength to save, heal, and guide.

TODAY: Have you ever wondered why some find it so easy to abandon the Orthodox Church? Could it be that they have been inoculated by a diluted witness of the Faith? How sad that we insist on potent medicines for our physical ailments but accept watered-down medicine for our souls. Truly, we must be willing to go to Him who offers us the full potency of wisdom, faith, and love. As the light of the world, we are to attract wounded people to the only city that safeguards the medicine needed for their healing.

Tuesday: Matthew 9:14–17
A Better Way

We are not speaking the same language

I FELT THIS WAY RECENTLY when I was discussing an important topic with someone. The other person and I had different backgrounds and perspectives, and I was frustrated that he couldn't see my point.

All of us are shaped by our past and personal opinions. We will either try to bully others into seeing things our way, or we will work to understand where the other is coming from and then agree on our common ground. This latter path is certainly harder and more time-consuming, but love demands nothing less. Much of our modern discourse seems to take the former approach; this will not end well for any of us.

In today's reading, Jesus declared that His very presence is everything. The Lord confronted the foundation of the religious system of His day through the common religious discipline of fasting. His disciples didn't fast the way John's disciples and the Pharisees did, and that was causing conflict.

Jesus told them that the problem wasn't fasting but rather the motivation and the timing of the fasting. The coming of Christ initiated what St. Paul called "a new and living way" (Heb. 10:20) that transforms the discipline of fasting. Rather than fasting out of mere habit, the faithful fast to participate in the deifying work of God. We fast not to please God, but because by training our desires we are empowered to become like our Lord. On the Last Day, the family resemblance will be unmistakable.

TODAY: Why are you an Orthodox Christian? Is it out of habit or the happy accident of your birth? Are you beginning to realize that this living way of Christ opens up a new life of faith? The new wine of this radical message of communion and transformation is not going to fit in the old wineskins of thoughtless habit. But if you have courage and humility, you'll find that the Spirit will truly make you into His new creation.

Wednesday: Matthew 9:36–38; 10:1–8
Too Much To Do

Is all this activity really accomplishing anything?

I SOMETIMES WONDER about all our modern busyness. Is this abundance of activity really necessary, or are we running from something? Just looking at our family schedule makes me want to hide from all the deadlines and appointments.

We all need to ask if our to-do lists align with our cherished life goals. Do we even know what those life goals are?

In our Gospel reading, our Lord Jesus chooses twelve disciples and reveals the steps they need to take in order to form the proper goals and priorities.

Before we can escape the trap of purposeless busyness, we first need compassion—the ability to see beyond ourselves and our own feelings and desires to consider others and their needs.

Compassion allowed the Lord to view people with selfless, caring vision. Those around us are "weary and scattered, like sheep having no shepherd" (Matt. 9:36). When we act from compassion rather than out of our expectations for others, when we cease to judge others and their actions, we are liberated from our self-centered thoughts and more able to see others' struggles and motivations. Remember the old saying? "Walk a mile in my shoes, and then you'll understand."

Our insight into people and our compassionate perspective will motivate us to action. The Lord tells His disciples, "The harvest truly *is* plentiful, but the laborers *are* few. Therefore pray the Lord of the harvest to send out laborers into His harvest" (Matt. 9:37, 38). There are so many around us today who need kindness and understanding. A plentiful, potential harvest of people for the Faith awaits us; so many are longing to be transformed by love and truth.

TODAY: Do you have the spiritual maturity to govern your use of time to align with eternal priorities? Let's use the precious, dwindling gift of time to become harvest laborers. Let's allow our Faith to truly shape our lives.

Thursday: Matthew 10:9–15
Shake the Dust Off

Nothing worked

I ONCE HIT A BRICK WALL in a relationship with someone. I tried everything: being nice, apologetic, funny. I tried being nonchalant, and I even tried being brutally honest. Everything I tried ended up making things worse. I didn't get it, was I really that ineffective?

Well, in this case, yes I was. I reluctantly concluded that I was not going to be the one to break down the wall between me and this other person.

The Lord knew about times like this. He cautioned His disciples that they were not going to succeed every time. When they hit a brick wall in ministering to someone, they had a choice: to keep beating their heads against it or move on. So move on, the Lord said.

How do we know when that time has come?

First, we should humbly realize that success isn't up to you or me. We are servants. We need to avoid the savior complex, because we can't and don't save the world. There are people we won't reach, and that's okay. Humility is so important: only God never fails.

Second, remember that you and those around you are truly free. As I was making my spiritual journey toward the Orthodox Church, a wise man told me, "You aren't free to say 'yes' until you are truly free to say 'no.'" The gift of human freedom means we must respect another person's freedom as much as God respects our freedom. He never forces Himself on anyone, and we shouldn't either.

TODAY: There are going to be times when you have to shake the dust off your feet and move on, but that isn't a failure. In fact, it proves that love and humility have won the day. If we can allow the Spirit to develop a peaceful calm in our hearts, then our prideful desire to be indispensable to people will melt into the freedom of love. With that freedom we are able leave all the results to God, who loves all of us more than we, ourselves, know how to love. Is it time to shake the dust off your feet with some people or situations in your life?

Friday: Matthew 10:16–22
Be Saved

Called to be, not to do

IT TOOK OVER A YEAR OF CATECHISM and then many years after that for me to complete the journey to the Orthodox Faith.

One catechism class was particularly eye-opening. We were told, "God is *being*, not doing; you are called to be a human *being*, not a human *doing*." My purpose wasn't to expend my time and energy reforming my behavior. No, it wasn't a self-help program that was needed to reform my behavior, my choices, and my priorities; it was a change of heart. My heart only needed to be so transformed that I discovered my true nature as a *being* created in God's image.

In our Gospel reading today, the disciples were tasked with carrying the message of the Good News of the Resurrection. But this message was going to be seen as a threat to the status quo, and there would be trouble. This same Good News is still challenging us today—when we make our faith the top priority of our lives, we are sure to face difficult consequences as a result.

In the face of persecution and rejection, the disciples were not told to do something but to *be* something: aware, fearless, trusting. A wise person doesn't just observe facts; he or she is awake to the challenges that come from being in the world, but not of it. In difficult circumstances, we can't allow fear and doubt to cause us to forget that God loves us and will be faithful. That awareness should govern our attitudes and actions.

TODAY: The practice of your Faith will help you be like Christ from the inside out. You were created to *be*, not just *do*. The *doing* is always the natural consequence of *being*. Don't settle for some self-help pep techniques; tap into the real transformation offered to you through a purposeful relationship with the uncreated God who made you to be like Him. Remember: "He who endures to the end shall be saved" (Matt. 24:13).

Monday: Matthew 10:23–31

You Are More Valuable

That hurts my self-esteem!

S OME SAY THAT current educational practices have created a "snowflake" generation in which every young person feels special and is emotionally delicate. The underlying philosophy of this approach is motivated by the best of intentions, but by attempting to correct a perceived flaw in our system, we have made matters worse. Nurturing self-esteem now takes precedence over other more important educational goals.

In today's lesson, we learn about the true source of healthy self-esteem.

Christ told His disciples to go everywhere spreading His message. He warned them they will be persecuted and driven from town to town. The disciples should understand that this rejection of Christ's message revealed the spiritual poverty in the world and shouldn't be taken personally. Opposition shouldn't discourage or dissuade them or crush their self-esteem.

After all, we are not to fear that which can merely kill the body. Doesn't our Creed declare the resurrection of the dead? Isn't the central message of our Faith the destruction of death by death? Therefore, our greatest threat to our true selves comes from anything that enslaves us to the fear of death.

Your Father sees every sparrow that falls to the ground, and you are worth more than many sparrows. In fact, even the hairs of your head are numbered by the Lord who knows you. This is where your real self worth lies—in your intimate connection with your Lord.

TODAY: No amount of self-esteem education will free us from our deepest fears. Only the esteem that flows from Love Himself will ever set us truly free to be who we really are. That is where our best and most purposeful work needs to be and where we will discover our true uniqueness.

Tuesday: John 14:21–24
Do You Love Me?

What's love got to do with it?

IF WE GET THE DEFINITION of love wrong or if we fail to constantly strive to fill up our understanding of love, the consequences can be disastrous. We can fall for a caricature of love and destroy our lives chasing after a false version of it.

We were made to know true love in our lives. In fact, the Faith insists that we understand God as Love Himself. Without real love, precious friends, you will never truly know God.

The Lord insists that the natural result of true love is obedience. But what is it about obedience that demonstrates our love for God?

First, obedience stems from trust. Fear of punishment can deter us from doing wrong, but you can't love someone you fear. When we love God, we trust that He wants what is best for us. This trust increases my love for God, so it's a positive cycle: obedience flows from trust, trust encourages obedience, and obedience grows love.

Second, obedience results in faithfulness. When we truly treasure the wisdom of God and love our Lord, we expend the energy, time, and resources to preserve and propagate His Word from generation to generation. Our greatest desire is to pass our devotion to God down to our children. A faithful person is an obedient person.

Finally, obedience creates communion. Eventually a branch becomes so like its tree trunk that one can't really tell the two apart. In obedience, I am moving in symphony with God so that the family resemblance is obvious. This is exactly what we Orthodox Christians mean by *deification*. Our love draws us deeper into the restoration of God's image within us.

TODAY: Do you love God enough to commit to greater devotion to Him through obedience? Do you desire to hold more of God's presence in your life? Perhaps now you can see why we must always be encouraged to a life of repentance and a growth in spiritual maturity.

Wednesday: Matthew 11:2–15
Without a Doubt

"Doubt is not the opposite of faith; it is one element of faith."
—Paul Tillich

IN READING THE PSALMS, I find great heroes of the faith questioning. The Psalmist asked why the wicked should prosper while he suffered and struggled.

People regularly come to me struggling with doubt. Some are in great distress, thinking their momentary doubt has offended God or undermined all their spiritual efforts. Of course, I remind them that no one can disturb God or cause Him discomfort. And when you pass through doubt, you are stronger than ever.

St. John the Forerunner, jailed because of his unflinching and bold message of truth, is in prison facing execution. In the face of this pressure, he wonders, "Am I wrong?" (see Matt. 11:2–3).

Jesus tells the men sent from John, "Go and tell John the things which you hear and see" (Matt. 11:4). Philosophy and mere intellectual arguments never overcome doubt without the aid of evidence of God's work in the world.

Second, Jesus teaches that doubt melts when the people witness changes in their own lives due to following Christ. The Faith isn't a spectator sport; we are meant to practice the Faith, because that unleashes its transformative power.

Finally, doubt melts in the face of knowing our identity. Our Lord reaffirms St. John's identity as the promised Prophet tasked with preparing the way for the Messiah. The reminder of his true identity eliminated his struggles with doubt.

TODAY: Are you struggling with doubt and fear? What are you allowing yourself to see? What are you doing to practice your Faith? Doubt doesn't become a spiritual disease until it's allowed to make its home in your heart and blind you to the evidence of God's goodness all around you. Your faithful practice of the Faith through prayer, fasting, and generosity will eventually dispel doubt. Don't allow these moments of doubt to last for a lifetime.

Thursday: Matthew 11:16–20
Why Aren't You Making Me Happy?

Petulant child

I WATCHED A MOTHER attempt to placate her toddler during his tantrum. Nothing seemed to work. He wanted the toy, and then he didn't want it. His mother gave him a treat; he threw it down. She held him; that didn't work. She was at a loss, and the look of frustration in her eyes was heartbreaking.

In our Gospel reading today, we see that petulance and perpetual adolescence aren't new. How do we stop the cycle of emotional immaturity once it starts? There is no easy way. If we want to walk on the straight path and leave selfishness and immaturity behind, we will always need to practice true repentance. "Godly sorrow produces repentance," noted St. Paul (2 Cor. 7:10).

Authentic repentance doesn't come about just because we feel badly that we've done wrong. No, true repentance always calls us to deeper spiritual maturity. It requires that I acknowledge that my attitude and actions are disordered and harmful. This is only possible if I have the humility to look into the recesses of my own heart.

Next, repentance calls me not merely to look at my disordered and wounded thinking, but to move beyond regret to action. Repentance insists that I allow the grace of God to reshape my mind so that I acquire the mind of Christ.

Finally, repentance transforms me so much that I become an example for others.

Look at the Lord's wisdom in the last statement He makes in today's reading: "But wisdom is justified by all her children" (Luke 7:35). In other words, wisdom is shown by deeds. We can argue with one another until we are blue in the face, but until we humbly learn how to live a life of repentance, we will never be a source of wisdom for others. As St. Isaac the Syrian declared, "This life is given to you for repentance. Do not waste it on vain pursuits."

Today: Let's say goodbye to childish ways and embrace the mature lifestyle of repentance.

Friday: Luke 1:1–25, 57–68, 76–80

Come to Prepare the Way

You might not know their names

YOU'VE MET THEM BEFORE. They aren't the center of attention, but they have the knack of recognizing where talent lies. They are the scouts who see the unusual skills of a young ball player, the acting abilities of a high school actor, the leader potential in the club president. There seems to always be a forerunner who clears the way so that the great leader who follows is able to succeed.

This was true of our Lord Jesus. Our Gospel reading describes the circumstances surrounding St. John's birth and miraculous naming, giving us a hint of what is to come.

God, working through the centuries before the coming of the Lord, had already established His *modus operandi*—time and again, He granted children to barren women. And the Lord had also given significant attention to the naming of the children who had a major role to play in our salvation history.

St. John's birth was another instance of God's wonderful habit of bringing about the seemingly impossible. We serve the God who created the universe, and it's good to be reminded of that regularly. As St. Luke declares in this very first chapter of his Gospel, "For with God nothing will be impossible" (Luke 1:37).

TODAY: St. John the Baptist served as the forerunner to the Messiah, fulfilling the promise God made to His people long ago that a prophet would come to blaze the trail ahead of the Lord. What people do you know who are ready to hear and embrace the life-changing message of faith? Are you able, by God's grace, to prepare your family and your home for the coming of the Messiah? Let's be available to Him. In turn, He will enable us to continue the ministry of St. John the Baptist in our world today. Follow in the steps of the blessed Forerunner.

Monday: Matthew 11:27–30
Take This One; It's Lighter

Come you who are weary

W HEN I WAS A BOY, my brother and I would visit a farm. I enjoyed seeing how chickens eggs were gathered and cows milked, but my favorite site was the mule, yoked to a plow.

The unending series of life challenges can make us feel like we are yoked to plows. There are times when the weight of the plow slows me down, when I simply square my shoulders and push on ahead. And then there are times when I just drop the whole thing and throw up my hands in despair.

Jesus tells us that there is a better way to deal with the burdens of life. In our Gospel reading today the Lord offers to lighten our burdens.

First, knowing God puts life in perspective, allowing us to release the mistakes of the past and the worries of the future.

Next, knowing Christ allows us to become like Him, and He is "gentle and lowly in heart" (Matt. 11:29). When we relinquish our expectations for Christ's perspective, we learn the way of mercy and patience and love. Jesus never carries the heavy burdens of false expectations or superfluous opinions.

Finally, the Lord's yoke is light because He lives to serve, not be served. He loves without expectation, and He doesn't carry the burdens of trying to accumulate worldly goods or acclaim. When we aren't focused on our selfish desires, we can entrust our lives unto Christ our God.

TODAY: Are your burdens too heavy to bear? The Faith once for all delivered to the saints offers you a trade. Accepting a purposeful life lived by the wisdom and disciplines of the Faith is much easier than going it alone in arrogance. Christ says, "My yoke *is* easy and My burden is light" (Matt. 11:30). Let your soul rest in Him.

Tuesday: Matthew 12:1–8
Freedom's Just Another Word

The land of the free and the home of the brave

THE SEARCH FOR FREEDOM is at the heart of most of human history, and the desire for it is ingrained in us. We were created in the image of God, the source of true freedom. God is beyond being and non-being because He creates being—now *that's* freedom.

But what is freedom? Is it the right to do anything I want to do? Try that and see how free you end up. No, freedom is the joy of becoming who you are in the light of who He is. All other pursuits toward false versions of freedom lead you to a dead end.

In our Gospel reading, our Lord Jesus is trying to communicate this message to the religious leaders of His day. He is criticized because his disciples plucked some grain in a wheat field on the Sabbath, a violation of Sabbath law. The Lord attempts to get past the stubborn blindness of these religious leaders and their unforgiving slavery to mere rule-keeping. "I say to you that in this place there is *One* greater than the temple," He says (Matt. 12:6).

Of course, the Lord refers to the very Incarnation of the free and uncreated God, who is standing right there in front of them offering them the freedom they have traded for something less. He asks them—and us—to give up our illusions and embrace authentic communion and freedom in Him. Learning how to embrace that path of true freedom is the only work you and I will ever do that is truly worth our best efforts. All of your gifts, all of your time, even all of your resources were given to you to learn this way of life.

TODAY: As we sing patriotic songs, shoot off fireworks, and grill hamburgers on the barbecue, let's have the courage to see beyond mere political freedom to the freedom offered to us by our God. Let us take the path of disciplined formation that teaches even our very bodies how to acclimate to that place of freedom we are all moving toward, and let us become Orthodox on purpose. Having done the hard work of becoming free, we will someday be able to join in speaking out these powerful words of Martin Luther King from our hearts: "Free at last, free at last, thank God Almighty, I'm free at last!"

Wednesday: Matthew 16:13–19
Who Do You Say that I Am?

First principles are important

FOR INSTANCE, if you don't build your life on the fundamental truth that when you say "God" you mean the Holy Trinity, you will wind up with a god who is too small. First principles are absolutely necessary in building strong foundations. Our Gospel reading lays out a significant first principle that is foundational for those of us who embrace the Christian Faith.

Our Lord wants to drive a critical, essential message deep into His disciples' hearts, so He asks them, "Who do men say that I, the Son of Man, am?" (Matt. 16:13).

The disciples give a variety of answers about the popular beliefs of the people of the day. Then the Lord asks the key follow-up question: "But who do you say that I am?"

"You are the Christ, the Son of the living God," answered Simon Peter, indicating that he understood this first principle (v. 16).

If we are going to successfully navigate our lives based on more than immediate stimuli, we need to know our first principles. An unexamined life ends up nowhere. The first principle of the Lord's identity reorders everything for us. If Jesus really is the Son of the Living God, then His promise that the gates of hell won't prevail against the Church is solid and true. You can build a real life on this solid foundation.

That's why the fight through the centuries has always been about the Lord's identity. The enemy has always tried to water it down ("He was a good man") or encourage the denial of His existence. If the Lord is who He says He is, then the Church is what He says she is. To the extent that my life is in harmony with this wisdom, I will be safe.

TODAY: Are you pressing out this significant first principle in your life? Are you willing to unpack the meaning of the identity of the Lord and His Church and its consequences for you? If you are willing to wrestle with this revelation, this first principle, you can watch as amazing formation begins to occur in your own life.

Thursday: Matthew 9:36–38; 10:1–8
He Gave Them Authority

Sheep without a shepherd

THIS ORTHODOX CHRISTIAN WAY is often the opposite of everything this modern world tells us and contradicts all the accepted ways of getting ahead to achieve happiness. Plus, if you do try to live out this life, you will constantly be misunderstood, seen as a threat, dismissed as a crank or a fanatic, and treated like an outsider.

True life looks crazy to a world gripped by the fear of death and existential angst. In this upside-down world, those who cooperate with the Spirit in an attempt to turn it right-side-up again look insane.

In today's Gospel reading, our Lord looks out over the crowd following Him. "But when He saw the multitudes, He was moved with compassion for them, because they were weary and scattered, like sheep having no shepherd. Then He said to His disciples, 'The harvest truly *is* plentiful, but the laborers *are* few. Therefore pray the Lord of the harvest to send out laborers into His harvest'" (Matt. 9:36–38).

How do we minister to this upside-down world as our Lord did? We need to operate from a place of deep commitment to the Faith and sincere humility, acknowledging our own spiritual sickness and hunger. This approach will create compassion in our hearts for those around us who are still gripped by the spirit of the age and the fear of death. We will truly desire true freedom and peace for those around us. Then we can pray with the Lord for laborers to reap the plentiful harvest of those who are seeking Christ and His Church. Regularly I ask myself: Am I simply going through the motions? Or am I truly and deeply moved with compassion, even for those who have wronged me?

TODAY: An honest diagnosis of your own soul always precedes true spiritual healing and growth. Today, make an appointment for confession. Sit quietly before your prayer corner and examine your own heart, not dwelling on this or that external matter. Meditate on what you've been given and then determine in your heart to do that which in the eyes of this world doesn't make sense: give your time and treasure away.

Friday: Matthew 10:1, 5–8
What Do You Mean?

The art of communication

EVERY DAY, we send multiple verbal and nonverbal messages to the people we encounter. Just the other day, my wife and I were enjoying a conversation in our home. As she was talking, a matter of concern in my ministry work came to my mind. It was something completely unrelated to our conversation. My facial expression changed, and my wife concluded I was upset about the subject we were discussing. That's the complexity, and the power, of communication.

In today's Gospel reading, the Lord gave His disciples some specific directions and then reiterated to be certain He wasn't misunderstood. He communicated clearly so they would grasp the importance of the task He was sending them out to accomplish. Go and preach and serve, He told them—go specifically to the lost sheep of Israel, those dear ones who have many spiritual advantages but grasp none of them.

It is critical that we who claim to follow Christ are clear about the central message of the eternal Kingdom. He has told us to go and proclaim our Faith to those who are open to the truth.

While sharing the message of the Gospel with authority, we also must remember that we are called to serve. Heal the sick, raise the dead, relieve the suffering of others: this is the task the Lord has given the Church. Often, we've reduced the Church to a social gathering or a school of self-help lectures, and our vision is too limited. People drift from the Church because we haven't done a good enough job of communicating our message in word and deed.

TODAY: All kinds of people are seeking the Kingdom of heaven, and we will have to be creative in using tools both old and new to communicate our message in a clear and compelling way. Let's never be confused about our main purpose and our chief calling.

Monday: Luke 1:39–49, 56
Blessed Are You Among Women

It is truly right to bless you

Let's look at our Gospel reading for today, where we read about the meeting between Mary and Elizabeth. Both women experienced miraculous pregnancies. Elizabeth got a taste of what is freely offered to all on the Feast of Pentecost, when she was filled with the Holy Spirit. Thus, her words were inspired by the same Spirit who was the inspiration for Holy Scripture. Three blessings follow:

Blessed are you among women. If I can put this in Southern slang—Ain't never been a woman like you, ever, and ain't never gonna be another like you.

Blessed is the fruit of your womb. This is far superior to that fruit that Eve ate in the Garden of Eden, for this fruit reverses the damage caused by the Fall.

Blessed is she who believed. In His desire to make us like Him, God allows us to freely participate in His love. We must choose Him, as Mary chose Him.

Our passage today reveals why Mary occupies a unique place in the Church. Elizabeth makes an astounding statement, coming as it does from the wife of a Jewish priest who knew the Scriptures, theology, and the warnings against idolatry in Jewish tradition. Filled with the Holy Spirit, Elizabeth calls her younger cousin "the mother of my Lord" (Luke 1:43).

Mary the Theotokos (or "God-bearer") deserves to be held in the utmost esteem and honor for her faithfulness, her devotion, her piety, and her love. Her title tells us why we honor her this way: in her womb, God Himself took on flesh to redeem all of humanity. To diminish her is to diminish Him and to diminish each other too. We are called to do exactly what Mary did: open our hearts so that Christ can be formed in us.

Today: For twenty centuries, Christians have asked for Mary's intercessions as the obedient mother of our Lord. Let's imitate her example by saying yes to God. Then henceforth, all generations may call us blessed as well.

Tuesday: Matthew 13:3–9
Good Ground

A sower went out to sow

THE GIFT OF DISCERNMENT and wisdom to see clearly comes through effort, attention, and years of experience. If we will be wise, we must be willing to be taught and patient enough to endure life's lessons.

How many times have you heard the parable of the sower? Yet this passage still holds power, because it teaches us about the acquisition of true wisdom.

The sower expects and desires a harvest. He wants the seeds he plants to grow and to produce. We too, desire to be productive—we are created in God's image, so naturally we desire the same things He does.

However, the seeds fall on all kinds of ground. God offers His love to all no matter who they are—to hearts ready to receive Him and hearts hard and stony. God the Sower spreads the seed not for His benefit—of course He already knows what kind of soil each heart contains. God spreads the seed liberally so we will learn the nature of what ground lies within us. And as we become wise, we will also develop discernment so that we can see where the most productive soil lies.

If we are willing to prepare the soil of our hearts through disciplined and focused attention to proper priorities—purposeful practice of the disciplines of the Faith and humble repentance and confession—we will be able to be that good soil where the seed of God's love, His Word, finds a hospitable home to grow and produce good fruit. As an added benefit, we will also learn to discern where the good soil is around us so that we can encourage good fruit in others as well.

TODAY: Do you cultivate good soil and encourage the growth of God's grace within you? The treasure of our timeless Faith, with all its necessary spiritual and physical tools, is available to you so that the Sower's seeds will produce good fruit. The Divine Liturgy, the prayers, the Church calendar, and Holy Scripture and Tradition all act as God's soil preparation so that you can be wise and discerning in your life. Let's turn over the soil of our hearts.

Wednesday: Matthew 13:10–23, 43
Dull Hearts and Heavy Ears

Glory to God for all things

WHY IS IT SO DIFFICULT at times to see God's purposes and plans for us? Life can be frustrating, confusing, and scary; when we are told that God is testing us, we aren't encouraged.

God knows the end from the beginning. He sees every consequence to every potential decision I could make from the biggest choice to the smallest. The God we adore is a God beyond being—He is the cause of being. He is beyond existing, and He is the cause of existence.

In today's Gospel reading, we learn God already knows all about you. There is no mystery to God about who you really are or who you could become. God even knows the number of hairs on your head.

What's the problem then, and why is it so difficult to know His will? Well, you don't know *yourself*. You don't know what you're capable of or what you are meant to be—you don't know your truest self.

Make no mistake, dearest, you need to know yourself—for your own benefit, not God's. Unfortunately, we don't always attain self-knowledge easily. How many times have we heard good advice and then promptly ignored it?

So our loving and gracious Lord places us in the midst of good, bad, and everything in between. Then we have to make choices and decisions, and we are forced to set our priorities. This, in turn, reveals to us who we really are and where our souls are most gripped by fear and slavery to our passions.

In this way, we mature, develop, and become who we really are.

TODAY: Are you willing to learn about yourself? The whole of the Faith is meant to bring you to the place of spiritual maturity where you can learn who you really are so that God can restore His image in you and make you into His likeness. Your whole life is meant to bring you to that glorious place.

Thursday: Mark 5:24–34
Your Faith Has Made You Well

Who touched Me?

In today's Gospel reading, a woman dying of a hemorrhaging disease came to Christ. No one had been able to help her.

She said to herself, "If only I may touch His clothes, I shall be made well" (Mark 5:28). She was hoping to stay anonymous, unnoticed and secret, yet she did that which always gets God's attention—she believed. Her faith changed everything, and generations of faithful Christians have heard her story.

When the crowd finally noticed this poor woman, the Lord used it as a teaching opportunity. "Daughter," He said to her, "your faith has made you well. Go in peace, and be healed of your affliction" (v. 34).

Here are several things to notice:

The connection between faith and love cannot be stressed enough—love makes faith deeper, while faith makes love stronger. Mere assent to religious philosophy always fails to rise to the level of true faith and love.

Christ tells the woman, "Your faith has made you well." Faith heals. Someday she will die, but her faith has brought her eternal health.

After the Lord heals us, he sends us into a hurting and broken world. We become His ambassadors for healing and peace. From that moment on, this woman shared her story with others. "Let me tell you about the day I met Christ."

Today: You are going to encounter Christ. You are going to meet Him in your prayers, in a pleasant conversation, over a meal with a friend, or perhaps even in a painful confrontation. Somehow, you are going to meet Him today. The only question is, will you recognize Him? Will you have the courage to say, "If only I touch the hem of His garment"? When you meet Christ today, have faith.

Friday: Luke 6:17–19; 9:1–2; 10:16–22
Your Name Is Written in Heaven

My car is stolen!

ONE DAY, MY HIGH SCHOOL FRIENDS played a practical joke on me and hid my car while I was at work.

I panicked. I looked everywhere while my friends pretended to help me look. Did someone steal it? Should I call the police? Thankfully, they didn't make me wait long before revealing their deed. They enjoyed a big laugh as they thought about those moments when they knew something that I didn't.

We love to be privy to secrets, don't we? We feel special and privileged.

In our Gospel reading today, the Lord Jesus was teaching a crowd of people who wanted to touch Him in hopes of receiving healing. The Lord then empowered the disciples to heal the sick and cast out demons to multiply His ministry.

The disciples were energized—honored, but also endangered by their excitement. Jesus rejoiced that their communion with Him and their obedience to His commands was enabling them to minister. But He also corrected them, reminding them that their real joy and source of power and self-worth lay in their connectedness to Him. If they lost that perspective, they risked the sin of self-righteousness and pride, undoing their good work. The real joy was having their names "written in heaven" (Luke 10:20).

TODAY: What is your source of self-worth? Where do you rejoice in your life—your career, education, accomplishments, or your children? Your relationship with God should be such a priority in your life that you draw your self-worth from that vital connection. He is the source of joy that will bring healing to every other relationship you have. Hidden knowledge might make you feel special, but the best things should be given to everyone.

Monday: Matthew 13:36–43

What You Have Here Is Weeds

"He who has ears to hear, let him hear." (Matthew 11:15)

EVERY TIME I'VE TRIED to create a garden, it has ended up overrun by weeds, eaten by critters, over- or under-watered. I just don't have the proverbial green thumb.

There is something significant in how often the Lord used gardening and farming illustrations when teaching us how to be faithful followers. Remember, the first job God gave our father Adam was to tend the garden.

Our Lord interpreted the parable of the weeds for His disciples by telling them that He is the One who is sowing seeds of His love and wisdom in the world. The good seed is those who hear and embrace the invitation of the Lord, while the weeds are ones who choose their own way. Ultimately, the useful seeds will survive, and the weeds will be burned.

We notice that weeds are growing side by side with healthy plants. The weeds and the good seed are growing side by side in my own heart, so I shouldn't judge others.

The Lord made clear that this state of affairs will not last forever. There will be a day of harvesting, and the Lord's angels will deal with the weeds. Christ used this apocalyptic language to wake us up and get our attention— we need to take our sin seriously.

Finally, the clear and unmistakable difference between the destiny of the weeds and the righteous is obvious. Both are going to be consigned to their proper place: one group to the fire of the furnace and the other to a place where they will "shine forth as the sun" (Matt. 13:43).

TODAY: Are you wakefully tending the garden of your life by embracing with joy the wise pathway of the Faith? Such treasures are readily available to you to help you deal with the weeds in your life now, while we still have this life to do so. When that time of harvest comes and we stand before the awesome judgment seat of Christ, will we have been good farmers? Let's care for our plot of land.

Tuesday: Matthew 13:44–54
The Treasure in the Field

Hunting for hidden treasure

EVERYTHING THAT IS MOST VALUABLE in our lives takes work. We have to learn to prioritize the most important things over the less important things. Being disciplined enough to do that is the main characteristic of a spiritually mature person.

In our Gospel reading today, first notice that it is out of *joy* that the man who found the treasure goes and sells all he has to buy the field that holds the treasure. It isn't fear or obligation or even sterile knowledge that motivates us to prioritize our faith above all other things in our lives. That joy flows from the ability to properly value this treasure. Too often we forget that our faith is the greatest treasure. Subsequently, we find it easy to allow our faith to fall from its proper place at the top of our priority list.

Notice also, it makes absolute sense for us to place our faith at the top of our list. After all, it has eternal worth. Once we assign it the proper valuation, everything else in our lives falls into its proper place.

Finally, those who have learned to discern their priorities have been properly trained for the Kingdom of heaven. These servants are wise enough to know how to use both old treasures and new treasures to enrich their lives with eternal values and wisdom (see Matthew 13:52).

TODAY: Are you wise enough to value treasures of faith old and new? Do you recognize the true value of your faith and practice it with proper dedication and a commitment to learn more? Make no mistake, the Kingdom of God is worth whatever price you have to pay in order to properly possess and enter into it. Your relationship with God and His Church is the greatest treasure you possess and the greatest inheritance your children will ever receive from you, by far.

Wednesday: Matthew 13:54–58
Because of Their Unbelief

Jealousy is the tribute mediocrity pays to genius

THERE IS NO OTHER VICE that destroys personal ties as completely as jealousy. But what is its source? Jealousy is caused by our feelings of fear and pride when we compare ourselves to others. It is the desire to even the scales of perceived injustice when we believe we've been treated unfairly or received less than we deserve. Many of the Fathers of the Faith warn against its soul-destroying effects.

St. John Climacus said, "Some people with a hot temper do not worry about it and ignore the remedies that would heal them. They forget, unfortunately, what is written: 'Surely anger kills the fool, / and jealousy slays the simple'" (see Job 5:2).

In today's Gospel reading, the Lord Jesus faced the jealousy and fear of His hometown.

Jealousy and envy are rooted in a lack of faith. When I compare myself to another and am envious of his or her achievements, insights, or gifts, I imply that I am afraid that my gifts and achievements aren't good enough—in other words, I doubt the grace of God for my own life. Insecurity and unbelief effectively block my ability to develop and grow my own gifts. I am frozen in my envy and jealousy, and it consumes my own soul. St. John Chrysostom rightly observed that "as a moth gnaws a garment, so does envy consume a man."

TODAY: Are you jealous of someone else? Does your heart ache with envy over someone else's achievements, gifts, abilities, and insights? Stop! Recognize that the jealousy and envy are secondary emotions driven by root causes. Discover those root causes and avoid this dead end. Let's rejoice in God's goodness to us and flourish in that place where He has planted us. We weren't meant to compare ourselves to anyone other than Christ.

Thursday: Matthew 14:1–13
They Kill Prophets

Master or servant?

W E ARE CALLED TO BATTLE and tame the passions. So, then, what are the passions? Some may think being a passionate person is a good thing, but it depends.

In the mentality of the Church Fathers, passions are forces in our lives that can ruin us—feelings, desires, and entrenched habits that have a strong grip on us and bend us to their wills. We frequently suffer from the consequences that result from giving in to our passions. A traditional list of such passions includes gluttony, lust, avarice, anger, despondency, envy, vainglory, and pride.

Look at our Gospel reading and discover the dangers of untamed passions. The story of the beheading of St. John the Baptist offers us a powerful warning about the dangers of unbridled passion. Herod was mastered by his passions—that's the nature of them, when they are untamed. They enslave and master us, when the truth is, God made us as masters of the passions rather than the other way around.

Father John Chrissavgis wrote, "Passions are our inner sounds, those deep marks in the space of our heart that require healing . . . our passions indicate not so much that we are doing something wrong, but that we are not in control" (*In the Heart of the Desert*). In other words, it's not so much that we're doing bad things or thinking bad thoughts but that we aren't in the driver's seat. Just like a powerful, beautiful horse can't do good work when it is wild, so our passions, meant to be our servants, run roughshod over us when we don't discipline them. What was meant to serve us destroys us.

Our Faith is geared to training us in how to tame these passions so that they will act for our good and not our destruction.

TODAY: Are you learning to master your passions? Let's watch as these passions are transformed into wonderful servants who usher in freedom and joy. The path to mastering them isn't easy. Hard work and childlike trust are needed. It's time to ask the Holy Spirit to enable you to be who you really are, not as the passions make you appear.

Friday: Matthew 17:24–27; 18:1–4
Childlike or Childish?

"Unless you . . . become as little children" (Matthew 18:3)

The great twentieth-century thinker Aldous Huxley once said, "Children are remarkable for their intelligence and ardor, for their curiosity, their intolerance of shams, the clarity and ruthlessness of their vision."

Of course, adults know that with maturity comes the ability to see life's nuances. Complexity sometimes means we have to adjust our desires, our timetable, and our behaviors.

But is it possible to exhibit the good traits of children while maturing into responsible adults?

In our Gospel reading today, the Lord used something as mundane and despised as taxes to teach Peter and the disciples about this powerful paradox of mature childlikeness.

Through this practical example, the Lord taught us how to keep the best of both worlds and grow in faith.

As adults, we learn to exercise the power of our will. We choose to be responsible and, in so doing, create a pattern of choices and behaviors that allow us to be at peace with our responsibilities. It is through letting go of our child*ish*ness that we grow up as leaders, examples, and trustworthy guides to the next generation.

But we are also called to hold onto the child*like*ness that allows us to retain the qualities of wonder, hope, and love. We are called to be like children in our dependence on God as our heavenly Father and provider. In truth, only by keeping the best parts of childhood will we ever be able to grow up and accept the responsibilities of adulthood.

Today: Are you able to cheerfully shoulder your responsibilities? Yet have you also retained the joy of life and an innocence concerning sin? Holding in tension the best of both of these stages of life is a key that enables you to embrace a purposeful Orthodoxy. A lifelong practice of the Faith is meant to help you stay childlike while also helping you to grow up to be Christlike.

Monday: Matthew 15:12–21

What Makes You Unclean?

Clean hands and hearts

ALL TOO OFTEN, people miss the connection between the physical and the spiritual dimensions of life.

To be sure, anyone stubbornly wedded to a solely scientific, materialistic worldview will certainly downplay or even dismiss any notion of a spiritual life. But how can we Christians miss the relationship between the physical and spiritual worlds? Our entire Faith hinges on the Incarnation, where God Himself married the physical to the eternal. For Christians, there is no division between the physical and the spiritual. Consequently, our worship has always been physical: we use candles, incense, icons, vestments, movement, bread, wine, oil, and water. We never allow that old and false division of the physical and the spiritual to enter into our understanding of the world.

In today's Gospel reading, the Lord Jesus drives this point home when He explains a parable to His disciples.

The Lord considered the Pharisees blind guides, not because they taught a strict observance of the Laws of Moses and Torah (especially the dietary laws), but because these Pharisees had forgotten the *why* behind the wisdom of the Law and the Prophets. They had forgotten that the purpose of all this wisdom was not just to clean the skin but to cleanse the heart. He was calling them out for divorcing the spiritual and physical from one another.

TODAY: Let's remember that God intends for us to truly clean our insides as well as our outsides. Our timeless Christian faith marries the physical and the spiritual aspects of life. There's no point in following the rules while remaining broken and self-centered in our hearts. God became flesh for us in our Lord Jesus, forever joining the physical and the spiritual.

Tuesday: Mark 5:24–34
The Wisdom to Know the Difference

"Youth is wasted on the young." —George Bernard Shaw

YOUTH HAS GREAT STRENGTH and potential, but when we are young, we are still too immature to take full advantage of our possibilities. When we gain the wisdom of years, we have less energy and time to take full advantage of our hard-won insights.

Yet—both in youth and old age—each of us incarnates our common human nature in an unrepeatable way. There isn't another you out there. How sad that we clutter that beauty with mundane passions and habits that slow us down and get us off track.

Our fallen world often threatens to reduce and empty our lives of uniqueness and mystery. But God has another path for us, one that leads to spiritual maturity and joy.

In our lesson, the woman touched the Lord with faith. In this amazing encounter, Our Lord was so aware of His own person that He knew someone had touched Him. His wakefulness about His own life allowed Him to be completely aware of His surroundings and the people around Him.

The woman with the issue of blood also possessed something powerful when she realized that her internal illness could only be solved by internal work. Ultimately, she was willing to make a desperate choice and risk everything. Perhaps because of her suffering, her life coalesced in a moment of faith and action that brought light, healing, grace, and power.

TODAY: Are even your moments of suffering becoming gifts to your life, revealing the powerful potential of your faith? If so, you are growing up instead of merely growing old. Learn to embrace this spiritual journey, knowing your unique person is meant to be both fully alive and mature so that you will be able to enjoy being with God forever. Do this, and you will not only witness your own transformation, but the grace of your faith will spill over to everyone around you.

Wednesday: Luke 4:22–30
A Prophet Without Honor

Familiarity breeds contempt

"HEY, I KNOW THAT BOY. I've known him my whole life. Who does he think he is?"

I was preaching one of my first sermons, and a family friend who'd known me since I was a baby was a bit put out by my sermon topic. I don't even remember what it was now, but I do remember his easy dismissal of my thoughts, simply based on the fact that he had watched me grow up.

Why does familiarity sometimes breed contempt? We are uncomfortable around events and people that challenge our sense of normalcy and equilibrium. But sometimes our normal world needs to be disrupted.

The Lord was familiar to the people who had known him from childhood. This was a stumbling block to them and caused them to ignore His powerful message. They were so disturbed by His words that they actually tried to kill Him.

What was His message? The same message he'd proclaimed elsewhere: "Repent, for the kingdom of heaven is at hand" (Matt. 4:17). Yet they were so blinded by their prejudice against the hometown son that they refused to accept His words. Sadly, the Lord told them, this barrier of mere familiarity would keep the very people who had been given this spiritual treasure *first* from holding this treasure forever. Their comfortable knowledge of the Faith became a stumbling block. They were so convinced they knew the Faith that they missed its fulfillment when it was right under their noses.

TODAY: Do you really know the Faith or are you just so comfortable with its trappings that you have become numb to its message? If you are confronted by your spiritual poverty in a way that disturbs you, don't resist that moment. If you have the humility and courage to embrace the momentary discomfort, you may discover a depth in the treasure of your faith you never really knew existed. What is merely familiar may become brand new all over again.

Thursday: Matthew 16:6–12
Spiritual Germs

Pride goes before a fall

IN 1546, ITALIAN PHYSICIAN and scholar Girolamo Fracastoro first suggested that unseen germs were the cause of infectious diseases. Centuries later, this theory was proven accurate.

Over and over again, we've seen a correlation between our physical world and our spiritual lives. Since physical diseases are caused by unseen germs, it stands to reason that there are also spiritual diseases caused by small things that grow into big problems.

In today's Gospel reading, our Lord Jesus used the common practice of baking bread as the perfect illustration to show that the "leaven of the Pharisees and the Sadducees" causes spiritual illness. You can't see it—it works inside the heart, and it makes one unable to enjoy intimacy with God.

So what is this leaven? The Sadducees were the elite and educated ruling class of Jesus' day. They were skilled in administration, in politics, and in diplomacy. The Pharisees, on the other hand, were meticulous observers of Jewish law. Yet both shared a common weakness and blind spot that festered in their souls. Russian Orthodox believers call it *prelest*, or spiritual delusion leading to pride. Both the Sadducees and the Pharisees were proud of their virtues and thus undid all their good works through their lack of humility.

We don't need to fear being educated or avoid pious and meticulous practice of the Faith. But we do need to remember that all good things come from God. The best way to avoid the sins of the Sadducees and Pharisees is to regularly partake of the Holy Eucharist. Through Holy Communion, we receive antibiotics that destroy the germs of pride.

TODAY: What daily practice keeps you focused on the truth that it is God who has given you your very life? Let's remember that God has given us this day. He has given us the breath we breathe. Thankfulness and gratefulness kill the germs that sicken the soul. No wonder the Church keeps the gift of the Lord's Eucharist as the central vision of a healthy Christian life.

Friday: Luke 8:1–3
They Provided for Them

God will provide

IS THIS A GOOD AND TRUE SAYING? Perhaps, but there is also a danger when we forget that while God does provide, He does this through people.

The Lord and His disciples were always focused on doing what they were called to do: bringing the Good News about the Kingdom of God. Surrounding them were their traveling companions, who believed in their mission so much that they provided for the disciples' needs out of their means.

We must remember, dear ones, that if we see a need and offer kind sentiments while withholding a remedy, we only practice half of our Christian Faith. It is so very good that we feel compassion, sympathy, and even empathy for those in need, but that is just the narthex of faith.

We mustn't stop there. We must see ourselves as God's hands and feet on the earth. St. Paul calls us the Body of Christ—we are His continued physical presence in the world, and He uses us to provide what people need. Each week, God feeds us with the precious Eucharist. He takes our work—our bread, which we have mixed, kneaded, shaped, sealed, and baked, and wine we have prepared—and fills it with Himself. This is what God does with all our offerings we bring to Him to provide for the work of the Faith. That's why being stingy creates such a small soul in a man.

TODAY: Do you believe in the continued ministry of Christ in His Church to provide for the disciples' needs out of your means? Do you see yourself as an active member of the Body of Christ, or are you a spectator? The truth is we have all the resources we need to accomplish everything the Church is called to accomplish. We never have a money problem; our challenge has always been a faith and love problem. Perhaps today is the day to decide that I am part of His work to provide.

Monday: Matthew 16:24–28

There's No Profit in It

We're not in Kansas anymore, Toto

MY CATECHIST IN THE ORTHODOX FAITH had just explained that the concept of paradox was not only a comfortable and necessary tension within Christianity, it was expected. This was something completely different for me, yet it somehow rang true. When we desire peace, invariably conflict is given to us. When we desire acceptance or belonging, we may face rejection and isolation. When we crave hope, we are given a hopeless situation to teach us.

I look back and realize that moments of pain and loss in my life have placed me at a crossroads of choice. Would I abandon the path or would I draw strength from that moment, thus receiving the very virtue I thought I was missing?

In today's Gospel reading, Jesus made it clear that the message of Christian faith is nothing less than the turning of all our expectations upside down. We live in a dog-eat-dog world in which we are counseled continually to look out for our own interests. Yet our salvation is found is adopting the exact opposite attitude.

Jesus reminds us if we try to save our lives, we'll lose them. But if we lose our lives for His sake, we'll find our lives again. We get what we need in life by passing through the door of its opposite. This profound bit of wisdom is both a comfort and a challenge—a comfort when I'm passing through a tough time in my life, and a challenge when I am ignoring the voice of the Lord.

TODAY: Your current struggles hold great potential for your spiritual growth. The most difficult circumstance you face is packed with glorious potential if you can see past the fear and pain toward the gift that waits for you. Do you see how this knowledge removes all the sting and fear even when our circumstances are dire, and instead fills up every challenge with God's grace? No tear is wasted, and no pain is worthless.

Tuesday: Matthew 17:10–18
They Could Not Heal Him

I need to speak with your supervisor

SOMETIMES WHEN YOU ARE WORKING with others and you encounter an obstacle for which there is no solution, you have to go to the top and speak to the person who can actually address the problem. Who's the boss? That's the one I need to speak to. Let's fix the problem, not waste time on false promises or attempts to placate my frustration.

Well, it looks like this same situation existed in the Lord's life.

The poor man with the sick son had already tried to get the disciples of the Lord to heal his son, but they couldn't. Isn't it fascinating that the disciples had been given power to heal the sick, raise the dead, and cast out demons, and yet that power would ebb and flow? There were some problems they simply couldn't fix.

I wonder why. Perhaps they were like me, and they wrestled with weak faith? Perhaps they were like me in that I, too, am distracted by the worries of life, and I fail to appropriate God's grace for my circumstances. Regardless, the disciples couldn't help this father and son.

In His response, the Lord calls our attention to the tendency toward inconsistency in our spiritual lives when He reacts as He does in this moment. He laments the "faithless and perverse generation" (Matt. 17:17), and He makes it pretty clear that a lukewarm mindset won't be tolerated forever. And of course, He heals the young boy.

TODAY: What lack of consistency in your faith is making you faithless and perverse? We are all so blessed to be living in the moment before the awesome judgment seat of Christ, and there is still time for us to learn to repent and reorient our lives toward greater faithfulness and wholeness. What a blessing! Perhaps it's time, today, to abandon the automatic pilot mentality regarding our faith and actually embrace this wonderful moment of opportunity.

Wednesday: Luke 21:12–19
Hang in There

"Every calamity is to be overcome by endurance." —Virgil

ENDURANCE IS A LEARNED TRAIT. Most of us know someone in our lives that just seems to be able to endure any challenge until it's overcome. How do they do it?

I knew a man a few years ago facing personal and professional tragedy. His career was falling apart, as was his family. When asked, "How are you able to keep going in the face of all this?" he answered, "What choice do I have? Others depend on me." The man endured great heartache and tragedy, but his circumstances eventually improved, and he emerged stronger and more resilient.

Endurance requires a noble vision. If a person has the grace to see beyond temporary setbacks and difficulties to deeper truths, then the winds of trouble may blow hard in his life, but he is rooted in a firm foundation. No wonder a tree with deep roots stands strong even in the face of a hurricane.

In our Gospel reading, our Lord warned His disciples that all who follow Him will face persecution and trouble. Yet, He promised that through patience, we will gain our lives (see Luke 21:19).

Oftentimes, we want magic over faith. Yet over and over again we learn that these quick-fix fantasies—even the religious shortcuts—all prove to be wishful thinking rather than lasting remedies.

The Faith is entirely different. Here, we learn about endurance, through reading in the lives of the saints, studying the Scriptures, working through difficulties with the help of our father confessors. There are no shortcuts, no magic—just the steady acquisition of virtues through endurance.

TODAY: Just like the long-distance runner, the man or woman of faith grows in endurance and faithfulness by applying consistent, daily spiritual discipline. In our quick-fix world, let's say no to the temptation to relax our discipline. Nothing should lead us away from Christ and His Church. If we endure, we will—in the end—gain our lives.

Thursday: Matthew 18:18–22; 19:1–2, 13–15
Are You Connected?

"Wise as serpents and harmless as doves"
(Matthew 10:16)

FROM POLITICS TO DISASTERS, culture change and social trends, and even local news events, I enjoy keeping up with the news of my world. Being informed about the news of our day is part of my responsibility as the pastor of a parish.

It's easy to feel overwhelmed by the pace of life today with its rapid societal shifts. However, we don't want to overreact by living in a walled-off ghetto where we watch the world from a distance and sink into despondency. We are called to be the hands and feet and mouth of Christ to our generation.

In our Gospel reading, Jesus teaches us that the path to being *in* the world but not *of* it involves three powerful connections.

First, we must be a part of an authentic community. The Eucharist, our central act of worship, is meant to foster communion between God and us, and between Christians as well: "For where two or three are gathered together in My name, I am there in the midst of them" (Matt. 18:20). This connectedness feeds our ability to stand in the midst of today's storms with the collective strength of the entire Body of Christ.

Secondly, we need abundant mercy. How many times should I forgive someone? As many times as they sin. The willingness to forgive is absolutely necessary so that I can stay connected to those around me and not be swallowed up by grief, disappointment, and bitterness. Lack of forgiveness drives us to isolation and self-protective actions, but where forgiveness is present, freedom is too. Finally, we need authentic humility. Real humility forgets wrongs done and refuses to notice insults and sins altogether.

TODAY: We are tempted to either run away from our world or be swallowed by it. With community, mercy, and humility, we'll be able to be a source of salvation to all around us, while also standing firm against the storms of culture and politics. Live out your faith purposefully and stay within the community of Faith—it is the home for your soul and the source of your strength.

Friday: Matthew 20:1–16
Is Your Eye Evil?

Where do I go to get my reputation back?

WHEN I BECAME an Orthodox Christian, I learned that there was a whole body of writing and even prayers against the so-called evil eye. The concept is that envy and jealousy have toxic power, and when they are present, an entire life, even an entire community, can be poisoned. Over and over again, envy has been at the root of destroyed relationships in which lives have been ruined and hearts broken by this spiritual cancer.

We know the story of our lesson well. The owner of the vineyard hires workers throughout the day to work His plot of land. He promises to pay the workers at the end of the day. The vineyard owner is generous, paying the men who had worked a short amount of time the same amount as He promised the men who had worked a full day. Here is where the trouble starts. The all-day workers grumble, complain, and cause trouble.

The hidden sin of envy and jealousy in our hearts is often revealed and uncovered in the face of generosity. God gives to those who don't deserve it (at least according to us). When we see His gifts bestowed on those we think are unworthy, we discover that there is a root of weakness and a poverty of soul within us. Our evil eye of jealousy blinds us to our own blessings and gifts from God and causes us to focus resentfully on the good things that happen to others.

How can we avoid this trap? First, let's be humble and honest, focusing on our own sins and weaknesses rather than the sins of others. Secondly, we can learn to love people as Christ loves them. This sets us free to rejoice at the blessings and successes of others.

TODAY: Where do you cast an evil eye on others? The envy in your heart is a barrier to your spiritual growth and freedom. Humble faith keeps your eye free from envy—it will only see your own sins and will be able to view the good that happens to others with rejoicing.

Monday: Matthew 20:17–28
Mom Wants Us to Be First

Me first!

S omeone once said that God has four answers to our prayers: "Yes," "No," "Wait a while," and "You've got to be kidding Me."

One of the blessings of being Orthodox is that the prayers of our Faith are expansive, not selfish and narrow. We end up praying for concerns we might neglect if we were making it up as we go along. We pray for our nation, for our civil authorities, for times of peaceful and temperate weather, and even for a good defense before the awesome judgment seat of Christ. These petitions keep me from childish prayers in which I focus only on my needs and desires. Indeed, I pray for the whole world, not just for myself.

In today's Gospel reading, we encounter two of the Lord's disciples learning about the dangers of self-centered prayer. James and John, the sons of Zebedee, were close disciples of the Lord who both became apostles. In this passage, they have requested a place of honor near Christ when he sits on His throne. We notice two things: First, they misunderstood the nature of Christ's mission, thinking he had come to establish a political kingdom. Second, they had no idea what they were asking.

"Are you able to drink the cup that I am about to drink?" asks the Lord, adding, "You do not know what you ask" (Matt. 20:22).

The other disciples are angry, but the Lord takes the opportunity to remind them all that leadership requires sacrifice and an attitude of servanthood.

TODAY: Are you praying with the help of the Church's prayers in order to be protected from a self-centered prayer life? When you attend liturgy, listen and participate in your heart when the priest prays the familiar litanies. Allow them to inform your priorities and requests.

Tuesday: Matthew 21:12–14; 17–20
Time to Tell It Like It Is

She did it, so why can't I?

THIS IS THE UNIVERSAL COMPLAINT of younger siblings—I've certainly heard it in my house on numerous occasions. The truth is, often the younger child isn't developmentally ready to take on the task her bigger sister is doing. Likewise, we followers of Jesus need to keep this in mind as we grow up in the Faith. We should show patience with those who are younger in the Faith than us.

In today's Gospel reading, Jesus cleanses the temple with absolute authority, but we shouldn't assume that we should go and do likewise. He is like our mature elder brother—He demonstrates for the temple worshipers, and for us, that God's house is primarily a place of prayer and not for the exchange of goods or to serve as a gathering place for friends.

Note also that the shops had been set up in the Court of the Gentiles, where foreigners were allowed to come and learn about the Jewish God. Clearly, Christ wasn't happy that the outsiders and foreigners were being exploited in this way.

Now before you go into church next Sunday and start driving out the money changers and all those folks who you think don't measure up, or before you start cursing any barren fig trees in your parish, stop and take a deep breath. And then do a difficult thing: think of those people as younger siblings, and turn that critical eye inward toward your own heart. The temple you must first cleanse is that of your own heart, and the fig tree you must first examine for fruit (or lack thereof) is your own soul. Only when you've matured to the point where those places are perfectly aligned with God's will can you ever be able to start cleansing others.

TODAY: Is there room in your heart for the stranger to find God? Is your life producing the fruit you were created to produce? Examine your own heart before pointing out the sins of others. The disciplines in the Church will help you grow into a mature believer. Then you will best know how to assist others in their walk with Christ.

Wednesday: Matthew 21:18–22
You Have to Have Faith

Is the intention to believe, belief itself?

WE LIVE IN A DAY AND AGE where the nature of faith is deeply misunderstood. Some suggest it is a tool to manipulate God into giving us what we desire. Others say faith instructs them to commit senseless acts of violence. Still others claim to have faith, yet their lives don't bear any real evidence that this is the case.

St. Paul declares in Hebrews 11:1 that "faith is the substance of things hoped for, the evidence of things not seen." While faith starts in my heart and mind, it should also impact my choices, priorities, and behavior.

In our Gospel reading today, the Lord confronts the empty fig tree, and the disciples marvel at the power of His words to wither the tree so quickly. The Lord wants His disciples to know that all obstacles and outward circumstances can be overcome with true faith; clearly this faith is active, and not just mental assent to a set of ideas or concepts.

The faith the Lord describes instills such confidence and hope in the heart of the man or woman who believes that no obstacle is big enough to block the faithful person's journey toward God's purpose and plan for his or her life. This isn't a faith that merely makes us happy and comfortable or blithely committed to a set of ideas. This faith actually defends the believing person, rather than the other way around. True faith is the actual living out of our beliefs rather than mere membership in a club. Belief becomes true faith when it is practiced and actually put into action.

TODAY: How is your faith? Your faith is meant both to reveal your real purpose in life and to give you the strength to live according to that purpose. When we live out our Orthodox Christian Faith, we cross that mental divide between *thinking* something is true and actually *acting* like it's true.

Thursday: Matthew 21:23–27
Wise or Shrewd?

He was all alone

A CANNY BUSINESSMAN TOOK PLEASURE in knowing he had gotten the better of his business associates. He seemed to know just when to strike and just the right words to say to get his way and get ahead. Of course, everyone around him felt like they were always being conned, manipulated, or cheated. Eventually, his business associates figured this out as well, and his short-lived success crumbled.

He was shrewd, but he wasn't wise.

When people have the gift of turning situations to their advantage, that ability needs to be tempered by love and wisdom, or it will lead to isolation and loneliness. No one wants to be around someone who is always manipulating others for selfish gain.

In today's Gospel reading, our Lord Jesus graphically illustrates the difference between being shrewd and being wise. Accustomed to negotiating with the occupying Roman army, the priests and the elders cleverly question the Lord. Shaped by their years in survival mode, they were looking for an angle, a way to entrap Christ. Sadly, because of their narrow focus on mere survival, they miss the very abundant Life standing in front of them.

Jesus lovingly uses their shrewdness against them, offering them instead a path away from their small, exclusive, and lonely existence. They ask Him the right question, to be sure. It really does matter what authority He appeals to, yet they ask, not wanting the answer, but to trap Him. He avoids the trap, exposing their true motivations. In doing this, He opens a door of escape to them, if they have ears to hear.

TODAY: Do you manipulate others to further your desires? Remember, the people in your life are icons of God. With the Holy Spirit supplying internal grace and fortitude, we can pass through difficult circumstances with love rather than desperate self-interest. We don't find peace by everything outside ourselves being perfect, but by acquiring an internal mindset that enables us to be wise rather than merely shrewd.

Friday: Matthew 21:28–32
No, You're Behind the Tax Collector

Is honesty the best policy?

I'VE NOTICED THAT SOME FOLKS appreciate straight talk, and some don't. In fact, there seem to be whole cultures where plain talk and honesty are discouraged, because bluntness is considered rude.

Honest communication is, admittedly, disconcerting at times. It's hard to hear straight talk, since we have a tendency to avoid conflict and unpleasantness. Yet sometimes the only way someone can get us out of neutral gear is to talk straight and plain, and use the power of that jarring moment to rouse us from our anesthetized stupor.

This is what Jesus does today in our Gospel reading. The Lord used plain talk and a stark comparison to wake up His hearers to the reality laid before them. It turns out those who think of themselves as good people have a harder time repenting than those who know they aren't good people.

The Lord's hearers condemned themselves with their answer to His question. They admit that the second son, who promised to go and work and didn't follow through, was disobedient to the call of the father, while the first son, who rebelled but later repented and went to the fields for his father, was really the faithful son. Clearly, Jesus was confronting those who manifest their outward piety for all to see while their hearts are proud, unyielding, and far from real faith.

TODAY: Do you work at developing humility and true honesty in order to avoid the twin traps of self-justification and self-loathing? Perhaps it's time to embrace the wise and timeless insight of our Faith. We are called to regular confession and a healthy distrust of our ability to accurately see ourselves objectively. We live out our faith in community, and true communion is achieved not through paying it lip service but by participation in an actual loving community of people committed to serving one another in spiritual growth. Your spiritual life will benefit more from humble confession than from an insistence on the "I'm not so bad" stance. Your ego will be healthier for it, and so will your soul.

Monday: Matthew 17:1–9
Transfigured

"There are no ordinary people. You have never talked to a mere mortal. Nations, cultures, arts, civilizations—these are mortal, and their life is to ours as the life of a gnat. But it is immortals whom we joke with, work with, marry, snub, and exploit— immortal horrors or everlasting splendors."
—C. S. Lewis, *The Weight of Glory*

IF THIS IS TRUE, then all our interactions today will be with immortal souls. We have a hard time accepting this cosmic reality that all of those we encounter every day are immortal beings. It is just so hard for us to believe that we are meant to be more than the sum total of our desires. As a result, we treat ourselves and others in a debased way that is not worthy of our calling.

The Lord's disciples got a huge wake-up call in today's reading as the Lord took His inner circle with Him to the Mount of Transfiguration. In our Gospel reading, three of Christ's followers have their worlds turned upside down. They have lived with Jesus, listened to His teachings, and seen His miracles. Now, at this miraculous moment, there is no doubt. Jesus is no mere prophet, guru, or religious teacher. He has conversed with Moses (the Law) and Elijah (the Prophets), and even God the Father's voice has revealed Him as "my beloved Son" (Matt. 17:5).

The Feast of the Transfiguration reveals *our* potential identity as well. Everything in the Church is meant to enable us to become like Him.

TODAY: Are you ready to press into this wondrous Faith with purpose and love? Are you willing to be made into His likeness by the acquired wisdom of twenty centuries of Orthodox insight, or will you be satisfied merely standing in the narthex of the Faith? At His Transfiguration, Christ revealed Himself and reveals what you could be.

Tuesday: Mark 9:2–9
Don't Tell Anybody Until . . .

Surprise!

I WAS TASKED WITH KEEPING A SECRET about a surprise birthday party for a dear friend. I was chosen to delay him until all the festivities were ready. The elaborate celebration included a convoluted journey and an unexpected guest. It was fun, but I was on pins and needles as I played my part.

Timing is everything and makes the difference between failure and success. As we mature, we learn how to be sufficiently aware of our surroundings, our own heart, and the hearts of those around us as we make decisions about careers, family, and our parishes.

In our Gospel reading today, the Lord commanded Peter, James, and John not to tell anyone what they had seen until after His Resurrection. Why?

First, the Lord knew they'd need time to process this revelation. Peter had denied the Lord, and James and John so misunderstood the Lord's ministry that they asked for places of honor in His Kingdom. All of them scattered once the Lord was arrested and crucified. If profound truths aren't given time to sink deep into our hearts, we often fall back on our weak and selfish ways.

Second, the Lord knew that without preparation through suffering, the disciples might misunderstand and misinterpret what they'd heard and seen. That's true of us as well. Many times we must pass through times of silence and suffering before we can speak with clarity. The Church Fathers say the language of heaven is silence of a profound and full nature. Adoration is the only response.

TODAY: Let's allow some time for silence so that this wonder can do its work in the deepest parts of our hearts. Only in that way will we be discerning enough to know the right time to speak.

Wednesday: Matthew 23:13–22
Lead, Follow, Or . . .

Get out of the way?

YOU'VE MET THEM. They stand on the sidelines and criticize, unwilling to jump in and help. The truth is, I've caught myself doing the same thing.

Often in parish life, folks offer observations rather than their hands and feet. What is the root cause of this common ailment of complaining? Jesus offers His insight in our Gospel reading this morning, when He tells us that the root illness that causes this affliction is hypocrisy. We don't like to think of ourselves as hypocrites, do we?

Fear and the lack of love produce hypocrisy. We are smart enough to see what should be done, but we shy away from getting involved for fear of failure and rejection. Our fear enslaves and isolates us.

Hypocrisy also flows from a lack of love. Remember, "there is no fear in love; but *perfect love casts out fear,* because fear involves torment. But he who fears has not been made perfect in love" (1 John 4:18, emphasis author's). Love sets me free so that I can be lighter and more accepting of all those around me. Love enables me to let go of my own expectations of response and behavior. Love enables me to act without regard for others' reactions, because I can take risks confidently, secure in the knowledge of God's unconditional love for me.

TODAY: As we learn to live in a healthy parish community and in healthy relationships at work, home, and church, let's fight the illness of hypocrisy with the medicine of perfect love. We see what should be done but fearfully stand on the sidelines offering advice without risking anything—this is the trap of hypocrisy. We never want it said of us that we stood in the way of others entering the Kingdom of God and that we wouldn't go in ourselves either. Let's embrace the risk in active involvement, knowing that God is our ever-present help. We are loved unconditionally. As the saying goes, "Lead, follow, or get out of the way."

Thursday: Matthew 23:23–28
In-N-Out

Looks can be deceiving

M**Y GRANDMOTHER LOVED** sayings about inner and outer beauty. She used to say, "Pretty on the inside means more than pretty on the outside."

We spend millions of dollars on treatments that beautify our outward appearance. The whole fashion industry is built on the premise that looking good is vital to our existence, and even the *Saturday Night Live* actor Billy Crystal used to quip, "It's more important to look good than to feel good." Although we condemn shallow existence with our mouths, if we are honest, appearance matters more than we care to admit.

When God in the flesh says "woe" to you, you better bet that's not a good sign. In today's Gospel reading, our Lord Jesus opposed a group of leaders who were absolutely committed to appearing pious, down to the details of their clothing. The Lord challenged them with a difficult truth: their outsides didn't match their insides. These men had gotten the prescription for true piety backwards.

The religious leaders acted as though clothes make the man, but true purity starts from the inside and works its way out. When we focus on true repentance and inner purity, authentic outward beauty follows. Our eyes are easily fooled by appearances, but our hearts reveal our true selves.

T**ODAY:** It is important to have self-respect and care for one's outer appearance, but the subtle trap is to stop there, neglecting our spiritual lives. We must pay at least as much attention to our spiritual beauty as we do our outward appearance. If the regimen you follow each day to prepare for work, an outing with friends, or a date isn't equaled by the time you spend beautifying your soul, your outside has become more important than your inside, which always leads to woe. Be beautiful, indeed, but be beautiful to God in your soul, and the outside will shine with true beauty.

Friday: Matthew 23:29–39
Bad Words?

The times, they are a-changin'

NO ONE CAN LOOK at current culture and not witness the coarsening of the language of our day. Between the mainstreaming of pornography to the debasement of women in popular music, our children are being exposed to words and phrases that simply do not nourish dignity and respect in their lives. As a police officer in the mid-1980s, I gave a citation to someone using foul language in public within earshot of women and children.

Yet plain language can be necessary, especially if your audience has gone deaf to subtler forms of communication. Often, for instance, those who are entrenched in leadership positions need a wake-up call.

Such was the case when our Lord confronted the leaders of His day. For the last several days, we have been reading the woes the Lord pronounced against the religious leaders who needed to be called on the carpet. This is strong language.

"Serpents, brood of vipers! How can you escape the condemnation of hell?" (Matt. 23:33). The sheer amount of deafness that our loving Lord observed in these leaders required that he be forceful in his language so these men would open their ears to His life-giving rebuke. How sad that a person could become so inaccessible to God's grace that our loving Jesus knew these harsh words were their only hope.

TODAY: Today, once again, God has given us a new day. The Scriptures promise us: "*Through* the LORD's mercies we are not consumed, / Because His compassions fail not. / *They are* new every morning; / Great *is* Your faithfulness" (Lam. 3:22–23). God once again extends all His love, mercy, and strength to you today. Perhaps you've drifted from His side. Perhaps you've grown so deaf to His loving voice that He will have to speak louder, with strong words to break through that distance you've created. He will, because He loves you so much. Don't shut out His voice. Join us in the constant prayers of the Church, and your heart will stay tender, able to hear His loving offer each morning.

Monday: Matthew 24:13–28
The End is Near

Do not believe it

G LANCING AT THE TABLOIDS in the supermarket, it is fascinating to think that people read the far-fetched stories printed there. The end of the world is a favorite topic.

Although the Church does believe that this world will end someday, that's where the similarity between our teachings and tabloid depictions ends. In our Gospel reading today, we are cautioned to be aware, "for false christs and false prophets will rise and show great signs and wonders to deceive, if possible, even the elect. See, I have told you beforehand. Therefore if they say to you, 'Look, He is in the desert!' do not go out; or 'Look, *He is* in the inner rooms!' do not believe it. For as the lightning comes from the east and flashes to the west, so also will the coming of the Son of Man be. For wherever the carcass is, there the eagles will be gathered together" (Matt. 24:24–28).

In teaching about His return, the Lord wasn't trying to satisfy our curiosity or give us a puzzle to solve. Neither was He creating new doctrine about a supposed secret rapture. The Lord and the Church offered these teachings so that we will persist in endurance, faithfulness, hope, confidence, and love. We are promised that "he who endures to the end shall be saved" (Matt. 24:13). In the end, none of the terrors of the world will harm you.

TODAY: While the world may experience earthquakes, war, famine, and various apocalyptic events, let's not be fearful. We are to stay faithful, regardless of the circumstances around us. We have all we need to finish life well and present a good defense before the awesome judgment seat of Christ. We don't need shallow sensationalist teaching, for it only distracts us from faithfully loving and serving God. So embrace the peaceful rhythm of the Orthodox Christian Faith. It will enable us to truly endure to the end, whether that is the grave or the Second Coming of Christ.

Tuesday: Matthew 24:27–33, 42–51
Anticipation

It's making me wait

A NTICIPATION IS A POWERFUL TOOL. As with any good thing, the purpose of the evil one is to distort and to derail the good aspects of anticipation with the counterfeits of fear and dread. When it comes to the Second Coming of Christ, Christians can be distracted by gossip-like speculation and fantasy-driven Hollywood productions about our Lord's return. All the while, our true goal should be preparing to meet Christ.

In today's lesson, the Lord used the literary language of Old Testament Hebrew prophets to describe His impending death to His disciples.

"Watch therefore, for you do not know what hour your Lord is coming. But know this, that if the master of the house had known what hour the thief would come, he would have watched and not allowed his house to be broken into. Therefore you also be ready, for the Son of Man is coming at an hour you do not expect" (Matt. 24:42–44).

St. John comments on this teaching of the Lord when he says, "Beloved, now we are children of God; and it has not yet been revealed what we shall be, but we know that when He is revealed, we shall be like Him, for we shall see Him as He is. And everyone who has this hope in Him purifies himself, just as He is pure" (1 John 3:2–3).

TODAY: During every liturgy when we say the Nicene Creed, we assert that "[Christ] will come again in glory to judge the living and the dead." Rather than worrying about what current world tensions were predicted in the Bible, the wise servant watches and follows Christ each day. Our disciplined lives are the best preparation for the Lord's coming, which can happen at any moment. Indeed, this is why the Church calls us to pray, fast, and give alms. Practicing these spiritual disciplines contributes to healthy anticipation, not fruitless speculation. There are so many spiritual medicines to help us be ready and at peace. We can be ready whether we meet Him through death or at the Second Coming.

Wednesday: Mark 1:9–15
The Time Is Fulfilled

The best-laid plans of mice and men

I COULD SUM UP most of my life by discussing events solely from the perspective of timing. For instance, when I approached the Orthodox Church, I was an ordained minister in a Protestant denomination and figured my days as a pastor of a flock were over. I planned to use my gifts as a layman, but several years later I found myself standing in the Greek Orthodox Cathedral of Annunciation in Atlanta preparing for my ordination.

Frequently, life throws us curves, and we make decisions as best we can. We always need to exercise discernment and be willing to see every moment of our lives as redeemable. Even the sad times, the hard times, and the scary times can be productive.

In our Gospel reading today, look at what preceded the start of the Lord's ministry to save the world: an amazing baptism, a time of temptation, and the company of both wild beasts and angels. Only after these events was the time right to announce the Kingdom of God.

Our lives are filled with amazing and challenging moments—sometimes we make the right choice, sometimes we don't. We will find peace if we embrace all the wisdom life teaches us moment by moment instead of being deceived by the voice that says, "I will never recover from that bad choice" or "That experience was a waste of time." The key to getting the timing right in my life depends on my willingness to awaken to each moment by God's grace and humbly learn both dependence on Him and confidence in Him. When I am most focused on Christ, I am most conscious of the rest of my life and all the people in it.

TODAY: Are you struggling with hitting the right stride in your life? Are you grieving over bad choices and wrong decisions? This godly sorrow will bring you to true repentance if you are willing to learn—even your bad choices can be instructive. Even when you struggle with temptations or are surrounded by wild beasts (indeed, maybe especially in those times), you can grow spiritually.

Thursday: Mark 1:16–22
It's Not Always What You Say

It's how you say it

SURVEYS SHOW THAT SOME PEOPLE are more afraid of public speaking than death. Yet although a well-delivered, compelling declaration of the Gospel may look like foolishness to some, for centuries it has drawn men and women to embrace our Lord.

St. Paul said, "For since, in the wisdom of God, the world through wisdom did not know God, it pleased God through the foolishness of the message preached to save those who believe" (1 Cor. 1:21).

In today's Gospel reading, we read that Jesus "taught them as one having authority" (Mark 1:22). What a contrast to, and indictment of, the teaching of the religious leaders of Christ's time.

What gave Jesus this air of authority in contrast to the teachers of His day? Was it the content? They were both drawing from the same revelation God had given the Jewish nation through Moses and the prophets. Was it their level of education? In a population where literacy wasn't the norm, the scribes and teachers were very well educated. Was it because Jesus was God in the flesh rather than a mere mortal? The people knew that the Lord knew what He was talking about, that's for sure. Beyond all these things, I believe the Lord's authority flowed from this: the scribes and Pharisees possessed information, but Jesus genuinely loved His hearers. Christ spoke out of love and compassion, and people listened.

TODAY: Good public speaking can be learned, and effective communication skills can be developed, but you can't fake love and concern. The Gospel is only preached powerfully when the speaker has both a deep conviction about the Christian message coupled with a self-sacrificing love for those who are listening. That is true preaching as one who has authority. This, dearest one, flows always from a heart transfigured by love for God and love for neighbor.

Friday: Mark 1:23–28
You Were Made for Freedom

Why the caged bird sings

IN HIS POEM "Sympathy," Paul Laurence Dunbar writes:

> *I know why the caged bird sings, ah me,*
> *   When his wing is bruised and his bosom sore,—*
> *When he beats his bars and he would be free;*
> *It is not a carol of joy or glee,*
> *   But a prayer that he sends from his heart's deep core,*
> *But a plea, that upward to Heaven he flings—*
> *I know why the caged bird sings!*

Instinctively, we know we are made for freedom, not slavery. Yet even if we enjoy every civil privilege, we can still be imprisoned in our souls. A prisoner may exit his cell, but the prison cell inside a man's heart is the deepest form of slavery there is.

No wonder the people of Jesus' day thought some "new doctrine" (Mark 1:27) had come among them when they saw the Lord liberate a man with an unclean spirit.

In our lesson today, we see that the Jewish people—even while enjoying the benefits God gave them as His chosen people—had abandoned the inner freedom that brings about true hope and liberation.

Jesus stood before them as the shining example of true freedom. In His encounters with the unclean spirits who had enslaved people to spiritual poverty and self-destructive habits, He demonstrated that the restoration of their true humanity and freedom was indeed possible. Jesus set people free.

TODAY: What fears keep you imprisoned? What weighs down your soul and keeps you from feeling hopeful or encouraged? You are meant to experience inner freedom that can't be taken from you, regardless of your situation. The freedom that you are given by Christ today doesn't depend on your outward circumstances, on congress, on the president, or on your net worth.

Monday: Mark 1:29–35

Perspective Matters

Perspective changes everything

Today's media love to hold up the anti-hero as someone to be admired. From Tony Soprano to Walter White of *Breaking Bad* fame, we are presented with the good side of evil actions. Yet today, we also live under so many regulations that the average person can't help but break at least four laws before breakfast.

Between the obsessive law-making of our modern world and the media's obsessive glamorization of law-breaking, we have become confused about whether we should follow the rules.

In our Gospel reading today, the Lord Jesus adopted a decidedly different approach to dealing with the common population of His day than the one He used with the religious elite. The Lord extended healing and forgiveness to the common people but confronted the Pharisees with stark, brutal honesty.

The religious leaders governed with rules, so the Lord gave them a taste of their own medicine. On the other hand, the everyday people were genuinely suffering. The Lord didn't pile on more demands but healed and consoled them, teaching us that the path to true holiness can be walked when our souls are made whole. Following the rules doesn't gain us the Kingdom of God; the presence of God does.

Today: We don't need to improve our ability to keep rules; we need to admit our sickness and check into the hospital. The truth is we are all ill in our souls, and the amazing grace of God offered to us within the timeless Faith invites us to trust the Great Physician in the spiritual hospital of His Church. Here, we can be healed and made fit for His eternal home.

Tuesday: Mark 3:13–21
He's Crazy

True sanity

WE SEE THE DAREDEVILS who participate in extreme sports and climb Mt. Everest, and we think they are crazy for risking their lives. Yet they love what they do. In fact, they feel sympathy for us, depriving ourselves of excitement and adventure.

As it turns out, in our Gospel reading this morning, the Lord's own family thought He was "out of His mind" (Mark 3:21)—too zealous for His own good. They thought He needed to be rescued.

I'm sure they believed they were only concerned for Jesus' safety and well-being, yet their reactions probably had more to do with their own fears and insecurities than their concern for Christ. The Lord's willingness to serve all who came to Him appeared foolhardy to those who felt threatened by his wholehearted commitment.

The lives of the saints illustrate this same tension. Many of the saints seem crazy to us. Remember St. Symeon the Stylite? He lived at the top of a tall pole on a platform year after year, exposed to the elements. When we contrast how much effort we expend to make our own lives as comfortable as possible with St. Symeon's choices, we'd prefer to say he was the imbalanced one. But the stark contrast between the saints' lives and ours challenges our assumptions and priorities about what's important.

What makes more sense? Pouring all our energies into a present life that will end at the grave, or laying up treasures in heaven (see Matt. 6:20) for a life that will never end? In the end, who is really crazy?

TODAY: Don't be surprised when people call you crazy for practicing your faith. All the saints and even the Lord Himself were sometimes perceived to be out of their minds because of their focused and purposeful life. People are often uncomfortable when they see sincere Christians living with integrity—it troubles their conscience. Follow Christ anyway. Dare to look crazy in a world where people pour themselves into temporal pursuits while ignoring the essential preparation for eternal life.

Wednesday: Mark 3:6–12
Even His Enemies Praise Him

"You have enemies? Good. That means you've stood up for something, sometime in your life." —Winston Churchill

THERE WAS A MAN who took great pleasure in insulting me. It used to bother me, but to this day I pray for that man by name before every liturgy. His animosity accomplished two invaluable things in my life. First, it served as a regular reminder that I am not perfect, and I need to acknowledge my faults. Second, I learned to pray for someone who hates me. I hope that someday I will be able to love that man perfectly, as Christ does.

In our Gospel reading, the Lord was surrounded by both spiritual and physical enemies. His way of dealing with them is instructive.

First, He removed the source of the drama by leaving His enemies and spending time with those who genuinely sought His help and presence. He understood that the best way to usher in a cool-down period is to get away from the source of conflict for a time. In my own life, my active absence has often worked peace in unstable situations.

Second, the Lord didn't waste time on those who were only interested in empty platitudes. Notice that He commanded the demons He cast out to quiet down, even when they were telling the truth. The Lord knew they spoke not from love or worship but from fear and envy. They praised Him to cause trouble. Sometimes, pleasant voices in our lives speak to us with selfish intent. The Fathers encourage us to avoid flattery so that the darkness of arrogance and pride won't find room in our hearts.

TODAY: Are you tired of the drama around you? Do false friends spend more time flattering you than helping you in the walk of faith? Maybe it's time to practice some active absence and peaceful silence to quiet the turmoil created by the enemies of peace. Perhaps it's time to embrace the spiritual disciplines of prayer, fasting, and almsgiving in secret so that the inward man can be renewed in the privacy of your heart.

Thursday: Matthew 5:14–19
Let Your Light Shine

Get out of the way!

MY DAUGHTER IN THE BACK SEAT was yelling at the cars that blocked us as we drove to her dance class. Apparently, she had seen someone else react in the same situation, though I won't say whom she was imitating.

Her frustration is familiar to all of us. We often feel that our agendas are more important than those of anyone else.

On the other hand, why am I not as frustrated when I am in my *own* way? Sometimes my choices and my attitudes prevent me from moving forward in my own life. What do I do then?

In our Gospel reading today, notice that Jesus doesn't say *make* your light shine. Instead, He commands us to *let* our light shine (Matthew 5:16). Letting my light shine indicates that the Light is already present and burning, and all I have to do is get out of its way so that it can be seen. Just put the Light where it belongs, says our Lord. Set it on a lampstand so that it can be seen. The Light was meant not only to show me how to walk, but to shine so brightly that those around me will see how they should walk as well.

How do I *let* my light shine? It's instructive that the Lord follows this command by teaching about the commandments.

TODAY: Are you hiding your light? Perhaps it's time to get out of your own way and follow God's leading. By embracing His wisdom, your light will be free to shine. Embarking on the wise rhythm of the life of faith preserved in the Orthodox Church, your light can be so polished that it will bestow light on the lives of all of those around you.

Friday: Mark 3:20–27
Meant to Be United

United we stand, divided we fall

THE YEARNING FOR UNITY is as old as humanity. It permeates the stories of history, where we read about the attaining of unity, the betrayal of unity, and the loss of unity. Printed on each dollar bill is *E pluribus unum*, "Out of many, one." Unity brings strength.

Secular science may say the drive for unity is due to survival of the fittest. Sociologists may suggest it flows from our fear of being alone, but these explanations only scratch the surface.

God Himself is three Persons in communion. As such, He created us in His image to struggle for that same kind of existence He has eternally enjoyed within the Holy Trinity. Jesus revealed as much when He prayed "that they may be one just as We are one" (John 17:22). At the heart of our Orthodox worship is the Holy Eucharist, our communion, the symbol and actualization of our unity. We who are many drink from one cup.

When our Lord's critics, in our Gospel reading today, accused Him of casting out demons by the prince of demons, they couldn't have been more wrong. True unity gives strength to a home, a community, and a nation. The presence of division always portends impending destruction. Our enemy always fosters division, first in our own hearts, then in our communities.

The healing of our divided hearts is the purpose of the spiritual disciplines we practice. No wonder St. Paul commanded us to "note those who cause divisions and offenses, contrary to the doctrine which you learned, and avoid them" (Rom. 16:17).

TODAY: Where are you at war with yourself? Find the divisions in your own soul, and you will discover the roots of what divides you from others. Embracing the remedies of the eucharistic life heals your brokenness and makes unity possible. Healing must first come to your own heart, and then it will be manifested in all your actions and motivations. When you approach the chalice next, pray for the unity of the Church and ask that it begin with your own heart.

Monday: Mark 3:28–35

The Delusion of Illusion

I'm okay—you're not okay

HAVE YOU EVER HEARD of the common human practice that psychologists call *projection?* This happens when, rather than owning up to my weaknesses, I perceive the same flaw in others and judge them for it.

As Christians we can be more honest with ourselves. The Spirit invites us to the grace of confession and repentance, and try as hard as we might, the loving grace of God urging us to spiritual health is hard to extinguish.

In today's Gospel reading, the religious rulers surrounding Christ react defensively when He tells them the truth. Instead of owning their attitudes, they accuse Jesus of the spiritual poverty that they themselves possess.

When He tells them the truth, they insist that it's really *He* who is possessed by an unclean spirit. If they were being honest, their true spiritual condition was obvious to them and to those around them, yet they revert to a childish attitude and projection of their flaws onto Christ.

We shouldn't be surprised by the reactions of others to the honesty of our Lord. Though He offers the truth in love, we often don't want to hear it. Yet we are invited by the Lord to understand the weaknesses in ourselves and others so we can be healed.

TODAY: Life is too short to whitewash our weaknesses and leave them hidden. It's better to hear the truth and, as painful and uncomfortable as it may be, allow the sweet and gentle wisdom of the spiritual medicine of the Faith to cleanse our hearts. It is worthy work—the Lord's true friends are those who do His will, not those who simply intend to do His will.

Tuesday: Mark 4:1–9

Listen

Um, sorry, what did you say?

MY YOUNGER BROTHER'S HEARING took a beating due to his years of work at a body shop. When we are surrounded by ambient noise, I occasionally need to repeat what I've said.

While making my journey to the Orthodox Faith, I was intrigued with a repeated command in the liturgy: *Proskomen!* (in English, "Let us attend!") This command is there because we humans can be hard of hearing in our hearts.

In our Gospel reading this morning, our Lord wanted make sure His hearers were really with Him, so He issues the command, "Listen!" Likewise, He ends the parable with a similar command, "He who has ears to hear, let him hear!" Christ calls us to listen—He knows how easily we are distracted. We focus on minor things and miss important things with our selective hearing. Our spiritual hearing loss takes a heavy toll on our lives.

Our spiritual deafness is caused by our lack of focus and purpose. We are so easily captured by the frivolous and the temporary. We avoid anything that might wake us up from our distractions, with all the strength we can muster. We avoid the confrontational moments of our Faith, knowing that if we really listen, our lives will experience holy disruption. That's scary, isn't it? Yet when we consider the substantial cost of our spiritual deafness, the cost of a purposeful life is easier to bear.

TODAY: The Church has purposefully designed the Divine Liturgy to help us overcome our spiritual deafness. All the disciplines of the Faith are meant to make us more able to hear the life-changing message of the Gospel of Jesus Christ. When you fast, you participate in the grace that opens your spiritual ears. And when you give of your time, talents, and treasures, you sensitize your spiritual ears to the still small voice of the Spirit.

Wednesday: Luke 10:38–42; 11:27–28
Tell Her to Help Me

They just go along to get along

MY MAWMAW USED TO DESCRIBE some people this way. She meant that some folks simply absorb the opinions of those around them without discretion. We can be so averse to conflict that we will say yes when we should be saying no. But that requires strength of character, and this isn't developed overnight. Sometimes people never learn to stand up for anything that's foundational and right.

Where do we go to build strength of conviction? How does one develop solid life priorities that are based on eternal truths rather than temporal goals of happiness or ego gratification? The only place to find lasting life principles is at the feet of the Master.

In our Gospel reading today, Mary and Martha were both doing good things. Martha was serving her guests as the hostess, but her sister Mary made another choice that bothered Martha a lot. Mary decided to sit at the Master's feet and be shaped and formed by His eternal wisdom. She said no to a lesser good so she could say yes to a greater one, and Jesus honored her for this.

Notice also how the Lord responded to the lady in the crowd who praised the woman who nursed the Lord: "Blessed *are* those who hear the word of God and keep it!" (Luke 11:28). The blessing of seeking the Kingdom of God first is greater than any other blessing and isn't dependent on genetics but on loving God's Word first, above all things.

TODAY: What do your priorities say about your character? Are you able to say no when the shortcuts in life are offered to you? Do you even know how to discern between these choices? The way to build strong character, one that resists temptations and models the path for future generations, is found in prioritizing God's truth over earthly pursuits for comfort or success. When given the chance to choose, will your decisions reveal a person who sits at the feet of Christ, choosing that better part which can't be taken away?

Thursday: Luke 4:16–22
Eatin' That Rainbow Stew

"You don't have to get high to get happy." —Merle Haggard

IN EVERY HEART, there lives the dream that all will be made right, that justice and righteousness will prevail for all people. It's a blessed hope but also terrifying. Why?

In our Gospel reading, we learn that a day is coming when all injustices will be corrected, all hurts will be healed, all lies exposed, and all wounds will be addressed and healed. However, this also means that every person I've mistreated, hurt, lied about, or selfishly taken advantage of will be avenged as well. On that day, I too will be standing in the light of the righteous judgment of my own faults and my own mistreatment of others. It puts a different spin on things, yes?

The spiritually mature person realizes that he or she must work diligently now to repent and ask forgiveness, thus opening the way for the grace of God to transform our actions toward others into righteous and peaceful love. No wonder the Church teaches us to pray for "a Christian end to our lives, peaceful, without shame and suffering, and for a good account of ourselves before the awesome judgment seat of Christ."

TODAY: Let's ask God for the grace to search our own hearts for our own faults, not even noticing of the faults of others. Let us become so gracious in our words, actions, and choices that when the Last Day comes, we will welcome the Lord's righteous judgments. Those who have already become practiced in humble forgiveness and repentance will naturally and quickly lay their burdens and expectations at the feet of Christ and cry out, "Lord Jesus Christ, Son of God, have mercy on me, a sinner."

Friday: Mark 4:35–41
Why Are You Afraid?

Our daughters are still very young

CHILDREN CAN BE AFRAID of the dark, and my girls are going through that phase now. My wife and I wake up to little feet crawling into the bed with us, because Mommy and Daddy make them feel safe.

Then I remember that I am also afraid at times. My fear doesn't manifest itself like the honest fear my little girls display. It usually shows up as anger, resentment, or despondency, but underneath it all, the emotion is fear. I'm afraid I won't reach this or that goal. I'm afraid this person will let me down. I'm afraid of what will happen to me as a result. I'm afraid.

We know the story in today's Gospel reading well. The Lord is in the boat with His disciples when a storm arises, threatening to capsize the boat. The disciples panic, but the Lord sleeps through the whole ordeal. They wake Him up and ask Him, "Don't You care if we die?" (see Mark 4:38).

I can imagine the Lord rubbing His eyes as He awakens to their cries of fear. He steps to the edge of the boat and commands the weather to calm down—and *it does*.

The Lord asks, "Why are you so fearful?" (v. 40). It turns out the disciples were afraid for the same reason I am: They were trusting in the boat instead of the Master of the sea. Too often, I trust in lesser things to fulfill my life and make me secure. When these unstable things don't bring joy and peace to my life, I'm devastated.

Eventually, I ask God, "Don't You care that I'm dying?" Then He reminds me that whenever I trust in these lesser things and people to provide for me what only He can provide, I am once again brought to the place of repentance. He knows His strength is greater than any challenge I may face. Why should I worry and fret?

TODAY: The reason we so easily become fearful is that we allow our walk with God to retreat into the background of our lives. When the storm hits, we cry out in panic. If, instead, we keep our faith front and center, we'll be ready when life throws us a curve. This is continual remembrance of Christ.

Monday: Mark 5:1–20

Our Desires: Master or Servant?

I scream for ice cream

M Y TONSILS WERE REMOVED when I was seven. Up until that time, I was a bit sickly and skinny as a rail. After surgery, I consumed copious amounts of ice cream. Interestingly enough, my lifelong struggle with weight began when I regained my health after that surgery. Weakness can be a gift, and overcoming a weakness can open the door to new temptations and struggles.

Our faith encourages us to come to grips with our passions so that they don't master us. When desires become masters, they lead us into slavery; untamed desires are *never* satisfied.

Our Gospel reading today features the demon-possessed man. All attempts to control him and protect him from himself had failed, and this is how it is when our desires rule our lives. This man in today's Gospel reading never intended to get to this point in his life, just as we never intend to indulge our passions to the point we find ourselves gripped by addiction.

What's the remedy? Getting free of our passions takes a lifetime. We need to prepare for the lifelong journey of knowing ourselves and being honest about our weaknesses. The more I learn about my passions, the more I see the depth of my own spiritual need. Yet, the Good News reminds us all things are possible with God, because His love and mercy are available to us without end. No wonder the Church teaches us to pray constantly, "Lord, have mercy."

TODAY: By God's grace, our passions can become our servants rather than our masters. The grace and mercy of God is lavished on us every moment, through a Savior who loves us more than we can comprehend—He will never reject us and provides all we need for healing.

Tuesday: Mark 5:22–24, 35–43; 6:1

Do Not Fear; Only Believe

That's impossible!

W HEN I FIRST PROPOSED the video teaching tool *A Journey to Fullness*, plenty of folks said it was a great idea—until I explained how I
was committed to producing them with a high level of professionalism. Then
I began to hear the objection, "That's impossible!"

Why do people dismiss goals and dreams that quickly? Maybe some don't
see the value in their dreams, or maybe they are so afraid of failure that they
never try difficult tasks, and are uncomfortable when they see someone else
go for it.

But what concerns me most is when the sense of impossibility is rooted
in a lack of faith. It's easy to pay lip service to a belief in the God who spoke
the universe into existence. But the declaration that something's impossible
sometimes comes from a heart that doubts whether God is as great as the
Church declares He is. We are defeated before we even start and achieve
far less than our potential simply because we can't bring ourselves to dare to
believe—how sad.

In our Gospel reading today, the people were overcome with amazement.
They laughed at Christ, crippled by their small imaginations—they couldn't
believe that grief could be turned to joy.

Yet for those of us who believe in God as Creator, in the miraculous birth
of our Lord Jesus, and in His Resurrection, we should never say, "That's
impossible."

TODAY: Are there mental blocks that are keeping you from living the free
life Christ has given you? Is your life governed by doubt and mediocrity that
comes with avoiding the impossibles? Perhaps it's time to embrace a God-
given dream and move forward with the glorious joy of a purposeful Orthodox life. Let's embrace the resurrected Christ and all He makes possible.

Wednesday: Mark 5:24–34
Eternal Healing is Best

It isn't all about me

THE POWER OF OUR TIMELESS FAITH is that it helps us gain freedom from our time-bound perspectives and narcissistic focus. The Faith reminds us of our slavery to time and invites us to see beyond our temporary circumstances to glimpse the Kingdom that is to come.

The tension between the *already* and *not yet* of salvation makes me both fully aware of the present moment—with all its joy and pain, suffering and peace, potential and loss—yet also keeps me confidently rooted in the Resurrection of Jesus Christ. This confidence allows me to remember that I am free in every moment of life; I don't need to worry about any temporary difficulties I might be experiencing. This doesn't make my troubles go away as much as it puts all my temporary circumstances into an eternal perspective.

In our Gospel reading, the Lord said to the woman, "Your faith has made you well" (Mark 5:34). He'd already healed her prior to saying those words, but the point is, there's more to healing than a physical improvement—we all need our hearts to be healed too.

True healing penetrates beyond the bone to the soul and heals the deepest wounds of our hearts—those wounds where a pill can't help and a scalpel can't cut. Our spiritual wounds keep us enslaved to our fear and delusion, make us selfish and stingy, and divide and isolate us from others.

TODAY: Are you ready to actively embrace the timeless wisdom of an eternal Faith designed to apply the medicine of immortality to your deepest wounds and illnesses? This active practice of our beautiful Orthodox Faith is meant to apply the balm that heals forever. Practicing the Faith in our everyday life sets us free from temporary worries and makes us totally present in the here and now. That sounds like paradise, doesn't it?

Thursday: Luke 10:38–42, 11:27–28
Happy Birthday, Mother

A mother's love

NO MATTER WHAT was going on in my life, I could always—and I mean always—count on my mom. No matter the tribe, the language, the politics, or even the passage of time, the bond between mother and child is hailed from one generation to the next. That's why stories of mothers who turn on their children are sensational and tragic—they are completely opposite to the norm.

Since this is true, what are we to think about God taking His flesh and dwelling in His Creation through a human mother? When we remember that He is eternal and rose from the dead, we are reminded that the relationship between Christ and His mother lasts forever. The Son of God, the second Person of the Holy Trinity, has an earthly mother. Amazing!

In today's Gospel reading, Martha is "distracted with much serving," and she asks the Lord to command her sister to help her. But Jesus answers in such a way that it turns the common social order on its head. The Lord blesses Mary, sitting at His feet to learn about the faith along with the men in the room. Another lady, hearing this, praises the mother who raised such a man.

But Jesus redirects this woman's praise of His mother, insisting it isn't the mere natural bond of family relationships that is most important. What mattered more was that His mother heard the word of God and obeyed it, thereby setting up the plan of redemption that made salvation possible.

TODAY: Mary is more honorable than the cherubim and more glorious beyond compare than the seraphim because she was the first to hear the Good News and invite Christ to live inside of her. Her free and loving yes made possible my relationship with Christ, the Son of Man whom I can love, follow, and embrace. His mother is worthy of veneration because of her humility, her courage, and her obedience.

Friday: Luke 8:16–21
Memory Eternal

United we stand

THE ANCIENTS KEPT THE STORIES of their past alive through story-telling and communal memory. Young people would memorize the tales of the tribe so that they could pass on this communal memory to the next generation.

One of the main things that drew me to the Orthodox Faith was the sense of living, communal memory experienced within the Church. This is an aspect of knowing myself as integrated by familial bonds—not just by imper-sonal concepts, ideas, or even rituals—to the whole Body of Christ and back to Christ Himself. Communal memory is absolutely essential to the Ortho-dox Christian and preserves a fundamental truth of our Faith: We are the One Body of Christ; the One, Holy, Catholic, and Apostolic Church. This is not because we repeat old words, practice old rituals, or agree to old ideas. It's a unity deeper than mere nostalgia and habit. Our unity and connection are because we are family.

Today, we *remember* (i.e., renew and rejoin an event of the past as if we were actual contemporaries of the event) Joachim and Anna, the Lord's grandpar-ents. We do this not out of some misguided confidence in ethnic or genetic connections, but because we are united in something deeper than mere blood ties. We are united through our living Lord. Jesus' victory over death forever transformed our faith from a mere tribal deity or family idol to the encom-passing Lord of all the earth and the source of unity of all peoples.

TODAY: As Orthodox Christians, we embrace our brethren from every tribe, kindred, and language, across the globe today and for all time. We are united by the loving Lord, who heals and calls us to the hard work of authentic com-munion. How is your communal memory? Are you working to know your holy lineage, and are you passing this on?

Monday: John 3:16–21

For God So Loved the World

"We all know that pleasurable rush that comes from condemning, and in the short term it's quite a satisfying thing to do, isn't it?" —J. K. Rowling

SHE'S RIGHT—I can't tell you how many times I've ranted at the news reports or a Facebook post and felt that pleasurable rush of righteous condemnation over the wrong ideas of others.

Yet our Faith isn't focused on being correct or even condemning wrong. In fact, the Scriptures declare that God the Father did not send the Son into the world to condemn it.

In today's Gospel reading, Christ didn't have to condemn—whoever rejects the life God offers condemns himself. Instead of condemning others, we should take pity and have compassion on those who are stuck in the self-imposed prison of their own condemnation. The merciful God the Father sent His Son to destroy sin, death, and Satan as an act of total love. God doesn't have to defend Himself, and He doesn't need to condemn us.

We who say we follow Christ are called to forgo condemnation, showing love and pity and faithfulness. This doesn't mean we excuse unhealthy behavior. Remember, those who reject Christ are already condemned in themselves.

TODAY: Why not abandon attitudes of condemnation toward others? Since God Himself refuses to do this, we who follow God should adopt His wise and loving ways. It's better for me to ask myself where my own sin condemns me. I ought to seek first to remedy my own distance from God and faulty thinking.

Tuesday: John 12:19–36
For This Purpose

"The answer is blowing in the wind." —Bob Dylan

Today, we are plagued by a loss of purpose. We grasp at anything and everything to fill the vacuum. We love the shortcut, the easy answer, the simple explanation, and we chase after fleeting, passionate causes with all the clever rhetoric we can muster. For all our posturing, where is the peace? For all our defense of prized ideologies, where is the joy? I have had to confess to my spiritual father on many occasions and repent for falling all too easily into the spiritual trap of getting stirred up about contemporary events and in the process, losing my peace and joy. This present age, like all others, is in the love and care of our Lord.

In our lesson today, Jesus is troubled by the events surrounding Him in this moment of truth before He is killed. Notice what comforts Him? A clear, abiding sense of purpose. Will He avoid the challenge, the pain, the Cross before Him for which He came? No, because His purpose is clear; it is the foundation of His life, and it glorifies God the Father.

The same purpose that kept Christ steady in the face of the Crucifixion also offers us hope and stamina as we stand in a world where the ground is shifting under our feet. When we are tempted to take the easy way out of our trials, or when we attempt to fix the world's problems by ourselves, we must remember that only when He is lifted up from the earth will He draw all to Himself.

TODAY: Are you tempted by the easy answers of this or that -ism? Do you find your soul troubled by the society around you? When that happens, remind yourself of God's purpose for you, and draw strength from our foundational and timeless faith.

Wednesday: John 19:6–11, 13–20, 25–28, 30
Lift Him Up

Save, O Lord, Your People, and bless Your inheritance. Grant victory to the Faith against the adversaries of the Faith. And protect Your People by Your Holy Cross!

WE'LL NEVER BE ABLE to tame our faith—there's no payoff without the pain. In today's passage, we read about the Crucifixion of the Lord, the moment in human history when the Son of God entered into the final battle with sin, death, and Satan.

This central message of Christ dying on the Cross for our salvation is a message that people have always tried to dismiss, diminish, or deny. The Jews of Jesus' time said He couldn't have been the Messiah because of the shameful way He died. Later, Muslim theologians would insist that Jesus didn't die on the Cross at all. They believed that through a miracle, Judas was substituted for Christ and died on the Cross instead. Today, there are those who either deny the existence of Jesus or believe the Crucifixion of the Lord proved He was a failure.

Why the wide range of reactions to the Cross of Jesus? We feel shame—if Christ was truly the Son of God, then we have perpetrated the greatest crime in history. The Crucifixion of Christ displays for all to see how ugly we are when we turn from God. We feel pride, because we refuse to take responsibility for His death. We feel hatred, because viewing Jesus on the Cross holds up a mirror in which we view our ugliness.

Of course, the Cross isn't the end of the story. The Resurrection places the Cross in the light of victory, as death is trampled down by death. That changes everything.

TODAY: Let's face it: we can't take the sting out of the Orthodox Christian message. Let's view the horror of the Cross with the Resurrection in mind. God loves us so much that He destroyed death by His own death. God liberated us from our human weaknesses and sin, destroying everything that keeps us enslaved.

Thursday: Matthew 10:16–22
You Will Be Hated

I hate this traffic

*H*ate IS SUCH AN UGLY WORD, one used too often, even by myself—Lord, forgive me. I've heard that word used about me, too. It was a shock and a wound.

Hate is a word used in all kinds of contexts. Some folks seem to think that every disagreement these days is based on hatred, and now we have the phenomenon of people who hate haters.

Our Lord Jesus promised that His followers would be hated by the people who hate Him. In today's Gospel reading, He lays out a troubling picture for His disciples. He promises them that when He's gone, they will be mistreated, dragged before the courts, and betrayed by their own families.

So, what is our reaction when we are hated? Pain, disappointment, fear? Sure, and other complex emotions as well. Yet there is a promise to us that salvation will be ours if we endure to the end, and endurance is based on exercise, focus, daily practice, and confidence.

Endurance isn't fostered when we respond to hatred with hatred. Doing so weakens us spiritually, and even physically. Instead, endurance is strengthened when we don't return evil for evil, when we refuse to hate those who hate us, when we actually love those who hate us. That's what makes it possible for us to be faithful. Love neutralizes the acidic and destructive power of hate.

TODAY: It matters *why* you are hated. If it's because you are selfish, meanspirited, disagreeable, and hardhearted, then no one but yourself is to blame. However, those who follow Christ will be hated because their lives shine a light on the spiritual poverty of those around them. That hatred is both promised and unsurprising. Just don't allow yourself to indulge in the debilitating and de-energizing emotions of returning hatred for hatred. Focus on Christ, practice the disciplines of the faith, and have confidence that God will give strength and endurance.

Friday: Luke 7:36–50
You Keep Using That Word

Life is difficult

O KAY, SO LIFE IS DIFFICULT—got it. Now what? How do I find a source of motivation that keeps me going, no matter how hard life becomes?

In our Gospel reading today, a Pharisee who seeks to follow God by obeying every detail of the Law invites the Lord to his house for a meal. The sinful woman, hearing the Lord will be there, enters the house and washes Jesus' feet with her tears, anointing His feet with ointment and kissing His feet.

Jesus then tells his host, "There was a certain creditor who had two debtors. One owed five hundred denarii, and the other fifty. And when they had nothing with which to repay, he freely forgave them both. Tell Me, therefore, which of them will love him more?" (Luke 7:41). Simon, the Pharisee and host, answered, "I suppose the *one* whom he forgave more" (v. 42). And Jesus said to him, "You have rightly judged" (v. 43).

Here our Lord reminds us of our need for repentance and spiritual healing. If I see only my own sins and refrain from comparing myself to others or making excuses, then I am on the path to finding my source of motivation.

Next, Christ teaches us that our response to Him reveals our hearts. If we approach Him in loving gratitude, we demonstrate our desire for real forgiveness.

Finally, He wants us to know that true forgiveness comes through admitting that we need His help and guidance. He will give us the grace to pass through the difficulties of life rather than always seeking to be rescued from these troubles.

TODAY: Instead of succumbing to despondency due to the challenges in your life, allow hard times to motivate you to confess your need to God and to ask for His grace. Train yourself to react to life's stresses with a heart of loving gratitude and service, and watch as grace and strength are given to you. The Lord says to you today, "Your faith has saved you. Go in peace" (Luke 7:50).

Monday: Mark 7:24–30

But You Are a Stranger

Who are your people?

IN MY EARLIER LIFE as a police officer, I was once sent to a local business in a small town to investigate a robbery. After asking some questions, I wrote up a report and continued my shift. A few minutes later, the chief of police of the small town called me and asked me if I'd encountered any problems while taking my report. Confused, I said that everything had seemed fine. But the police chief explained that the store's proprietor called to complain about me. Since I wasn't a hometown boy, he was uncomfortable giving me any information, despite my uniform and official status.

As a lifelong southerner, I understood that attitude toward outsiders. When someone from my town told you, "Excuse me, darlin', but I don't believe I know your daddy," you weren't to be trusted.

In today's reading, the lady the Lord dealt with was a Gentile and a woman. According to the culture of Jesus' day, she was not to be touched or even acknowledged. She was (in Greek) a *xeni*, or stranger.

So why did the Lord speak to her this way? Was He being rude, or cruel? No, Jesus is reminding us that we must never view anyone as an outsider unworthy of our attention and help. This woman cared nothing for her own ego; her only concern was for her child. Christ saw her heart and healed her little girl.

TODAY: Is ugly prejudice present in your heart, your parish, or your community? Is an attitude of "us versus them" clouding your heart and blinding you to the truth that we are all created in God's image and His likeness? Let's say no to our egos and fear and yes to trusting our neighbor as a child of Christ.

Tuesday: Mark 8:1–10
Gratitude Multiplies

Thank you!

A T THE HEART OF THE CHRISTIAN FAITH is the response of gratitude. We often fail to appreciate and embrace this attitude. Yet when
we do, we experience freedom from the fear of death and from the trap of
regret.

How do we actualize the attitude of gratitude in our lives? Well, for this,
God has given us the Holy Eucharist, or "the medicine of immortality" as
St. Ignatius described it in his epistle written in the earliest centuries of the
Faith. The word *Eucharist* is based on the Greek word for "thanksgiving." By
partaking of Christ regularly, we set our hearts free—no matter what our
outward circumstances are.

In today's Gospel reading, our Lord took what little the people had and
multiplied it so that they were satisfied.

Yes, the circumstances were bleak. The crowd had been following the Lord
for three days. They had submitted to the task of learning from Him and
being fed spiritually by Him; yet now they were in a deserted place, and there
was no food. The provisions available to them weren't enough to feed one
family, not to mention the thousands who were in the crowd.

Yet the Lord didn't leave them hungry and stranded. He took what they
had and made it enough. When Christ is with us, we don't need to focus on
what we *don't* have. Gratefully, we make available what we *do* have, and God
multiples it so it is sufficient.

TODAY: Every person who dares to trust God will find that He creates
enough out of the provisions we offer Him in childlike trust. In the Divine
Liturgy, we hear the call of Christ when the priest calls out to the faithful,
"With the fear of God, with faith and love, draw near!" Let's embrace the
Eucharist with gratitude, knowing that it is God's eternal invitation to us to
abandon doubt and fear.

Wednesday: Luke 3:19–22
The Heaven Was Opened

My beloved Son

OUR LIVES ARE FILLED with open and closed doors—with crossing over thresholds to move into the next room, the next opportunity, or the next challenge.

What does it mean for us when God Himself opens a door? In today's Gospel reading, we see people cross several significant thresholds.

Our passage today deals with both darkness and light: Herod's evil and Christ's Baptism. The Scriptures often set light and darkness side by side so that we can understand what's at stake in the struggle between good and evil. Even when we're not aware of it, every moment of our lives presents us with the choice between the two.

St. John is baptizing the people with the "baptism of repentance" (Luke 3:3), enabling repentant sinners to move over a threshold into a new life. Christ Himself submitted to baptism, not because He needed to repent, but so that a door for all could be opened. At His Baptism, heaven was opened, and the Father's voice was once again heard by His creation. Adam heard God's voice in the Garden of Eden, calling, "Adam, where are you?" (Gen. 3:9). Now, we hear the Father's loving voice speaking to His Son: "You are My beloved Son; in You I am well pleased!" (Luke 3:22).

All the hope, all the joy, all the strength we will ever need are available if we walk through this open door.

TODAY: What darkness do you face in your life? Do you realize that heaven's door has been opened by Him who pleased the Father on your behalf? What will it take to wake you up to this cosmic invitation to love, joy, and peace? What needs to happen in your life to move you across the threshold of this open door into a purposeful practice of your Faith? Christ has made it possible for us to live in His Kingdom of the Church.

Thursday: Luke 3:23–38; 4:1
Oh No, Not the Family Tree!

You can pick your friends, but you're stuck with your relatives

BEING IN COMMUNION IS HARD, really hard. If church is meant to be more than a social gathering, it shouldn't surprise us when conflicts arise. If that's true for parishes, it's true to a greater extent within families. The moments of disagreement and tension challenge and stretch us.

In today's Gospel reading, we are reminded that even the Lord, in His flesh, has a genealogy. He took His flesh from one of us and accepted all that entails, even being a member in a family tree that has its warts and flaws. By doing so, He invites us to see beyond the difficulties of family life; He wants us to see how families are the context for His grace and mercy.

How should we view our family members? We are called to embrace our families, even those members who aren't very lovable. Remember, sometimes we're not very lovable, either.

God only asks me to confess my sins with my family, not theirs. In our families, our pride often is confronted, and our expectations are tested. There, we are often asked the hard questions about our lives. Rather than analyzing the problems of others, I'm called to acknowledge my own spiritual weaknesses.

Finally, I am called to confess my love and need for my family. The truth is, I wouldn't be the man I am today without them. Even when it's hard, real spiritual benefits have flowed to me through sharing my life with these precious people. Every difficulty has invited me to become more serious about my faith and more honest about my own weaknesses.

TODAY: Let's do the hard work of communion. The spiritual treasures offered to us today through living in close quarters with our families are many.

Friday: Luke 1:5–25
This Medicine Tastes Horrible

The grass is always greener

ALL TOO OFTEN WE DISCOVER that the real answer to our longings is right under our noses. Some of my life's most surprising revelations have come when I awoke to what I already possessed.

Our Gospel reading today features Zacharias, the father of St. John the Baptist. He was visited by the angel Gabriel, who told Zacharias that he and his barren wife were to have a son who would prepare the way for the Messiah. Zacharias didn't believe the answer was right in front of him, so the angel announced a period of silence in his life.

This mute period of time wasn't meant as a punishment but an invitation for Zacharias to embrace spiritual healing through silence.

God works in amazing ways to wake us up from the lethargy of our own self-sufficiency. He does what is unexpected. He uses what is close to us to invite us to enter into His life and His peace. He offers us a way through, not a way out, so that even difficult times won't destroy us. The unexpected is only unexpected if we are blind to God's goodness to us.

When we dare to believe that He truly is everywhere present and filling all things, we discover right under our noses the absolute joy of His provision for every aspect of our lives. Not even the devil's best shot can withstand His power to turn every moment into a revelation of His love. Thanks be to God.

TODAY: Where does your life feel barren and lifeless? Look more closely. Pray and immerse yourself in the life of the Church, and you might find that God in His eternal love for you uncovers a path right in the middle of the challenges you are facing. Let's trade our spiritual blindness for His loving presence. Let's see Him and Him alone so that with His help, we can see all things.

Monday: 2 Timothy 3:10–15

Endurance

Not a philosophy, but a calling

St. Timothy was a young spiritual son of St. Paul, who placed him as the head of a local Christian community. St. Paul wrote to Timothy, encouraging him as he served in his first parish.

"All who desire to live godly in Christ Jesus will suffer persecution. But evil men and impostors will grow worse and worse, deceiving and being deceived" (2 Tim. 3:12–13).

St. Paul revealed three insights about endurance. First, he emphasized communion as a path to spiritual strength, reminding Timothy to pay attention to how he had endured persecutions (vv. 10, 11). The Christian life isn't a philosophy but a calling to be lived. We manifest this Christian life in real relationships and lean on our Christian friends in times of trial. When we read the lives of the saints and deepen our connections with our brothers and sisters in Christ who are faithful in trials, we are given strength to endure.

The second quality that contributes to a steadfast faith is the discernment to see the difference between truth and deception.

Finally, Paul tells Timothy to keep doing what he's always done and to stay on the path (v. 14). When we follow the scriptures and faithful people who've gone before us, we'll be planted firmly in the soil of truth. We know *what* is true, and more importantly, we know *who* is Truth. If we don't deviate from the wisdom given to us, we will have the strength to endure.

Today: Whatever you face today can be approached with confidence through the strength of God's grace. Be it illness, emotional heartache, even the consequences of your own mistakes, you can stand firm in the truth and live in the light that has been shed in our lives through Christ Jesus our Lord.

Tuesday: Ephesians 4:17–25
Put Off Your Old Nature

Breaking up is hard to do

IF YOU'RE LIKE ME, you tend to hold on to things too long sometimes. It might be a ratty recliner or an old jacket that we cling to, but sometimes it's a bad habit or sinful addiction that we won't put behind us.

In today's epistle reading, St. Paul makes no bones about what this new commitment to Christ means for the Christians in Ephesus: "You should no longer walk as the rest of the Gentiles walk," because their understanding is "darkened," they are "alienated from the life of God," and they "have given themselves over to . . . all uncleanness" (Eph. 4:17–19).

St. Paul doesn't equivocate: we *must* put off this way of life. This is why we call newly baptized and newly chrismated Orthodox Christians "the newly illumined." When we put off the ways of darkness, we begin to see clearly for the first time as we acquire the mind of Christ.

When we embrace the Gospel, we learn to think in a new way, and our minds are renewed. Isn't it interesting that this kind of wisdom always starts with a change in our thoughts? As time goes on, we find that our old and new natures are always incompatible with each other, since in putting on our new nature, we take on the likeness of God.

This process is what we Orthodox Christians call *theosis*—it isn't simply behavior modification but the means by which we truly become, in our natures, like Jesus.

TODAY: Are you still trying to wear that ratty old nature or perhaps trying to wear both natures at the same time? How's that working out for you? Perhaps it's time to let go of the old ways of thinking and embrace with purpose the Orthodox way of life. We are called to be like Christ in every way. It's the most important thing you will ever do.

Wednesday: Luke 6:17–23
How to Be Blessed

Bless his heart

WHEN YOU HEAR THIS PHRASE from a Southerner, you must parse it correctly. Said in a certain context, it is a genuine prayer. Other times, it is used to baptize gossip—context is everything. We use the word *bless* so much that it has lost its true meaning.

When I was in seminary in Boston, we were honored to have two precious monks from Greece taking classes with us. One day, I took the monks to the airport and, while I was helping one monk get his bags out of the car, the other monk put a twenty-dollar bill on my driver's seat. When I spotted the money he'd placed there, I was chagrined. How could I take money from the monks who'd shared so much with me? I grabbed the bill and ran after them, imploring them with tears to take it back. One of the monks took me by the shoulders and repeatedly said, "May it be blessed!"

In our Gospel reading, the Lord's compassion for the crowds around Him provides us insight into the true meaning of being blessed. The crowd is desperate, hurting, suffering, and they all press in to touch Him. Power is present in and through Him, power that heals and makes whole. Yet paradoxically, our Lord then provides a deeper understanding of what it means to be blessed. It is not just those who receive physical healing who are blessed, but those who are poor, hungry, weeping, and hated. Why is this? It is because when we are weak, we draw near to God, who is the Source of every blessing.

TODAY: Are you focused on your pain, your fear, or your difficult circumstances? If so, I imagine you don't consider yourself blessed. Yet if your hardships are drawing you close to Christ and to His Church, then even your pain is a blessing. When you are near to Him, you can see clearly—when you are weak, then you are strong, as St. Paul says (see 2 Cor. 12:9).

Thursday: Luke 5:12–16
Go to Church

Let us attend!

IN ONE OF THE RETREATS I offer in parishes around the country, I suggest a series of antidotes that can heal those of us afflicted with the weaknesses of our modern age. My presentation contains examples from sociology, psychology, science, and even religion. But then I get down to the most basic, timeless prescription for spiritual health available: "Go to church."

The practice of the Orthodox Faith has produced saints for centuries. Before there were Sunday schools, before there were multimedia presentations, before the advent of the internet or sound systems or videos, there was only this: the community of the faithful, gathered in worship. The Church year, with its a robust liturgical schedule, provided the means by which people followed our Lord in both good times and bad. The local parish provided the spiritual food that formed men and women, boys and girls, rich and poor in the likeness of Christ.

In today's Gospel, Jesus heals a man from leprosy, but He doesn't send him home. He sends him to the temple—the miraculous healing needed to be recognized by the community. Lone Ranger spirituality always leads to weak theology. As St. Cyprian said, "He cannot have God as his Father who does not have the Church for his mother."

When our habit of gathering together declines, all manner of spiritual illness grows. A recent study found that less than twenty-five percent of all Orthodox Christians attend liturgy weekly. We must stay connected to each other in the services in order to stay connected to our Faith.

TODAY: Is your occasional Christianity letting you down? Don't be surprised—the spiritual leprosy of our hearts can be cured by God's grace, but never forget He will then turn to you and send you to His Church for that healing to grow and be maintained. The answer to most of your spiritual challenges today is simple, though not easy: go to church.

Friday: Matthew 24:42–47
Will You Be Surprised?

Even so, come, Lord Jesus!

W HEN THE LORD TAUGHT His Church that He would return, he promised that there would be no schemes, no hidden agendas, no blood moons, and no gnostic secrets to be revealed only to the ones in the know. He only counseled us to be wakeful and ready. And in our Gospel reading this morning, we learn that we won't be told *when* Christ will return, but we'll know *what* the times will be like.

Jesus Christ is going to return, and that's all we really need to know. He is the object of our love and devotion, and the rest is for God alone to know. His coming might be preceded by a great tribulation or the ever-present antichrists who have always tried to usurp the Lord's place. Or, His coming could be when we meet the Lord in our own falling asleep. Either way, we love Him and desire to be with Him, and so we watch for Him.

This is the difference between what the Church teaches concerning the Second Coming and sensationalist theories that lack sobriety and peace. Don't be captured by rapture-mania and all the complicated popular theories promoted by those who are obsessed with the last days.

TODAY: In your spiritual life, are you motivated by love or by fear? To be sure, our fear of the future can initially motivate us in our walk with Christ. Nevertheless, as we mature spiritually, we are drawn toward God because of His love for us and our love for Him. The message of the Orthodox Faith is never sensationalist or fearful but always centered on God's eternal and unchanging love for you and me. If we walk with Him, we won't be caught off guard by His return or by our mortal appointments with death. Let's work so that our Christian faith progresses from being about something we know to being about Someone we *love*.

Monday: Luke 6:12–19

What Are Your Priorities?

Good night, sleep tight

OVER THE COURSE OF OUR LIVES, there are a handful of times the weight of a decision keeps us up all night. One such moment for me was when I was to be ordained as a deacon in the Orthodox Church. As I contemplated the implications of the changes that were about to take place in my life, I felt compelled to stay awake and focus on the holy ordination before me that would alter my life forever. Similarly, I've known friends who've stayed up all night when preparing for a major presentation or meeting or before an important event like a wedding.

What keeps us awake at night presents an interesting litmus test of our priorities. From our nights of insomnia, we learn whether our priorities are misplaced, disordered, destructive, or life-giving. Wakeful nights remind us of our need for God's grace.

In our Gospel reading today, the Lord entered into solitude for a night of prayer, during which He decided who would form the nucleus of the leadership for the Church. It was a momentous decision for Christ. Just as Israel was led by twelve patriarchs, the Church was led by twelve apostles God chose to shepherd the spiritual Israel. *Apostles* means "sent ones." The implications were clear: these men were being sent on the most important mission in the history of the world—Christ instituted His new and holy nation for the salvation of mankind.

TODAY: Are you aware of your own purpose and mission as a follower of Jesus Christ? Where does that mission fall in your list of priorities? I pray you are able to stop, even for a moment, and take stock of your priorities. Be honest: where does your faith fall in that list? Perhaps it's time for the practice of your faith to move up a few spots.

Tuesday: Luke 6:17–23
Blessed Are the Poor

Trouble with a capital "T"!

I LOVE THE SCENE in *The Music Man* when con man Harold Hill warns the good folks of River City about the pool hall in their little town. "Ya got trouble!" he sings, "with a capital 'T' / and that rhymes with 'P' / and that stands for pool!"

In this world, troubles come to us unbidden. Sometimes they come in clusters; sometimes they trickle in, sapping our strength slowly and weakening our resolve. Other times our troubles seem to come out of left field, catching us by surprise. However, in time, troubles come to all of us. So how are we to view them?

In our Gospel reading, the Lord taught that people going through troubles are blessed. Did we hear that correctly? Yes—blessed. The poor, hungry, weeping, and hated are blessed and should rejoice.

We don't rejoice in our troubles themselves, Christ says; we rejoice because they offer us the opportunity to view life more clearly and to be more dependent on God. Difficult times remind us that we are eternal beings, and there will come a time when these difficulties will be nothing but a distant, irrelevant memory. Our lives are not temporary and flimsy. We were created in God's image and in His likeness to live with Him forever. If our troubles can remind us of this, we are blessed indeed.

TODAY: What troubles are you facing today? Our Lord invites you to embrace this counterintuitive truth: You are blessed. These troubles are temporary and unable to destroy you, as long as you remain close to Christ. If your heart is aching, and your troubles are hard to bear, flee to the embrace of the Church. Stand in the midst of the eternal peace that dwells there, and watch as your troubles find their proper perspective.

Wednesday: Luke 6:24–30
Do Good to Those Who Hate You

It's opposite day

GRAMMAR WASN'T MY BEST SUBJECT in school. I've always been impatient with rules and process, and yes, that has caused me problems. Yet now that I've studied other languages, I've acquired a healthy respect for the rules of grammar. Take antonyms, for instance, which are words that mean the exact opposite of another word.

Antonyms are one grammar concept that has helped me as I teach the Faith. Our Orthodox theology is filled with antonyms—paradoxes, if you will. To save your life, you have to lose it; to be rich, you must become poor; to live, you have to die.

In today's lesson, our Lord Jesus has just explained the paradoxical teaching of the Beatitudes. You are blessed if you are poor, weak, and despised.

Now He is declaring woes, which are the opposites of blessings. If the hungry are indeed blessed and can look forward to being filled, then woe to those who are full, because they will end up hungry. Woe to those who think they have it all—they are actually poor in spirit. Woe to those who laugh now, because they will weep later.

Given these paradoxes, how do we live? Christ teaches that we should turn conventional wisdom on its head. Conventional wisdom says to hate those who hate you. Conventional wisdom says possessions equal prosperity. Conventional wisdom says being popular equals being good.

Our Lord calls us to do the opposite: Love your enemies. Do good to those who mistreat you. Do not return physical violence. In this way, we will be free rather than enslaved by feelings of revenge, hatred, greed, and self-centeredness. If this is your attitude of life, you will be blessed and joyfully free.

TODAY: Are you tempted by the illusion of prosperity, thinking that happiness lies in worldly success? Instead, let us embrace the paradoxes of the Faith and find Christ in the midst of poverty, weakness, and loss.

Thursday: John 20:19–31

St. Thomas the Believer

He's a doubting Thomas

WHY DO WE HARBOR DOUBTS about people or about our faith? Sometimes, past experience is a reliable indicator of future performance. It isn't wise to rely on someone who has broken promises in the past. But neither should we always expect the worst. So where's the balance?

Today's Gospel reading reacquaints us with that great apostle, St. Thomas. Do you notice how the Lord deals with Thomas's doubts? He doesn't scold him; instead, He invites Thomas to examine his heart. "Because you have seen Me, you have believed" (v. 29).

Three approaches can help us when we struggle with doubt. First, we can gain valuable insight through life experience. It is completely legitimate to look at a track record of behavior and postulate future performance. I give myself a C minus, for example, when analyzing my ability to stay on a strict diet. It's fair to say I will continue to struggle with this aspect of my health.

Secondly, we can embrace the power of expectation. We are never beyond God's grace and mercy, and if we forget that, we can end up giving into despair, doubt, cynicism, and sadness. As long as we have breath, we can joyously expect the best from ourselves and from others, because God's healing and power are accessible.

Finally, to rise above doubt, we can remember that God has given us the power to choose. Because we have that power, there is hope. Every day, you and I can make choices toward God and the good. God's grace makes up for our deficiencies.

TODAY: We all have doubts. They are natural, understandable, and expected. But doubt doesn't have to have the final word in your life. Doubt can be kept from becoming a paralyzing influence on your spiritual progress if you keep doubt from growing into disbelief. Through wisdom, and by embracing worthy expectations and remembering our power to choose, we can rise above our doubts, as St. Thomas did.

Friday: Luke 6:46–49; 7:1
Simple? Yes. Easy? No.

The wise man built his house upon a rock

IN A WORLD where we've come to expect easy answers and convenience, we are in danger of expecting that our walk of faith will be easy as well. To be sure, many household chores are now a snap, and we all benefit as a result. But when we struggle for spiritual maturity, we can't look for quick and easy answers.

Today's religious gurus want us to believe that attaining spiritual maturity is easy. All we have to do is succumb to their exclusive tutelage and listen only to them, and then we will progress. Spiritual wolves in sheep's clothing abound in our world, but spiritual maturity can't be earned so easily.

In our Gospel reading today, our Lord Jesus confronts us with a challenge: do our words match our actions?

An indication that we have built a true foundation in our spiritual lives is that we have made a singular commitment to Jesus Christ. If He is Lord, then He *is* Lord. This is simple, but it isn't easy, for we are plagued with many distractions and temptations.

The consequences of this singular focus are several. This singular focus means I must regularly inventory my own motivation. This singular focus means I must always remember that my spiritual life isn't a life of isolation. This singular focus means I must remain aware of the many potential interruptions that can sidetrack my spiritual progress. And this singular focus means that I must be within the Church, because I cannot and will not be able to do this by myself.

TODAY: Is the foundation of your spiritual life strong? What is your life built upon? Are you trying to do this work by yourself? Perhaps it's time to admit this isn't an easy undertaking and that you need to trust yourself to the arms of the Church. Only then will you be able to avoid being tempted by the easy spiritual paths.

THE HISTORY OF THE CHURCH is filled with the lives of saints who were holy fools. Two towns were situated on opposite sides of a river, and there was a bitter rivalry between them. In their love for their brothers and sisters, the saints decided to stage a morality play that would demonstrate the folly of this mutual animosity. The first saint would cross the bridge to the other side; the second saint would loudly berate him and use force to push him back to his own side. Then they switched roles and repeated the scenario. These holy fools demonstrated in this way the folly of this bitter rivalry.

In our Gospel reading today, St. John the Baptist lived as an extreme example in order to shake up and wake up his generation. Our Lord Jesus praised John for his holiness, then said, "but he who is least in the kingdom of God is greater than he" (v. 28). The saint prepared the way for salvation by Christ and for His Body the Church. Important as St. John was, what he ushered in was of incomparable significance. In the new community of the Church, all barriers of culture and language would dissolve into a oneness the world had never seen.

TODAY: We see the extreme example of St. John the Baptist and are offered a chance to embrace just a bit of the spiritual labor or ascesis that makes our radical faithfulness to God and others possible. Starting today, can you make a daily commitment to being faithful to this message of new life and eternal peace and joy? The disciplines of the Church offer us that kind of opportunity.

Tuesday: Matthew 9:36–38; 10:1–8
The Seasons of Life

Daddy, when will the leaves change colors?

I LOVE THE FALL. When autumn rolls around, I'm flooded with warm memories of stirring boiling water in large pots and helping my grandmother snap beans and put them up in Mason jars. The time of reaping after a spring and summer of growing and sowing was fruitful and satisfying.

Harvest time teaches us about spiritual principles, too. Just as there is a right time to pick the tomatoes, dig up the potatoes, cut the corn, and gather the fruits of the earth, there are harvesting seasons in the Christian life, too. We become ready to move forward in response to the call of the Lord of the harvest to enter the field already white and gather the most important fruit in the universe: the repentant person.

In today's Gospel reading, we find that the Lord was "moved with compassion" (Matt. 9:36) when He saw the people—they remind Him of lost sheep. Even though the Jewish people were given the Scriptures, the prophets, and temple worship, they had wandered from the fold. In response, Christ tells his newly harvested apostles to go and share the message of the Kingdom.

Jesus didn't just send the disciples forth to preach—He also empowered them to heal. He was strategic, directing them to minister to the Jews first; the harvest of the Gentiles would come later, after Pentecost.

Christ, as Lord of all, knows all about the harvest, and His call to us is clear: the fields are white, and the grain is ready—we are to work in the fields so that the harvest doesn't rot, God forbid.

TODAY: What season of life are you in? Where in your own life can fruit be harvested for the benefit of others? Let's do our part as we actively and purposefully cultivate, fertilize, and prune the fields of our hearts to prepare them for planting and harvest. Then we will be ready and able to assist the Lord of the Harvest in His work in the world.

Wednesday: Philippians 2:12–15
Work Out Your Own Salvation

With fear and trembling

ONE DAY, my little brother and I were fighting. My mom came into our room, looked at us both sternly, and said, "Work it out."

Work it out. There are situations in life that will not have easy answers. We have to use our minds and refer to our spiritual principles in order to figure out what to do.

In today's epistle, the Apostle Paul reminds us that the walk of faith places unique demands on each of us. We struggle with varying degrees of spiritual illness that require our active awareness of the problem and active participation toward healing. To work out my own salvation (Phil. 2:12), I must have insight into the deepest needs of my soul.

Of course, I'm not doing this work by myself—God is at work in me. I need to actively cultivate and deepen an intimate connection with God. He invites me to regularly cooperate with His work within me so that I can become more like Jesus Christ. It is amazing to think that the uncreated God is at work in me. Lord, have mercy.

Finally, as I work out my own salvation, I realize this creates a singular focus, not on other people's sins, but on my own. This liberates me from grumbling about others and opens the way for Christ to shine in my life, offering hope to others in need.

TODAY: Are you working out your own salvation with fear and trembling? Are you intimately aware of God's work in your life? Sometimes we become spiritually numb, making our active participation in our own salvation difficult. It's time to rise to the occasion and work it out as mature believers.

Thursday: Philippians 2:16–23
I'm Glad—You Be Glad Too

"Don't worry, be happy!" —Bobby McFerrin

THIS SONG CAPTURES an important principle. Happiness is a choice, just like love is. While there are emotions attached to these choices, happiness and love are not emotions but choices we make every day. If we allow our perspective to be governed by outside circumstances, we will be enslaved to powers beyond our control and at the mercy of outside forces. We weren't made for slavery. If happiness and love are always dependent on events and people, then we will be as unstable as the shifting sand.

In today's epistle, we read about St. Paul's wise advice to the Church at Philippi. The apostle is addressing the Philippian church from jail, having been arrested and placed in custody. He writes to Philippi after the community had sent their priest St. Epaphroditus to St. Paul for encouragement and assistance.

Clearly, St. Paul's circumstances shouldn't have been conducive to a happy existence, yet he told the believers, "I am glad and rejoice with you all" (Phil. 2:17) because he had not "run in vain or labored in vain" (v. 16).

St. Paul was able to rejoice because his joy didn't depend on his circumstances. Rather, he fixed his gaze steadily on his ultimate purpose and destiny. His love for the parish at Philippi and his confidence in their faith were all the assurance he needed that his life was worthwhile. Therefore, St. Paul was free to be at peace in the midst of his imprisonment. He could even love his captors. Happiness was his choice, and he was content.

TODAY: In the wisdom and beauty of our Faith, we are offered a way to choose freedom and peace, regardless of our circumstances. Today is the right moment to appropriate this wisdom in your life. You can be reoriented so that you *choose* happiness and joy.

Friday: Philippians 2:24–30
God Had Mercy

The best-laid plans of mice and men

MOST OF US at least try to achieve a planned life. We plan for college. We plan our careers. We plan our relationships. We are forever warned against haphazard living, and rightly so, because a haphazard life tends toward chaos and misery. Even our faith has all the earmarks of a clear path, a way of life guided by instructions and guidelines.

Although my favorite phrase is "Orthodox on purpose," I have to admit that life very rarely goes according to my plans. My best intentions invariably get disrupted—they fail. The plans of others conflict with mine. This doesn't mean I don't plan ahead, but I do try to remember that God has His plans, too.

In our epistle reading today, St. Epaphroditus—the priest sent to help St. Paul—has became gravely ill. I'm sure this ailment wasn't on his agenda.

There are three things we learn about disrupted plans from this passage:

First, don't panic—the only way to survive a significant disruption is to calmly and openly acknowledge the difficulty. Don't overreact.

Next, assume God's mercy. St. Paul always urges the Philippians to rejoice. Even when our plans are disrupted, we know God is present. He loves us and will be gracious in this momentary challenge. In our surprises and tragedies, our faith carries us through.

Finally, rest in grace. Frenzied activity only indicates a lack of confidence in God. Rest and be still. There is a great deal of wisdom available to us through the Church—let's never forget that, even for a moment.

TODAY: Have your plans been disrupted? Have tragedy, aggravation, or fair-weather friends turned your hopes and dreams upside down? Acknowledge the reality of your situation, remember God's mercy, and rest in His grace for you. "I lifted my eyes to the mountains; / From where shall my help come? / My help comes from the Lord" (Ps. 120/121:1–2 OSB).

Monday: Philippians 3:1–8
I Count All Things as Lost

It was amazing

A MAN ONCE TOLD ME his life story. He built his first company from the ground up when he was twenty-four years old and made his first million dollars at age twenty-eight. Then he started three more companies that he then sold for millions more in his mid-thirties.

But then he met a monk who had nothing. The monk so affected this millionaire's life that the millionaire turned his back on his fortune and entered the monastery.

I couldn't help but ask him, was it worth it? The monk's eyes shimmered with tears. All he was before becoming a monk was nothing compared to the joy of an intimate relationship with God, he told me. I was uncharacteristically speechless.

In our epistle reading today, St. Paul says the same thing. As he encourages the faithful at the church in Philippi, he tells them that while his faith in Christ has cost him, he was glad to pay that price. In fact, he considers all his accomplishments before Christ to be nothing in comparison.

Serving Christ is worth the labor, worth the challenge, even worth saying goodbye to temporary comforts that seem to consume the time and priorities of many around us. When you possess faith in Christ, that faith expands your horizons so that they extend into eternity. Indeed, this faith makes losing all things bearable.

TODAY: Are you willing to suffer the loss of all things for your faith in Christ? Really letting go of other temporal things will be impossible until Christ is in His proper place. Let's always remember to keep Christ in first place, and then the rest of our priorities will line up accordingly.

Tuesday: Philippians 3:8–19
That I May Know Him

"Now Adam knew Eve his wife, and she conceived." (Gen. 4:1)

ISN'T IT INTERESTING that the Holy Scripture describes the most intimate connection between husband and wife this way? In our closest relationships, there is a kind of knowing that transcends just knowing about someone. This kind of intimacy goes to the heart of what it means to be in communion.

God knows Himself as Persons in communion. In God's inner life as Father, Son, and Holy Spirit, the Holy Trinity consists of co-equal and co-eternal Persons in loving communion for eternity. Since we are made in His image, we are called into true communion with Him and each other as well.

In our epistle reading for today, St. Paul tells the people in Philippi that this kind of relational knowing is what knowing Christ means to him. He has lost his place in the Jewish community, he has lost his freedom and is in jail for his faith, and he has lost his reputation as a faithful and zealous follower of the Jewish Law. Nonetheless, St. Paul counts all these previous accomplishments as rubbish when compared to the singular joy of knowing Christ (Phil. 3:8).

Knowing Christ, explains St. Paul, means knowing His death and His Resurrection. When we join Christ, we die to our old life and ways and are resurrected to new life in our Lord. "As many as have been baptized into Christ have put on Christ. Alleluia!"

Then St. Paul notes that he continues to grow into this knowledge, pressing on to make the death and Resurrection of Christ his own (vv. 10–12).

TODAY: Do you know Jesus Christ in this way? Are you pressing on to know Him more? Let's focus on Him so intently in our lives that everyone else around us will be able to see that our relationship with Christ is our first priority. Let's grow in our communion with the living God.

Wednesday: Luke 9:18–22
Who Do You Say That I Am?

I can see clearly now

THE MORE I STUDY the Fathers of the Church, the more I allow the rhythm of the liturgy and prayers of the Church to wash over me. The more I live the Orthodox Faith in a purposeful way, the more I am convinced of this: the primary result of faithfully living this way is that I am gaining a clearer vision as to who God is and who I am.

In our Gospel reading today, we see a critical tipping point is reached in the lives of the disciples of Jesus. Jesus asks them the million-dollar question, "Who do you say that I am?" (Luke 9:20).

The truth is, I—as His modern disciple—will *never* know myself until I know in my heart the right answer to that question. "Who do *you* say I am?" And your answer to that question determines whether you'll be able to access all the spiritual resources given by the Holy Spirit to the Church.

Mere nostalgia or thoughtless repetition will not help us know Christ. Our hearts must really be centered on who Christ is and what He has done for us. If Christ really is fully God and fully man, "begotten, not created, of one essence with the Father," as we insist in the Nicene Creed, then I must know Him before I can know myself. Then through Him, I am able to love even my enemies, and my life will begin to more closely resemble His. The truth is, I'll call eternity "hell" if I don't do this important work now. It is only when I resemble Jesus that I will be able to call His home my home.

TODAY: What concrete and practical steps will you take today to know Jesus better? Will you pray? Will you stand before His icon and gaze into His Face so that His image can be imprinted on your heart? Then we can learn to see Him in those around us and deepen our capacity for love and compassion.

Thursday: Luke 9:23–27
I am Ashamed of You

"What will it profit a man if he gains the whole world,
and loses his own soul?" (Mark 8:36)

SCIENCE STRUGGLES WITH PARADOX. In our world, we want things neat and in order. We want to be able to predict how our world will behave and what comes next.

Yet look at the nature of light. Science has discovered through quantum physics that light is both a particle and a wave—yes, *both*. There are many such paradoxical principles in the natural world, eliciting from us a sense of humility and wonder.

In our Gospel reading today, our Lord is once again offering His disciples insight and wisdom into how to become truly free and truly human. The only real way to gain real freedom, he says, is through a great paradox: "Whoever desires to save his life will lose it, but whoever loses his life for My sake will find it" (Matt. 16:25).

Since this is true, we can't afford to put our faith on automatic pilot. The Fathers insist that our keen wakefulness is always necessary if we are to ever break the gravitational pull of our selfish world. To live, we must first cease our pursuit of our own pleasure. This may feel like death for a time as we let go of our worldly goals for success and achievement as measured by this world. Yet in this death, we'll find life, and we'll be able to fellowship with the uncreated God. To achieve this goal, it is worth abandoning the fantasy of success and achievement that ends at the grave.

TODAY: Entering into the life of faith with all its paradox is a daily struggle. Sometimes it's even a moment-by-moment struggle. Don't be discouraged, but turn instead to Christ—in so doing, your authentic self will be revealed. Faith in Christ is often seen as foolishness, but embracing it wholeheartedly will enable you to be unashamed of the paradox of Jesus Christ and His wisdom in a world that seems always to offer us the exact opposite of His wisdom.

Friday: Luke 9:44–50
Missing the Point

*"I know you think you understand what you thought I said
but I'm not sure you realize that what you heard
is not what I meant."* —Alan Greenspan

THE ABILITY TO COMMUNICATE EFFECTIVELY can be hindered by so many factors, and we often miss the point of what others are trying to say. In our Gospel reading today, the Lord said to His disciples, "'Let these words sink down into your ears, for the Son of Man is about to be betrayed into the hands of men.' But they did not understand this saying, and it was hidden from them so that they did not perceive it; and they were afraid to ask Him about this saying. Then a dispute arose among them as to which of them would be greatest. And Jesus, perceiving the thought of their heart, took a little child and set him by Him, and said to them, 'Whoever receives this little child in My name receives Me; and whoever receives Me receives Him who sent Me. For he who is least among you all will be great'" (Luke 9:44–48).

Here, Jesus is telling His disciples quite plainly that He is going to be crucified, betrayed, and killed. They missed the point entirely. Instead, they began to argue about which disciple held the highest position.

How can we avoid making this same mistake? Two things will help us: First, embrace humility. Assume the simplicity of acceptance. Don't be cynical. Second, rejoice with others when they do well. This keeps our hearts tender.

TODAY: Do you find yourself missing the point on a regular basis? Are you too busy promoting your own agenda to be able to hear the still, small voice of the Holy Spirit? If you return to the path of humble obedience and a joyful attitude, you will be able to stay focused on the main point rather than wandering off the road.

Monday: Luke 9:49–56

The Enemy of My Enemy

… Is my friend

THIS IDEA IS EMBRACED in politics and warfare to justify the strange bedfellows that certain alliances have created in the pursuit of political and military goals. But is there any spiritual benefit to this attitude and political tool?

In our Gospel reading today, the Lord's disciples came to Jesus to report their good work. They were seeking His approval for their actions. They had encountered a man casting out demons in the name of Jesus and told him to stop doing that, since he wasn't part of their company.

"'Master, we saw someone casting out demons in Your name, and we forbade him because he does not follow with us.' But Jesus said to him, 'Do not forbid *him*, for he who is not against us is on our side'" (Luke 9:49, 50).

The Lord turns this concept on its head to teach the disciples a valuable lesson. He wants the disciples to abandon in-group favoritism and adopt a wider perspective. The grace of God is given to all who sincerely seek to know Him. Today, we will need to overcome the temptation to stay in our spiritual cliques. Jesus reminds His disciples that our God is loving, giving, and humble, gracious to anyone who seeks to embrace Him. We should imitate His example.

This, by the way, isn't equivalent to universalism, the philosophy that all faiths are the same. Jesus is present in His world through His Church. In His Church, grace is given to love people regardless of whether they are in or out of the Faith.

TODAY: Instead of maneuvering people in your life to create maximum benefit for yourself, ask the Lord to help you bring His presence into every situation in your life. Let's transform by grace our relationships, acquaintances, and surroundings into humble opportunities for the presence of Jesus in His Church.

Tuesday: Matthew 13:54–58
Easily Offended

I'm offended

TODAY, PEOPLE SEEM TO BE offended for all kinds of reasons. Our Gospel reading today tells a familiar story: the hometown boy who has made good came home to a resentful community, incited to jealousy by his success.

Why is it that we are offended by others' success?

In Jesus' case, his hometown villagers thought they knew Him. Yet His teachings challenged their assumptions and pride. No matter who you are, that isn't easy or pleasant. Sadly, their unbelief meant that the ever-present grace within Christ could not and would not penetrate their hard hearts and heal them. Nursing their offended feelings, they blocked God's mercy.

How can we avoid a similar fate? We have to allow our assumptions to be challenged without getting defensive. Let's confess our need for Christ. Rather than being offended by the Lord's insight, let's acknowledge our deep need for a true relationship with God, not giving in to our fear and disbelief.

TODAY: Do the teachings of the Faith offend you? Before you cavalierly dismiss them, submit to honest self-reflection. Humbly assume that this wisdom just may be absolutely necessary to break up all those defensive walls around your heart so that true relationships can occur. Don't remain ill when there is healing right at your fingertips.

Wednesday: John 15:17–27; 16:1–2
Connected, But with Consequences

"In this world you will have tribulation." (John 16:33)

CLOSE RELATIONSHIPS can either blind or enlighten you. Codependency enslaves us, but healthy relationships nurture and fulfill us. God created us for communion and connection.

In today's Gospel reading, our Lord Jesus told His disciples how they will be treated after He has ascended into heaven. He warns them that they will be treated as the world treated Him, due to their connection with Him. This is because the world has forgotten the meaning of true communion and so is lost in a sea of confusion about right and wrong and the nature of true relationships.

These are the life-altering consequences that come from not knowing God. Jesus reminded His disciples of this: the world didn't know Him. Some thought of God the Father as a kind of cosmic terrorist. Others expected the Messiah to be a political figure, rescuing them from the Romans. Instead, He came and died a death on the Cross.

The greatest consequence of blindness toward God is a profound confusion about our own identity. This confusion ripples out, impacting every relationship we have and guaranteeing that we'll not be at peace. Without the right connection to Christ, we reduce our relationships to a quest for selfish satisfaction, and we engage in counterfeit communion. This is what the world understands and why it rejects Christ and His disciples, even today.

TODAY: If you desire healthy relationships in your life, you first need to strengthen your relationship with God. All other relationships in your life are, to varying degrees, a mirror of that primary relationship. The effort you give to knowing God, loving God, and coming to know yourself through Him, will bear good fruit. Today, seek Him. He wants to be found by you.

Thursday: Luke 11:1–10
Ask, Seek, Knock

You have to want to

Today, we are fond of creating systems for everything. "Ten Ways to Boost Your Metabolism!" "Four Steps to a New You!" "Eight Days to a Clean House!" promise the website articles. We simply can't resist clicking on the links, hoping to find the key that will finally unlock success for us in our failed endeavors.

But the truth is, we already know how to be happy in life and what it takes to succeed. We already know how to lose weight, grow a business, or pass a test. What we really need is the *want to*, so that we can accomplish what we already know. We need the relationships that foster and support good choices. What we need is communion, community, and intimacy with God and others.

Look at the familiar Gospel reading for today. Ask, seek, and knock, it tells us. It's as simple—and as difficult—as that.

Asking means that there is desire for something. Tell me what you truly desire, and I'll tell you who you really are. Jesus was constantly asking others, "What do you want?" As Christians, we are taught to desire God's will as the key to everything else.

Next, we must actively seek, pressing in and laboring toward the pursuit of His will. We must practice spiritual disciplines, patiently and steadily.

Finally, we must knock at heaven's door. We don't burst through the door as petulant children. A person who wisely seeks God's will knocks in humble love and obedience with full confidence that if this is the right door, it will be opened for him.

Today: Do you know what you really want? Are you actively pouring your best energies into looking for this? And, are you willing to humble yourself to knock with full expectation that the right door will be opened for you? If so, get ready to live the life you were meant to live.

Friday: Luke 10:38–42, 11:27–28
Keep It

"In the future life the Christian is not examined if he has renounced the whole world for Christ's love, or if he has distributed his riches to the poor or if he fasted or kept vigil or prayed, or if he wept and lamented for his sins, or if he has done any other good in this life, but he is examined attentively if he has any similitude with Christ, as a son does with his father."
—St. Symeon the New Theologian

To BECOME LIKE CHRIST should be the focus of all Orthodox Christians. All the disciplines of the Faith, all the liturgies, all the prayers, are aimed at this goal. If we are like Christ, we will bear the family resemblance we will desperately need on that Last Day. But how do we become like Him? Two verbs provide the key: to hear and to keep.

In our familiar Gospel reading, the blessed ones are they who both hear the Word of God and keep it. To truly hear God's Word means we desire to listen, and we come with a humble willingness to practice the things we hear.

Of course, Jesus Christ Himself is the Word made flesh for our sakes. "In the beginning was the Word, and the Word was with God, and the Word was God," writes St. John in the first words to His Gospel.

Then we must keep the Word of God. There have been many times when I have experienced a moment of spiritual clarity only to have it drowned out by the cares of everyday life. The Faith gives me daily disciplines so that I can keep what I have heard rather than losing precious treasure in the rush of daily life.

TODAY: Are you keeping God's Word? This is done through daily attentiveness to the disciplines of the Faith. Daily, make the choice to turn toward God. Today, take an icon of Christ and keep it before your eyes. Say to yourself, "This is my model and template."

Monday: Luke 11:14–23

Binding the Strong Man

"Some glory in chariots, some in horses,
But in the name of the Lord our God we shall be magnified."
(Psalm 19[20]:8 OSB)

MANY PEOPLE TODAY trust in strong men to guard their homes, families, and lives. Forgetting the name of the Lord, we put a great deal of faith in the stock market, politicians, our careers, our insurance policies, or our possessions, hoping some combination thereof will keep us content and safe.

Why do we so easily forget that it is *Jesus* who is Lord? Sometimes we are simply absentminded, and hours go by without our giving Him a second thought. Sometimes our faith is weak in the face of a skeptical world. Regardless, as soon as we become aware of our forgetfulness, we can repent and reaffirm our faith. Let's not listen to the evil one's voice, condemning us for our weakness. Rather, we can thank God for these moments of forgetting, because they can become stepping stones to greater faith.

In our Gospel reading, we learn that the true Strong Man has come among us, binding the power of the old strong man that used to enslave us to fear and doubt. Christ's name is powerful, and His love is unquenchable. He has indeed risen from the dead, trampling down death by death, and upon those in the tombs bestowing life. In His mercy, God brings us back to this truth time and time again. My faith is not just a mental affirmation of a set of facts, but a daily, life-altering relationship with our risen Lord. Behold, the strong man has come!

TODAY: Are you facing a challenge in your life that seems impossible to overcome? Do your fears cause you to forget that even physical death has been emptied of its power? Let's band together and enlist the spiritual tools of our Orthodox Faith to help us increase our faith and remembrance of Christ. Today, the strong man has come, and He is your eternal ally.

Tuesday: Luke 11:23–26
Simple, But Not Easy

Life is simple

L ife is not complicated. That doesn't mean it's always easy, but it is simple. However, I complicate my life in all kinds of ways. At its core, life is simple because God created life and is Life. God's simplicity is woven into all of creation. We are the ones who complicate our lives with our delusions and excuses.

But why do we do this? Why do we seem to end up being our own worst enemy? Well, just look at the first man and his stumble. Our parents in the Garden of Eden, with all their God-given advantages, exercised their freedom to turn away from God. All their Creator had asked was that they refrain from eating of *one* tree. Adam and Eve chose the complicated approach. They doubted God and suspected Him of hiding something from them, and then they chose to take matters in their own hands. The rest is (a very sad) history.

In our Gospel reading today, the Lord said, "He who is not with Me is against Me, and he who does not gather with Me scatters abroad" (Matt. 12:30). This statement is simple. The Author of our lives knows better than we do the path to peace and happiness. He invites us, "Walk with Me and be free, or walk by yourself and descend into the slavery of your desires." Responding the right way to God in each moment is not always easy, but the path is straight and simple. If I stay close to my Creator, I will live in freedom. If I strike out on my own, chances are my life will get complicated pretty quickly, and the free fall will continue as I spin out from His orbit.

Today: Are there desert places in your life—barren, dry, and void of joy and life? It's time to leave the desert and return to the source of living water. This is the life we were all meant to live, and we were created to enjoy it forever. There is no reason for your life to spiral downward. It's time to turn, to change your mind, and to embrace the simple life offered in Jesus Christ.

Wednesday: Luke 11:29–33
You Should Have Known Better

"For what I am doing, I do not understand.
For what I will to do, that I do not practice;
but what I hate, that I do." (Romans 7:15)

ALL TOO OFTEN, there is a difference between what I know and what I do. I make the same mistakes over and over again. Maybe you've experienced similar frustration to one degree or the other. St. Paul expressed these feelings too, in the Book of Romans.

What gives? Sadly, each of us has inherited a broken will. While we are aware of what we should be doing, we can't muster the willpower to follow through. We are our own worst enemies, and yet because we are free agents, we know in our heart of hearts that we are completely responsible for our actions.

In today's reading, Jesus confronted an ever-growing crowd of people who were following Him, absorbing His teaching, and receiving healing from Him. Rather than basking in His growing popularity, He opened His remarks with a convicting proclamation: "This is an evil generation" (Luke 11:29).

TODAY: To strengthen and heal our broken wills, we need to be completely honest with ourselves. We are an evil generation indeed, and we need to repent and come clean. Let's admit that we are broken and unable to do the things we ought to do. No wonder the Church prays "Lord, have mercy" throughout the liturgy. This isn't a prayer in which we beg God to be kind to us, for God is always kind and merciful. No, this is the Church's way of reminding us we continually should acknowledge our need for His mercy and grace. If we aren't alert to our peril and are numbed by daily distractions, we'll continue in a state of slavery to our weak wills.

Thursday: Luke 11:34–41
Distracted Again

Let us attend!

I CAN TRACE most of the challenges in my life to the times when I began to focus more on trivial distractions rather than on my spiritual life. In Orthodox Christianity we are taught attentiveness, which, simply put, is a continual wake-up call regarding the proper ordering of our priorities. Clarity and focus are the virtues that enable me to align the rest of my loves as they should be—if I am attentive, I find it is much easier to be selfless and generous.

In our Gospel reading, the Lord confronted the religious man who invited Him to dinner. Do you think the Lord forgot to wash His hands? Not a chance! The Lord knew this man needed to be confronted with his distracted life.

The Lord's host thought he was finished with his spiritual duties merely because he went through the motions. But Christ wasn't about to let him off the hook. He challenged the man to realize that an important spiritual ingredient was missing from his distracted life: the presence of an attitude of gratitude.

The key to living a life free of distractions and filled with clarity, purpose, and focus is the cultivation of gratitude and generosity. A grateful, generous person is a focused person. Gratitude and generosity equal spiritual health.

TODAY: Where are you most sidetracked by distractions? Lay aside all your excuses and justifications and look closely at your life. You might discover at the heart of the disorder lies a weakened sense of gratitude and an inability to be generous. Strengthen your ability to be grateful to God and those around you, and watch as the distractions melt away and order returns to your relationships, your career, your priorities, and your faith. It is precisely a healthy sense of gratitude to God first, and then to those around you, that will enable you to stay focused on the most important tasks: Loving God and loving your neighbor as yourself.

Friday: Luke 11:42–46
Forgetting Our Why

"Having a form of godliness but denying its power"
(2 Timothy 3:5)

A S A NATION, we are now obsessed with individual rights and freedoms at the expense of common sense or moral boundaries. When anyone dares to question this new orthodoxy, he or she is labeled an enemy of free choice. This perspective has been adopted by nearly all of our political leaders, and we thus have lost our shared understanding about our democracy's meaning and purpose. But can our society really survive without a social contract in place or agreement as to the underlying principles that govern our nation?

Our Gospel reading is instructive. Jesus again called out the religious leaders, lamenting that while they'd outwardly maintained the traditions of the Faith, they had lost sight of their *why*. He insisted that this was a dangerous situation—once the understanding and commitment to inner reasoning breaks down, outward practices are rendered meaningless. The Pharisees *loved* the attention they received: being seated at the best tables and being greeted as exalted leaders in the marketplace. The Lord knew that their outward practices had become an empty shell, and they had long since lost their sense of purpose.

Likewise, Orthodox Faith will lose its potency if we forget our *why*. We need to constantly renew our hearts and minds so that in our practice, we don't forget the purpose of our Faith. We too can slip into the mindless and heedless rote repetition of old words and old ways, having "a form of godliness but denying its power" (2 Tim. 3:5). Only God's Holy Spirit can truly transform us.

TODAY: Has your life been reduced to a mere set of personal choices you guard with religious devotion? Are the core purposes of the Faith—union with God and salvation in Christ—informing your daily actions and spiritual practices? Let's renew our *why* as Orthodox Christians!

Monday: Luke 11:47–54; 12:1
The People of God

"God is wondrous in His saints" (Psalm 67[68]:36)

A BRITISH JOURNALIST was visiting the library of an ancient Mt. Athos monastery. The old monk giving the tour was telling the reporter about the saints and authors represented in the library's stacks. The journalist remarked that it seemed to him that the monk actually *knew and loved* these people, since he described them as though they were still alive.

"We spend our lives not just knowing the ideas of these writers but they, themselves," replied the monk. "They are our brothers and they are with Christ, and Christ is not dead, so neither are they. Don't you folks believe Jesus rose from the dead?"

In today's Gospel reading, Jesus condemned the Pharisees, who while outwardly following a set of rules and regulations had lost the virtues of mercy and love. In their rigid observation of external practices, they had neglected to maintain the proper attitude in their hearts. "Woe to you!" Christ said (Luke 11:42).

God-filled faith always engenders connection and communion. When I submitted to the Orthodox Christian Church, I became a part of the communal memory of the great cloud of witnesses (Heb. 12:1). Being in actual communion with my brothers and sisters in Christ became more important to me than expressing my own insights and perspectives. None of us is saved alone—we are all saved in community.

TODAY: Let's repent of the hypocrisy in our hearts and be vigilant against the loss of love for God and others. We are stewards of the irreplaceable gift of the memory of the saints, who have preceded us in an unbroken chain forged by love, communion, and fellowship. Stand in front of your icons and declare, "God is wondrous in His saints!"

Tuesday: Luke 12:8–12
How Not to Be Anxious

Fear not!

GIVING IN TO WORRY and fear cripples us. In our Gospel reading today, the Lord tells us not to worry when we are called to stand up for our faith in a hostile society. Easier said than done. So how do we overcome our natural resistance to troubles and challenges?

The first thing we can do to fight our fear of speaking up for Christ is to be willing anywhere and everywhere to acknowledge our allegiance to Him. A lukewarm life—our hearts divided between our faith and worldly cares—never works. When challenged as a Christian, the temptation will be too great to back down.

Next, we need to accept that we Christians are marching to the beat of a different drummer. We will never been seen as friends of a world that often blasphemes against the Holy Spirit. We need to let go of concerns about what people think of us and be willing to be called bigots or simpletons. Let's face it—we will never be the cool kids, so let's stop trying.

Finally, we can embrace our position in this world, knowing that if God is with us, who can be against us? When moments come when we face rejection by those who also reject Christ, the Spirit of Christ at work in us will give us the words to say.

TODAY: Are you worried, scared, or overwhelmed by the challenges of following Christ? Today is the day to renew your focus on building intimacy with God through the spiritual disciplines of prayer, fasting, and almsgiving. If you practice the Faith with love and patience, you'll not only have the right words to say when the world challenges you, but you'll also set an example for others to follow.

Wednesday: Luke 12:13–15, 22–31
The Temptation of Misplaced Trust

Our Father, who art in heaven…

REMEMBER THE OLD TV SHOW *Father Knows Best?* It featured actor Robert Young as a wise, good-natured father who provided daily wisdom and guidance to his family. In one sense, the show was a winsome reminder that we all have a heavenly Father who yearns to be our model and guide as well.

However, we tend to lose our way. We focus on lesser things and travel down bunny trails and useless paths. Sometimes, without the guidance of our heavenly Father, our lives even spiral completely out of control. Like the Prodigal Son we are left asking, "How did I get here?"

In our Gospel reading today, Jesus reminds us we aren't going to be fulfilled by focusing on worldly success, possessions, or achievement. Instead, we should aim for the spot down the road that helps us travel in a straight line so we can reach our destination safely.

If we worry about all the interruptions and obstacles along the path, we'll be like the farmer who looks at the ground while plowing his field: when he looks up, the row is going to be a crooked as a dog's hind leg. The only way for us to reach our destination peacefully is to keep our eyes fixed on God our Father, who knows and will provide what we need. Remember, God takes care of His world and the children He has created. As long as we keep Him as our reference point along the journey of life, we will find our way safely home.

TODAY: Every event, no matter how pleasant or difficult, is a moment where we can be reminded of our ultimate destination. If we keep our eyes fixed on that point down the road where we join our Lord for eternity, we will stay on the path. We can trust God's love and guidance. Indeed, He loves us even more than we love ourselves—our Father knows best.

Thursday: Luke 12:42–48
Your Hunger Reveals Your Heart

You are what you eat

THE SEARCH FOR FOOD and daily bread has been at the top of the priority list for most of human history. Until the twentieth century, eating nourishing food every day was a privilege reserved only for the very rich and powerful.

Eating and hunger are at the very heart of true Orthodox theology, too. In *For the Life of the World*, the late Protopresbyter Alexander Schmemann wrote, "In the biblical story of creation man is presented, first of all, as a hungry being, and the whole world as his food."

In today's Gospel reading, we learn that if an impatient steward tries to satisfy his hunger before the Master gives him his portion "in due season" (Luke 12:42), he will end up consuming others, improperly indulging his hunger and becoming a slave to it. Only spiritual food truly satisfies the real hunger of our hearts.

Then the Lord adds this phrase: "to whom much is given, from him much will be required" (Luke 12:48). The physical and spiritual blessings we enjoy bring with them greater responsibility to use our advantages wisely and well. Truly, we must admit that all the wealth we enjoy and the ease with which we acquire our daily bread has only made it easier for us to be ruled by our passions. Today, we are no different from the millions who have come before us in earlier times. More than ever, we need mercy and grace to overcome the temptation to satisfy our hungers in an unfaithful way.

TODAY: Only love can satiate our hunger. On a daily basis, let's enter into a relationship with our Lord, who is Love Himself. In this way, we will able to wholly trust the Master who gives us this day our daily bread.

Friday: Luke 12:48–59
To Whom Much Is Given

"Refuse to listen to the devil when he whispers to you: give me now, and you will give tomorrow to God. No, no! Spend all the hours of your life in a way pleasing to God; keep in your mind the thought that after the present hour you will not be given another and that you will have to render a strict account for every minute of this present hour."
—St. Theophan the Recluse

THE WORD *account* has various meanings. In a mundane sense, it refers to fiscal practice and a responsible use of our finances. In a sober, spiritual sense, it refers to our eventual reckoning, where we will be required to give a good defense before the awesome Judgment Seat of Christ.

In our Gospel reading today, our Lord Jesus used some—some might even say incendiary—language. Whenever this happens in the Gospels (and it happens often), it's important for us who are serious students of God's Word to really explore *why* the Lord feels He must speak like this.

In this case, the Lord desires us to be rescued from the burning building of a life spent chasing after temporal—rather than eternal—pursuits. Sometimes Jesus speaks so plainly and emphatically that we are shocked into the realization of what is at stake, here and now.

What He is trying to remind us of is our responsibility to account for the gifts of time and talents God gave us in this life. We are called to make the most of these for the benefit of others. If we are living selfishly and ignorantly, the Lord loves us enough to speak sternly to us. May we be set on the path of what the Fathers called *nepsis*, or wakefulness.

TODAY: Are you aware of the gifts of time and talent you possess, and for what reason you have been so blessed? It's high time to wake up and see the responsibility you have to steward these treasures wisely, for the good of your soul and those of others.

Monday: Matthew 5:14–19

Relax! Wait, Maybe Not

*"Beware the barrenness of a busy life." —*Socrates

THESE DAYS, we scramble to fill every waking moment with working toward our goals. We hate to feel we are wasting a minute, yet how do we order our days so that our lives aren't just busy, but meaningful and pleasing to God?

In our Gospel reading today, the Lord made it clear that He hasn't come to undermine or replace the timeless wisdom of God's Law (Matt. 5:17). He warns against relaxing the wisdom of the Law to pave an easy path filled with worldly activities and goals. That's why He reminds the apostles that they are the light of the world. As such, they ought to lead meaningful lives that draw others to Christ. As lights, we aren't shining for our personal gratification and glory but so that others can see clearly and be pointed to our Lord. We aren't supposed to be celebrities, but servants.

Sounds challenging, doesn't it?

However, we aren't called to mere goal setting or list making. Instead, we are meant to make Christ's life—His priorities and wisdom—the standard for our activity and efforts. As our loving Father, God provides grace and love to shine through us as His lights to the world. His strength compensates for our weakness, enabling us to accomplish meaningful and eternal tasks rather than purposeless busywork.

TODAY: Are you tempted to be busy for no reason? Perhaps it's time to follow the path of wisdom and repentance that leads to lasting, eternal work rather than ephemeral tasks that won't outlive us. Let's learn the full meaning of Christ's command to be the light of the world.

Tuesday: John 10:9–16
A Mere Hireling

Every priest carries not only the burden of his own sins,
which are countless, but also the sins of everyone
whom God has entrusted to his spiritual care

D ID YOU KNOW that October is Clergy Appreciation Month? Those
of us in the clergy do. (October is also International Walk to School
Month too, lest we think it's all about us.)

It is wonderful to be appreciated, but we should never demand or seek recognition. Every time I see a brass plaque on a church building announcing a
donor's contribution, I reflect on the subtle temptations that come from that
kind of praise.

In our Gospel reading today, the Lord warns His people against the hireling, the one who serves God's people only for payment or recognition. When
trouble comes, the hired help is the first to bail out, since his loyalty is shallow.
He will only give if he can receive recognition and won't participate unless he
knows his gift will be acknowledged.

In contrast, a true shepherd lays down His life for the sheep. When trouble comes, he doesn't abandon his post but risks his life to protect the sheep
he loves. The true shepherd thinks of his people before he thinks of himself.
He makes it his business to know his sheep, and this relationship comforts
them.

We will only be able to be like the Good Shepherd when we relinquish our
rights to be praised and noticed. Whether we are a member of the clergy or
laity, we can emulate the selfless attitude of Christ, our Good Shepherd.

TODAY: Our goal should be to practice both forgetfulness toward ourselves
and thankfulness toward others, particularly those who serve us as good
shepherds. The twin virtues of humility and gratefulness protect our hearts
from the attitude of the hireling, who expects praise and compensation.

Wednesday: Matthew 9:9–13
Tax Collectors and Sinners

Behold, the tax man cometh

THERE ARE TIMES IN LIFE when conflict is unavoidable. You know the situations I'm talking about: a difficult confrontation can't be put off, a struggle with bureaucracy is inevitable, or a troubled relationship has to end or change.

So, how do we face such moments in life as believers? Our Gospel reading today provides direction.

Frankly, I can't think of anything more unpleasant than taxes. Tax collectors in the Lord's time were feared and hated, since they were collaborators with the occupying Roman government. Additionally, their income was based on how much they collected from people, so not only were they not trusted, they were considered to be traitors to their own people.

Yet St. Matthew the tax collector immediately responded to the Lord's call. How did he manage to overcome the obstacle of his profession to become a faithful disciple?

First, we read that St. Matthew "arose and followed Him" (Matt. 9:9). Embracing an attitude of obedience simplifies even the most complicated situations. We never improve anything by trying to negotiate with the right course of action. Simple, straightforward obedience is key.

Second, we must approach difficult decisions by being cognizant of our own spiritual illness and need for God's healing mercy and grace. When I try to work out my problems in my own strength, I fail. Repentance, on the other hand, brings help and peace.

Finally, remember mercy. Those who hurt us, even those we have to say goodbye to, are also in need of God's mercy and grace, just as we are.

TODAY: Are you putting off making a difficult decision? Like St. Matthew the tax collector, summon your courage and, with humility and prayer, walk the path of obedience, repentance, and mercy. Then you will have the strength to do what is called for in your difficult circumstances.

Thursday: Luke 14:25–35
Salt Makes People Thirsty

"You are the salt of the earth" (Matthew 5:13)

WE OFTEN SUFFER from self-inflicted blindness that robs us of our peace and joy. We tell ourselves that we control our own destinies, but as soon as we do this, we lose the ability to see ourselves and to understand others with clarity. The truth is, of course, that none of us is in control of our lives: God is.

In our Gospel reading today, our Lord addresses this spiritual blindness and delusion head on. He insists that to live in right relationship with others, we have to get our relationship with God right first. In fact, even my relationship with myself is not right until my relationship with Him is restored. As His followers, we must realize our purpose for being: to be the salt of the earth.

I love that phrase the Lord uses. By referencing the preservative so necessary for everyday life, He strikes a chord of understanding and recognition in his hearers. Salt was a commodity so valuable in the time of Christ that they would actually use it as currency. It preserved food, added flavor, and was used as a disinfectant. Even to this day, one of the time-honored traditions of greeting our bishops when they come to our communities is to offer them bread and salt.

The properties of salt are the same properties we need in order to live a spiritually productive life. We should flavor the lives of those around us, and we should help preserve the faith and the truth. Yes, we *are* the salt of the earth. But if the salt loses its saltiness, what good is it? So too, someone who is a follower of Christ in word only has no zing or zest or preserving power.

TODAY: Are you providing salt in your world? Are you wise enough to embrace all the spiritual tools so abundant in our Orthodox Faith to help you keep your saltiness? As we fast during this Advent, remember that the goal of the disciplines of the Church isn't to make your life hard or to make you feel guilty, but to help you to remain true to your real identity in Christ.

Friday: Luke 15:1–10
The Legend of Narcissus

"Those who are well have no need of a physician." (Mark 2:17)

NARCISSUS WAS A MAN who was exceptionally handsome and knew it. His actions reflected his utter disdain for those who loved him. He walked through life proud of his appearance and dismissive of those who admired him. Eventually, Narcissus was lured to a pool where he could see his reflection. Enamored with the view of his face and form, Narcissus couldn't tear himself away, and eventually he drowned in the pool. To be clear, Narcissus's sin wasn't that he was handsome. It was his self-love and disdain for others that killed him.

In today's reading, the religious leaders had grown so entrenched in their spiritual practices that they simply dismissed anyone outside the fold. They were meticulous in their religious observances but had forgotten that they'd been given this treasure in order to be a light to the world so that others would be drawn to the Faith as well. In their pride, they had hardened their hearts against those who were in need of spiritual healing. Instead of cultivating hearts of mercy and love toward outsiders, they viewed them with pride and suspicion.

Christ upended this system, spending His time not with the people who mistakenly thought they were healthy and whole but with the folks who knew they were lost. God's chosen people had closed their hearts to the spiritual seekers at their gates. They ignored them, feared them, and even hated them. In the end, the narcissistic religious leaders were the unhealthiest people of all.

TODAY: Does your Faith make you loving or fearful toward outsiders? Does your parish welcome the stranger, or do the faces in your congregation reflect suspicion and disdain? God's love makes us more welcoming and loving, while counterfeit spirituality only feeds the false notion of our own specialness. Let's seek the lost sheep rather than being satisfied with our comfortable group of insiders.

Monday: Luke 16:1–9

Make Friends for Yourselves

Daddy, I don't have any friends!

IT WAS A HEARTBREAKING MOMENT for my daughter in her young life, and my heart was broken too. She was learning a lesson that we all have to learn: "A man *who has* friends must himself be friendly, / But there is a friend *who* sticks closer than a brother" (Prov. 18:24 NKJV).

We humans crave companionship, and yet we are so afraid of being hurt that we draw back from connecting in a real way with others. Thus, we find ourselves either lonely or trapped in toxic, unhealthy relationships. Then we struggle in our relationship with God as well.

In our Gospel reading today, the Lord once again is telling a story. Having squandered his position through poor choices, the unfaithful steward of the rich man's possessions is finally called to account for his poor work. In desperation, he shrewdly goes to all the rich man's debtors and makes a deal, in hopes that when he is out of a job, they will show him kindness in his need.

When we face the consequences of our bad choices, we can either choose despair, or we can reach out for God's mercy. By the way, protecting our children from having to face reality and the consequences of their actions always does them more harm than good. We short-circuit the opportunity these temporarily painful moments present to them and delay the inevitable moment when there is no protection possible.

TODAY: Do you allow the consequences in your life to teach you, or do you find yourself constantly crying for rescue? Let's learn valuable lessons from our failures and not perpetuate destructive behavior patterns.

Tuesday: Luke 16:15–18; 17:1–4
Only the Violent Enter

Taking the Kingdom by force

OUR MODERN WORLD is awash in violence. But the Scriptures mention another kind of violence altogether, a purposeful, determined struggle for salvation.

In today's Gospel reading the Lord Jesus reminds us we *will* face temptations—they shouldn't come as a surprise to us. We live in a world where it's easy to sin and hard to do right, where we are constantly tempted to compromise with the truth in the name of getting along. Yet, of course, we know that those who want us to water down the Faith will never be satisfied until we capitulate all together.

Sometimes, Christ reminds us, we aren't satisfied with our own sins; we want others to join us.

Then the Lord tells us "everyone is pressing into [the Kingdom]" (Luke 16:16), almost in a violent way. This isn't to say we are called to be violent toward others, of course, but to bring our best efforts to the fight against our own weaknesses and sin.

Finally, the Lord insists that we take responsibility for our brothers. We are to love them enough to help them see the destructiveness of their rebellion and then to forgive them every time they ask.

TODAY: Are you resolute enough to enter God's Kingdom by violence, if necessary? Do you remember the words at each baptism, that we are called to keep the baptismal garment spotless? If so, know this will take a violent embrace of wisdom, repentance, spiritual struggle, and faithfulness when all around you tempts you to give up or give in. To enter the Kingdom of God, we need to be resolute.

Wednesday: Luke 17:20–25
Right in Front of You

"Of His Kingdom there will be no end" (Luke 1:33)

THROUGH ALL OF HUMAN HISTORY, people have endeavored to create the perfect society. Try as we may, we stumble to create heaven on earth. Just ask the millions slaughtered in the name of the workers' paradise promised by communism.

What if we have this all wrong? What if this perfect Kingdom isn't a place but a Person?

In our Gospel reading today, our Lord Jesus reveals the principles of the Kingdom of God to the Pharisees and His disciples. He tells them the Kingdom that will finally satisfy the best intentions of humanity will not come in the way we expect. The Kingdom meant for all humanity isn't a hereditary monarchy, a system of democratic government, or even a benign dictatorship. It isn't dependent on the next election cycle or on a political party platform.

No, this Kingdom is "within you" (Luke 17:21). In other words, the Kingdom of God is a Person, not a place.

This means that all our seeking to make the Kingdom about this or a policy or a political system will always disappoint us. The rule of God is found in the hearts of those who have willingly allowed Him to be the ruler of their lives. The transformation of human society doesn't start with a politician or a political ideology. Only when we are transformed into faithful subjects of the Heavenly King who died and rose again will we experience the lasting Kingdom.

TODAY: As we rightly struggle to do what's right and have a just and honorable society, we shouldn't fall for the utopian rhetoric of lesser kings who worship power. We worship the only King able to establish His governance in our hearts, and in Him we place our confidence. Indeed, we are committed to the only Kingdom that ultimately matters.

Thursday: Luke 17:26–37; 18:8
Will He Find Faith on the Earth?

Take up your cross

IN OUR GOSPEL READING TODAY, the Lord reminded His disciples that when human history begins winding down, it isn't going to be so obvious that people everywhere will be alarmed. In Noah's time, people were living their lives day to day as they always had. They watched Noah construct the ark, but people didn't repent. Rather, they ridiculed Noah and went about their business. The same scenario played out in the story of Sodom and Gomorrah. People kept on living their lives, ignoring the opportunities to repent until destruction rained down upon them.

What do we learn from these examples?

Can we take our courage in hand and do the hard work of examining our hearts? Can we die to the false notion that we are the center of the universe? Can we learn to die to the temptations of fulfilling all our desires in a selfish way? Then we will enter into the life God offers us through the Resurrection of His Son, our Lord Jesus. If we selfishly try to save our lives, we will watch them slip away. Remember paradox?

But if we enter into the disciplined life followed by believers in Christ, we will learn that saying no to temporary things allows us to say yes to eternal joys.

No wonder the Church, under the gentle and loving tutelage of the Holy Spirit, leads us to a time of fasting before the great Feast of the Nativity. If I teach my stomach to discipline its desires, I'll have a head start on teaching my whole self how to die to my selfish wants in favor of eternal life.

TODAY: Don't look back. Look forward. Look inward. Look upward. Let's discover how to die to the soul-killing patterns of behavior that don't save us and don't change us. Let's reach forward to Christ, who is Life Himself. Fast, pray, worship. This leads to real life.

Friday: Mark 5:24–34
Keep on Being Healed

"Youth is wasted on the young." —George Bernard Shaw

WHEN WE HAVE GREAT STRENGTH and potential, we are still too immature to take full advantage of them. With age comes wisdom, but then we have less energy and time to appreciate of our hard-won insights.

However, later in life we do sometimes act more purposefully as we see time running out. Of course, it is indeed sad when the passing of years doesn't mean that we grow in wisdom, rather that we just grow old.

God has created us as free, unique, and unrepeatable people. How sad when we lose sight of that mystery as the years go by. If we can but grasp it, we can live our days with purpose and meaning, even as we age and move toward eternity.

So how do we progress on the path toward spiritual maturity while preserving the childlikeness of faith?

In today's reading we encounter the woman who has been ill for some time. She hears Christ is coming through her town and says to herself, "If only I may touch His clothes, I shall be made well" (Mark 5:28). Subsequently, she does touch the hem of His garment, and she is healed. Notice: in the midst of this, Christ asks, "Who touched my clothes?" (v. 30).

Our Lord didn't ask this question because He didn't know the answer. He asked the question to teach His disciples a powerful lesson in spiritual maturity. Jesus was so alert at every moment that when something significant happened, He knew. In fact, both Christ and the woman provide an example for us. Both brought their faith to bear, enabling the miracle to take place.

TODAY: Let's acquire a deeper understanding of our hearts. As we mature in Christ, let's remember that each one of us is unique, created to be with God forever. We are meant to be so filled with grace and love that these qualities will spill over to everyone around us.

Monday: Luke 18:31–34

Shamefully Treated

He who has ears to hear

A CONFRONTATION WAS COMING, and it was unavoidable. As I sat in the office, I waited my turn to offered feedback as requested. I was struck—not for the first time—by how difficult it can be to handle unpleasant conversations.

Yet sometimes in hindsight, we have to confess that these uncomfortable moments were absolutely necessary. How we handle these moments reveals our character and our mettle.

In our Gospel reading, the Lord tells the disciples the truth about what is coming in His life and in their lives as well. He is going to be shamefully treated and eventually executed. Then He will rise from the dead on the third day. Yet somehow His disciples miss His message.

To comprehend hard news like this requires three characteristics of the serious disciple. The first thing we need is an openness to hear the Lord's voice. Often, we just aren't ready and willing to even listen to loving feedback. Second, we need to trust the one telling us the truth, implicitly. Third, we must remember that the temporary pain of the confrontation isn't the end of the story. The Lord's sufferings and death were temporary—His Resurrection is eternal.

Let's strengthen ourselves for the difficult moments of life. Let's keep our ears and hearts open to our Lord's voice, and for the joy set before us, endure the cross.

TODAY: Let's embrace the eucharistic life wholeheartedly and refuse to allow temporary setbacks to knock us down. Let's look beyond our momentary struggles and conflicts to the eternal joy of resurrection.

Tuesday: Luke 19:12–28
Ready, Set, Shop

Fight, fight, fight!

EACH YEAR BLACK FRIDAY sales and the hoopla associated with them are the most dismal part of the holiday season. The sales, the markdowns, the deals all are conspiring to get us to spend. The competition is hot, the deals are incredible—knock down that person ahead of you. Reach across that lady and grab that item first.

The emphasis on spending money reduces us to being nothing more than consumers of goods. It taps into the part of our souls where we are easily numbed and medicated by purchasing stuff.

Our Gospel reading for today—the parable of the talents—is appropriate. A master gives several servants the same resources and then leaves for a time. When he returns, he is confronted with a wide disparity between how well the money has been used.

This parable presents us with an opportunity to take stock of how we have invested our lives and used our gifts. Have we squandered our time, talents, and treasures? Have we been too afraid or too forgetful to make the most of what God has given us?

Let's remember what the Incarnation means. When I come to grips with the truth that God took on flesh in Christ Jesus so that I may by grace become like Him, then I am reminded of just why my time, talents, and treasures are so valuable in the first place, and I'm motivated to use them for eternal return.

TODAY: In our consumer culture, you will undoubtedly be tempted to reduce your value to what you can purchase or receive. Avoid this reduction of your real self by taking the courageous path of a purposeful Orthodoxy.

Wednesday: John 1:35–52
We Have Found the Messiah

What do you seek?

THE ENTIRE CHRISTIAN FAITH is all about helping people reconnect with God and restore the relationship lost by our first parents, Adam and Eve. When we draw close to God, we won't be able to cover any imperfections, either. Perhaps this is why we are afraid to be near Him: we fear He will let us down, or maybe we'd rather not expose *our* imperfections. The truth is He already knows everything about us and loves us still.

In our Gospel reading today, Jesus asks a probing question to test the motives of those around Him. And this is the question the Lord asks us today: "What do you seek?" (John 1:38). To develop a healthy spiritual life, we will always need to answer that question truthfully. What do we really desire?

The disciples' reply is interesting: "Where are you staying?" Notice, our desire to be where Jesus *is* indicates what it is we truly seek. "Come and see," the Lord responds (v. 39). We must trust that when we follow Christ, He will lead us to His home. In time, as we dwell with Him, we will be able to become *like* Him. Occasional visits will never have the same effect.

Ultimately, what does abiding with Christ produce? It engenders faith. "We have found the Messiah," declared the disciples (v. 41). When we spend time with our Lord, we begin to recognize Him as the Savior, the Promised One, and we begin to change. In the presence of our Lord, it is impossible to remain the same.

TODAY: Do you desire to know where the Lord lives? If you do, be assured that if you come and see, your life will be changed as you follow Him. And this change will transform not only your own life but those around you as well. It may even ignite a flame of spiritual desire in the hearts of others who previously didn't even realize they needed to know God.

Thursday: Luke 19:45–48
An Integrated Life

Your actions speak louder than your words

WE WERE NEVER MEANT to divide the spiritual from the physical. This separation is a result of the Fall. The spiritual and the physical are all part of God's creation and reflect His glory. When we separate them, we create all sorts of practical barriers to authentic faith and practice. In essence, we assert we believe, but don't put that belief into practice. But as St. James has pointed out, faith is no good unless it is accompanied by our works (see James 2:14–26). If you don't practice the faith, do you really believe it?

In our Gospel reading today, our Lord observes commercial transactions going on in the Court of the Gentiles, a section of the temple reserved for outsiders who wished to learn more about the God of Israel. But the people of Jesus' day had transformed this into a place where insiders could buy their animals for temple sacrifice and exchange their currency for temple currency used for offerings. They had completely perverted the original intent of the porch.

Jesus decried the loss of evangelistic outreach, calling the religious leaders out for their inconsistency. Of course, in our Lord's life, actions and words always lined up perfectly, which gave Him an unmatched air of authority and integrity. In His life, Christ demonstrated time and again that our words and actions do matter. He acted and He spoke, and the religious authorities couldn't weaken the impact of His words, because His life was absolutely consistent.

TODAY: It can be a challenge to live an honest life where our actions and words match. Do your actions ever betray your words? Let's be faithful in our spiritual housecleaning and reinforce our good and just actions through prayer, fasting, and almsgiving.

245

Friday: Luke 20:1–8
I'll Tell You If You Tell Me

Can I trust you?

W E ALL STRUGGLE with being honest about our true motives, but the sad truth is many times we don't even stop to consider what those motives are. We simply act selfishly, and then wonder why our relationships suffer or why we are misunderstood. If I turn a blind eye to how self-interest, greed, and fear are corrupting my own purposes, I will use those around me for my own gratification.

In our Gospel reading, our Lord appealed to this aspect of our hearts when confronted by the religious leaders of His day. In a session of verbal jousting with the temple leadership, they were revealed for the hypocrites they were. Jesus knew the religious leaders weren't really interested in hearing about His true identity or His authority; they were just trying to trap or shame Him— or at least cover up their own spiritual poverty. It didn't work, of course, and ultimately they had to admit, "We don't know."

They weren't capable of knowing the truth, due to their egos and their pride. That same fate awaits us if we don't spend time in honest reflection, spiritual discernment, and humble confession. This is why the Faith offers you and me this precious Sacrament. We can't trust our own motives—we will either be too easy or too hard on ourselves. When we approach our confessors, those given the grace by the Holy Spirit to bind and loose our sins, God's searchlight will shine a light on those hidden parts of our personality that need healing.

TODAY: When is the last time you went to confession? Having heard confessions and gone regularly to confession myself, I can attest to the joy and liberty that it brings. Guess which question about confession I get asked the most? "Father, how often should I go to confession?" My answer is always the same: "Every time you need to." Try it!

Monday: Luke 20:9–18

The Stone the Builders Rejected

W E E K 49

"Christianity, if false, is of no importance, and if true, of infinite importance; the only thing it cannot be is moderately important."
—C.S. Lewis

THE CHRISTIAN FAITH isn't merely a set of moral teachings; it centers on the Person of Jesus Christ and the claim that He is God in the flesh. It might not be politically correct to say this, but the Christian Faith, if true, isn't merely one of many religions, it is the Faith for all mankind. If it is true that God has taken His flesh from one of our own, then that message alone is absolutely vital information for every man, woman, boy, and girl alive.

Look at our Gospel reading today. The Lord declared that if humanity rejects the heir, the Son, they condemn themselves. The Lord's audience understood the ramifications of this and responded, "Certainly not!" (Luke 20:16). They saw what was at stake—rejecting the Son was their own destruction. This is exactly what happened in AD 70, when the Roman army destroyed the Jewish temple and the city of Jerusalem. On that day, Judaism ceased to be a religion with a temple—priests and temple worship were over.

Jesus continued, "The stone which the builders rejected / Has become the chief cornerstone" (v. 17). He added a final warning: "Whoever falls on that stone will be broken; but on whomever it falls, it will grind him to powder" (v. 18).

TODAY: The Christian Faith is meant for everyone; otherwise it is useless for everyone. As we approach the commemoration of our Lord's Nativity, when God Himself stepped into human history, let us abandon the foolish notion that the Christian Faith is merely a preference. It's time for us who say we follow Christ to share the Good News of His Incarnation.

Tuesday: Galatians 3:23–29; 4:1–5
A Slave or a Son: Which are You?

It's hard being a grown-up

THE YOUNG MAN BRISTLED under his father's rules and regulations. He hated knowing that while he was under his dad's roof, he had to buckle down and do what he was told. As he grew older, his impatience to gain his inheritance mounted. When he was finally of age, his father announced that he was the heir to the family fortune. From that day on, he began to realize that the responsibilities of his new position were many. Inwardly, he often longed for those carefree days when he was still under his dad's wise tutelage.

Isn't that always the way? We think we know it all when we are in our teens, but our responsibilities increase as we mature.

Let's look at our epistle reading today. St. Paul tells the faithful in the Galatian church that putting on Christ in baptism means they have become heirs of Christ. They have graduated from being servants of God to being actual sons and daughters, and that distinction changes everything. What a contrast to Islam, where all people can ever hope for is to be an obedient servant of Allah. The Christian Faith even dismantles the distinctions between Jews and Greeks—God dismisses any notion of second-class citizenship based on gender, language, or economic status. We are all heirs to the Kingdom of God.

What does this mean? We should never take this for granted. We are invited by God to inherit all He has, and He owns everything. It doesn't matter how much money or prestige we have. It doesn't matter if we have the proper pedigree. God accepts and adopts us as His own. What then do we owe Him?

TODAY: In approaching the manger in Bethlehem, we see that God Himself has become powerless so we might be saved. The angels were amazed by the love and grace of God freely given to save His creation. Let's thank Him for His love and grace and offer him the gift of our faith in return.

Wednesday: Luke 20:27–44
Why Did You Ask Me That?

What the Dickens?

I LOVE *Oliver Twist*. It's a great story about people confronting an inhumane system. During the industrial revolution, the story's hero challenges the status quo at the workhouse by asking for more food. The entire plot unfolds based on this one inconvenient request.

Uncomfortable questions can force us to look at our deep-seated prejudices or our hidden sins. Once we ask the questions, are we willing to hear the answers?

In our Gospel reading today, Jesus was challenged by a group of religious leaders called Sadducees. The Sadducees were the intelligentsia of their day and the most influential group in the leadership of Israel at the time. They insisted the Jewish religion limit its teachings to the books of Moses, the first five books of our Old Testament. Because of this, they had no beliefs or teachings about life after death—in fact, they made fun of any notion of a resurrection. According to them, focusing on life after death distracted people from the present. (Turns out the here and now is where we prepare for the later on. But I digress.)

Using their own Scriptures, the Lord Jesus turned their challenging question into an embarrassing silence. He also confronted their misplaced confidence in their sense of superiority, saying that only "those who are counted worthy" will attain the resurrection (Luke 20:35). As He challenged these proud leaders, He also invited them to let go of their pride and really listen. He invites us today as well to leave behind our egos so that we can hear His voice.

TODAY: On our journey to Christ's manger, we are challenged to ask ourselves hard questions about our priorities, our motives, and our desires. If God really has united our human flesh to His divinity, how will we respond to such unfathomable love?

Thursday: Luke 21:12–19
People Talking Without Speaking

The best defense of the faith is silence

A T A RECENT SPIRITUAL RETREAT, I was asked how one should prepare to deal with questions about the Faith. It's a reasonable question and points to a deeper challenge, as most good questions do.

While it might help us to memorize some basic talking points about our Faith, or even receive some training so we can articulate our reasons for following Christ, my counterintuitive reply is this: our best defense is silence.

This requires explanation, especially since it's coming from someone who loves to talk. What I mean is, the best testimony will always be the power of our transformed lives. The best defense of the Faith is faithfulness itself.

This doesn't mean we shouldn't perfect our communication skills, since our love for our neighbor calls us to share the Gospel. And it doesn't mean we neglect the intellectual work and serious development of our minds in studying the Faith. But it does mean we keep the limitations of all that good work in mind.

In today's Gospel reading, crafty rhetoric wasn't sufficient. No debate tactics or apologetic skills will ever be as effective as a heart prepared for the message of Christ. In the world, people don't want to hear the message. Instead, Christianity is the most persecuted religious group on the planet.

So how do we prepare for questions? We practice the disciplines of the Church and strive to love God and others. Nothing else has nearly as effective an impact as this.

TODAY: This world has never understood Christ. Whether in your office, within your families, or even in your parishes, loving others is difficult. The way to approach others isn't better rhetoric or more skilled communication tools. Instead, practice the Faith and allow your silence to communicate louder than words.

Friday: Luke 8:16–21
He Who Has Ears to Hear

Did you hear that?

IN TODAY'S GOSPEL READING, this question assumed eternal signifi-cance. Christ warned his listeners—and us—to "take heed *how* you hear" (Luke 8:18, emphasis author's). In that phrase, the Lord revealed that *how* we hear the truth reveals the real state of our souls and whether or not we have integrity, courage, or humility.

So, how can we learn to hear well? First, it's important to understand that hearing takes attentiveness. In a world of crescendoing noise, we must pri-oritize listening to God through His Word and His Church over our many other distractions. Also, to hear well, I have to love the speaker. It's easy to ignore someone you don't love, but make no mistake: learning to love God is the first commandment. If you're ever going to love Him enough to making hearing His voice your top priority, you are going to have to actively pursue Him where He is found.

Did you hear that? Our willingness to hear well and obey the message we receive will determine whether or not we will inherit the wisdom and spiri-tual treasures available to us in Christ.

TODAY: Do you long for the fullness of wisdom that will fill your life with spiritual treasures and joy? Be careful how you answer that question, because we gain these treasures the hard way. The message of the Gospel will chal-lenge all our superficial goals, but the peace offered in exchange sets us free. This freedom is costly if we cling to ease and comfort. Eternally, though, we will be far the richer if we live as a true family member in the household of our Lord, who holds history and eternity in His hands.

Monday: Luke 21:28–33

Signs of the Times

Keep Christ in Christmas

A S USUAL, the stores are putting out decorations, sale signs, and merchandise for Christmas before Halloween. Our culture certainly does telegraph what's important to the masses. Yet this emphasis on material possessions has no place in the Kingdom of God.

In our Gospel reading today, "these things" (Luke 21:28) the Lord mentions refer to the signs He talks about earlier in the chapter. Most of what the Lord was saying anticipated the years following His Resurrection, when the Roman army would destroy the temple and the city of Jerusalem. So what does all this have to do with us today?

First, we need to focus on the Kingdom of God. Our faith needs to move beyond just being a Sunday ritual so that we can see our surroundings in light of God's Kingdom. Second, our awareness of God is heightened by the active practice of our faith in daily prayer, fasting, and almsgiving, frequent confession, and frequent communion. When we expend our energy this way, we'll see God everywhere. Finally, we need to center our lives on His words, His wisdom, His way rather than our changing circumstances. The enemy of our souls wants us so focused on temporary circumstances that we lose sight of the Kingdom of God. He wants to flood our minds and hearts with fear, confusion, and doubt so that we miss the coming of our Lord, even at this time of year.

TODAY: Let's not allow holiday distractions to numb our hearts and minds. Let's make sure that in the moments of this day, we are awake to the signs that Jesus Christ is active in our lives through our participation in His Body, the Church. And, in so doing, we won't be surprised when it turns out it is much later than we think. In fact, we'll be ready for whatever comes our way in life.

Tuesday: Luke 21:37–38; 22:1–8
Don't Blame the Person

"Never confuse the person, formed in the image of God, with the evil that is in him: because evil is but a chance misfortune, an illness, a devilish reverie. But the very essence of that person is the image of God, and this remains in him despite every disfigurement." —St. John of Kronstadt

IN THE ABOVE QUOTATION, St. John of Kronstadt calls us to focus not on the evil that men do, but on the image in which those men are made. On the Cross, after He was slandered, tortured, stripped, and nailed to the tree, Christ said, "Father, forgive them, for they do not know what they do" (Luke 23:34). In the face of injustice, cruelty, pain, and even physical death, Jesus still saw the image of God in His murderers.

How do we see our neighbors, our family, even ourselves? As we approach the Feast of the Nativity, it behooves us to ask this question.

In our Gospel reading today, Judas approached the leaders of the Jews to betray Jesus. Notice how St. Luke describes what happened to Judas: "Then Satan entered Judas" (Luke 22:3). The question here is, who chose to leave the door of his heart unlocked in the first place?

St. John of Kronstadt invites us to contemplate profound truths. First, everyone is created in the image of God to be made into His likeness. Before we make one good or bad choice, our infinite worth is established and cannot be erased. Next, all kinds of influences will shape us if we don't guard our hearts. A man or woman left to develop by himself or herself will be a mere shadow of what God intended for him or her. Finally, God has not left humanity in our fallen state. He condescended to be "born of a woman, born under the Law" (Gal. 4:4) to restore and elevate our humanity to His divinity.

TODAY: With the help of God's wisdom, His love, and His life, we will never view another person as a monster, even if they act like one. Let's dare to believe that God has become a Man for our sake so that we can, by His grace, become what He is.

Wednesday: Mark 8:11–21
Why Don't You Understand?

I should be more patient

I CONFESS TO A DEEP SENSE of frustration when I'm trying to explain something like how Wi-Fi works to someone who doesn't understand.

Why do we struggle so much sometimes to understand each other? It has everything to do with our different upbringing, life experiences, and personalities.

But what if there was a fundamental truth that was misunderstood by everyone? The consequences would be tremendous.

In today's passage, Jesus warned His disciples about the "leaven of the Pharisees" (Mark 8:15). Immediately the disciples think He's talking about the fact that they have no bread. Before we are too hard on the disciples, we should be honest: how many times have we also misunderstood spiritual truths? The Lord is warning the disciples not to become so enamored of doing things for God that they forget to love God.

What keeps us from understanding the central message of our Faith—that is, that we love the Lord our God with all our hearts, souls, and minds? First, we become distracted. Then, we view life in relation to ourselves rather than in relation to God, and our vision becomes distorted and truncated. Finally, we misunderstand and become confused when we forget all God has done for us in our lives. Remembering God's faithfulness helps us to maintain the attitude of gratitude that is foundational to understanding spiritual truth.

TODAY: Are you distracted by the cares of this world? Are you missing the big picture by focusing on trivial concerns? You're not alone—we all do this. Let's all stop, take a few minutes, and reorient ourselves toward the One who knows and loves us and desires that we gain true understanding. Let's enter into this period of festal preparation and, once again, rejoice that God has come in the flesh to make us whole.

Thursday: Mark 2:23–28; 3:1–5
Is It Lawful to Do Good?

The spirit of the law rather than the letter of the law

As a police officer, I had to memorize the road rules so that I could properly enforce them. Though I knew the laws were on the books for people's safety, I can't tell you how tempting it was to make the law into an end in itself. There's a world of difference between an officer who rules by the spirit of the law and the one who only thinks of the letter of the law.

We do this because it's easier to know the rules than it is to internalize the wisdom behind the rules.

In our Gospel reading today, pious religious leaders rebuked the Lord for allowing His disciples to break the rules of the Sabbath. They were furious that the Lord refused to buy into their point of view, thus exposing their own spiritual poverty. Then Christ makes two very important distinctions about God's wisdom for humanity.

First, the rules of spiritual life are made for man, not man for the rules. In our Orthodox Christian tradition we don't even refer to the disciplines of the Faith as rules. Rather, we refer to this body of teaching as *wisdom*. The Lord makes it clear that Sabbath disciplines were meant to change our thinking, not to become straightjackets that keep us even from doing good.

The second distinction is equal to the first. The Lord reminds these Jewish leaders that even King David allowed a higher law to govern his behavior when he and his men were hungry and ate the bread in the temple that was exclusively reserved for the priests. When the Lord healed the man with a withered hand in the synagogue, He demonstrated that the law of love trumps all laws.

TODAY: We are called to be purposeful in our relationships with God and one another. Let's not take the easy way out by reducing our love for God to the mere keeping of rules.

Friday: Mark 8:30–34
The Road to Hell

Is paved with our good intentions

EVERY TIME MY LIFE spirals downward and I go the wrong way, I can trace the problem back to a moment I began to rely on my own good intentions rather than on God.

In our Gospel reading today, our Lord told His disciples that things were going to be get very difficult for Him very soon. St. Peter didn't take this well, of course, and quickly protested. Imagine Peter's surprise when the Lord reacted as He did: "Get behind me, Satan!" (Mark 8:33). I'm sure Peter was completely flabbergasted that the Lord rebuked his good intentions and considered them obstacles to His mission of salvation.

How can we make sure our good intentions aren't the enemy of God's best for our lives? Simply, through devoted and single-minded love for God. That love enables me to be humble about my own plans and ideas, and it sets me free to trust my circumstances to Him. Love for God causes me to let go of my own desires and dreams in favor of His will for my life, and this love must be nurtured if I am going to avoid paving a road to hell with my good intentions. This love isn't a feeling. Rather, it is my willful choice to embrace honest intimacy with God. All the prayers, incense, liturgies, fasting disciplines (and the feasting joys), all the lives of the saints, and especially the mystery of confession have this aim: that I learn to love God and then my neighbors as myself. Orthodoxy is the science of spiritual labor that produces love for God.

TODAY: Can you see how good intentions aren't enough? As we move toward our Lord's Nativity in Bethlehem, let's remember that all our pious practices are aimed at two goals—that we will love God and our neighbors.

O UR DAUGHTERS LOVE the books that depict various hidden items bur- ied in drawings or photos. Invariably as we look together for the dis- guised object, a little voice will say, "Daddy, help me find the sock." When the object is found, we both say, "Aha! It was there all the time."

The spiritual life is like that. When our eyes are opened, we see truth in a deeper way, and it is a paradigm shift—we never return to our former ignorance. Once I decided give the Holy Orthodox Church the benefit of the doubt in regard to truth, I could never trust anything less. You just can't unlearn a truth the Holy Spirit has given you the grace to embrace.

In our Gospel reading today, the disciples of Jesus ask about the first com- ing of the Messiah. (This has a contemporary ring to it—today we are still speculating about the coming of Jesus.) The Lord guides His disciples to a deeper understanding of the Scriptures, predicting His Resurrection while they are still musing about Elijah the prophet. Our Lord says, essentially, the Messiah is already here, so don't keep looking for Him. Their eyes are opened to understand the meaning of Scripture, and their lives are changed forever.

Many Christian groups today claim to know the Bible, but their compet- ing ideas don't satisfy spiritual seekers. Those who find the treasure hidden in the field of right Faith and practice are blessed indeed.

TODAY: As we prepare to mark the first coming of Christ and await His Sec- ond Coming, let's remember that the fullness of the Christian Faith is found in the Church of our Lord Jesus. Let's ask God for the eyes to behold the true meaning of the Incarnation.

Tuesday: Mark 9:33–41
Who's the Greatest?

Power corrupts

NOTHING IS MORE CENTRAL to our faith than the acquisition of true humility. This virtue will change every aspect of our being as it guides and tempers our thoughts, words, and actions. Humility frees our beliefs from the whim of others' opinions and enables us to harness our convictions in the service of love rather than of power. Our Lord Jesus taught His disciples that true authority rests in service to others, not in being served.

In today's Gospel reading, our Lord Jesus challenged His disciples, who were discussing among themselves who was the greatest in their group. When the Lord confronted them, they were reluctant to come clean. (If we're embarrassed when we're overheard, what does that tell us?)

Jesus used this moment to teach the disciples about real authority and power. He gestured to a small child—tradition tells us that he would grow up to be St. Ignatius—and said that we must be like children, humble and simple. Humility sets us free to be servants, and in receiving a child, we receive the Lord Himself and the Father who sent Him. We can receive the fullness of God because we've made room for Him in our hearts.

Think about it. The power of humility is that it offers us what we could never hope to receive by demanding our rights or asserting our authority over others. The acquisition of humility enlarges the soul so that it holds all the blessings and joys of the All-Holy Trinity—Father, Son, and Holy Spirit. Imagine souls so enlarged that they hold the entire universe. Who in his right mind would trade these blessings for mere power?

TODAY: Let us trade our insane desire for power for the pursuit of humility. As we approach the Feast of the Nativity, in which we see the depth of God's humble embrace of our humanity, let's give up our lust for control and rejoice in God's gift to us of His Son.

Wednesday: Mark 9:42–50; 10:1
Everyone Will Be Salted with Fire

"You are the salt of the earth" (Matthew 5:13)

SINCE THE MOST ANCIENT TIMES, salt has been an important mineral. It has preserved and seasoned food, cured illness, and is a symbol of hospitality.

In today's Gospel reading, we are told, "Everyone shall be seasoned with fire" (Mark 9:49). Whoa, wait a second. Everyone? Yes, everyone.

This passage explains that we are called to take sin so seriously that we are willing to embrace the fire of God's love. His fire will purify us so that we won't be tormented in eternity because of our willful rejection of His love. Imagine the torment of having salt in a wound that never heals, all because we refuse the healing.

For the Orthodox Christian, sin is seen as a disease, and repentance is the cure. The fire of God's love can make you salty now and able to preserve and season and make your life as it should be. As the Lord promises, everyone *will* be seasoned with fire. But God has made us free to choose whether that will happen in this life, to purify our hearts, or whether we will foolishly put off this seasoning until the last day, where the same fire will torment us rather than make us whole.

So, the metaphors of salt and fire aptly describe the purpose of the life of loving discipleship to our Lord Jesus for us now, today.

TODAY: Let's not continue to make excuses in sin. Otherwise, the growing infection in our souls will eventually prove fatal. Let's allow the salt of truth to be rubbed into the wound of our repentance. When we are healed, those around us will be thirsty for the water we drink.

Thursday: Mark 10:2–12
This is Not a Game

You think this is funny? This is not a game, young man!

COACH GOT HIS POINT ACROSS by making me run laps until I wasn't smiling anymore.

Sometimes we don't take things seriously when we should. Other times, we go overboard on things that ultimately don't matter. Marriage is a good example—our culture has been desacralizing the true value of this sacred mystery for decades. The current state of marital relationships certainly reflects this.

In our Gospel reading, our Lord challenges the religious leaders to see beyond mere rules to the eternal wisdom that has infused the marriage relationship since the beginning of time. Certainly, Moses gave this commandment for divorce, notes Christ, because of our tendency toward hardness of heart (Mark 10:5).

What is God's eternal design for marriage?

First, we are created for communion. This is why believing in the threefold nature of the Holy Trinity is a non-negotiable requirement for Christians. God made us in His Image, and He is three in one. This is the foundational truth about God Himself—we were made for communion, but we fail, and our hearts are hardened by this failure.

Next, God designed male and female to be one flesh. God took the woman from the side of man in the beginning. God separated male and female, but for a deeper purpose: To train us in the hard work of becoming "one flesh" (v. 8) as a reflection of the Holy Trinity's life of communion.

Christ's teaching had little to do with keeping a set of marriage rules. Rather, we were meant to learn the purpose of the divine mystery of marriage.

TODAY: As we approach the mystery of the Nativity in which God, the uncreated one, takes flesh from His creation and comes among us, let's pause in wonder and reverence. The world has turned this into a shallow celebration, but we mustn't do the same.

Friday: Mark 10:11–16

This Makes Jesus Mad

Indignant: feeling, characterized by, or expressing strong displeasure at something considered unjust, offensive, insulting, or base

I STRUGGLE WITH ROAD RAGE—I admit it. As a former police officer trained in the rules of the road, I frequently observe drivers ignoring the conditions, traffic flow, and sound guidelines for safe road behavior. I have also participated in high-speed chases in which I've had to chase down irresponsible drivers, and these were terrifying. So I know what it means to be indignant.

In our Gospel reading, Jesus was indignant because the disciples were blocking the people from bringing their children to the Lord. Jesus knew how important children are—they are pure and haven't been hardened yet by disappointment. The Lord knows that we need to embrace the very difficult task of being child*like* without being child*ish*. If we can do this, we will be able to enter the Kingdom of Heaven. In childlikeness we find spiritual maturity. This is one of the greatest paradoxes of the Christian Faith, and we must embrace it to truly celebrate Christmas.

When we forget this, we forget something essential to our salvation. Christ is calling His disciples back to the spiritual basics—their first principles, if you will. His shortsighted disciples forgot that the Kingdom belongs to children and those who are childlike.

This is why I invite parents to keep their children in liturgy—I don't want our community to be guilty of the same attitude. Children remind us of God's Kingdom and how to obtain it.

TODAY: Let's keep our first principles at the very front of our thinking so we don't fall into the trap of forgetting the only goal worth living for in the first place: the acquisition of the Kingdom of God.

Monday: Luke 2:1–20

Let Us Go To Bethlehem

It's the most wonderful time of the year

TONIGHT'S THE NIGHT. Our daughters go to bed after the liturgy bursting with excitement. In the morning, we're going to Mawmaw's house, and that means chocolate cake and presents. As an Orthodox priest, I am also filled with joy as I celebrate the Gift of God with prayers and worship.

In today's Gospel, the angel visited the shepherds and announced that the Messiah was born in Bethlehem (which literally means "House of Bread"). The shepherds' response was to tell everyone the good news. It isn't enough to simply witness the arrival of Jesus: like the shepherds, we too must respond. In Christ's birth, we witness the greatest mystery of all: the heavenly bread that satisfies our deepest hunger has been given to us. Christ becomes a second Adam who will grow up to destroy sin, death, and Satan for all time.

No wonder the Church offers a series of beautiful worship services during this festal season. How else could we respond but with joy, adoration, and wonder?

We mustn't hoard this joy. The shepherds made known what they had witnessed. If you knew how to make sure no one around you would ever be hungry again, would you share that knowledge? God has come to satisfy our spiritual hunger, so let's share the Bread of Life with others.

TODAY: We are entering into the season of Christmas, and for twelve days we will bask in the glory of God's love for us. Enjoy your family feast and make merry—just don't forget to be Orthodox on purpose.

Tuesday: Luke 14:25–35
Counting the Cost

Take up your cross

THIS IS THE TIME OF YEAR we normally spend some moments reflecting on the previous year and looking forward to the next. Some will make some New Year's resolutions; others will systematically set goals and benchmarks for the coming year. I do a little bit of both, but I also make every effort to be fully present in the moment so that I don't miss what's right in front of me. I do this by counting the cost (see Luke 14:28). What do I mean?

In our Gospel reading today, our Lord Jesus reminds us that being His disciple will cost us something. As His followers, we make His priorities our priorities so that our lives will follow the same trajectory. Being Christ's disciple means that my New Year's goals should match up with His plans for me. In fact, my love for God is so great that all other loves will look like hate in comparison, according to this passage. Now that's costly.

I also count the cost when I am willing to bear the cross. No one in the Lord's audience that day missed His meaning. The cross was an instrument of death, and that was our Lord's intended point. I have to be willing to die to the world's priorities if I am following Him.

No one starts to build a house without first sitting down to count the cost. This is true for those of us who are disciples of Jesus Christ. It's summed up in a saying found written on the wall of a monastery on Mt. Athos: "If you die before you die, then when you die, you won't die." The only way to deal with our past, plan for our future, and actually be present in our now is to remember our own mortality and live lives of repentance. Our Lord trampled down death by death, and so He will trample down ours as well, if we follow Him.

TODAY: As we look forward to a new year, let's create resolutions that align with the wisdom of the Lord we claim to love. Then perhaps those around us will want to follow too when they see the beauty of a purposeful Orthodox life.

Wednesday: Matthew 2:13–23
Rachel Weeping

"Refusing to be comforted for her children, Because they are no more" (Jeremiah 31:15)

THE ORTHODOX CHRISTIAN FAITH IS meant for every man, woman, boy, and girl everywhere and at all times. If it's not offered to everybody, it will eventually belong to nobody. However, this truly catholic Faith which was "once for all delivered to the saints" (Jude 1:3) requires us to commit our whole lives unto Christ our God. God "desires all men to be saved and to come to the knowledge of the truth" (1 Tim. 2:4), but that doesn't mean following Him is easy.

In our Gospel reading today, a terrible scene unfolds. The ancient prophecy of Jeremiah is fulfilled as Herod slaughters innocent children in an attempt to kill Jesus.

What are we to make of this slaughter, this unthinkable evil? Why is this here? Why does the Church wish us to retain such a nightmare in our memories?

Certainly, we are called to remember this so that we won't repeat it. When we speak of the Holocaust during World War II, we say "never again." Yet although we have advanced in technology and medicine, we still continue to slaughter innocent children in the womb. Have we really progressed at all? The Orthodox Faith has been clear throughout its history: life begins at conception. As of old, Rachel still weeps for her children.

Whenever our society is ruled by utilitarian aims, we will always end up choosing convenience over life. No matter how advanced our technical and scientific skills become, we will still miss the value of each human life if we don't honor the Creator of life.

TODAY: As we remember with joy that God sanctified every aspect of human life by taking flesh and passing through every stage of human growth and development, let's treat our unborn children with respect and care. God loves us and will always forgive every sin, so let's winsomely and gently show the world a better way.

Thursday: Mark 11:22–26
Faith in God

Just have faith

IT'S NEVER THAT EASY, IS IT? The so-called prosperity Gospel would have us believe it is. Yet in our Scripture reading today, we learn what it truly means to "have faith" (Mark 11:22).

When Jesus spoke of casting a mountain into the sea, He wasn't reducing the Christian life and the struggle for holiness to a "name it and claim it" style of theology. Instead, the Lord goes on to talk about the internal, deeply difficult spiritual struggle of forgiveness and relationships.

In fact, the Lord associates great faith with spiritual maturity and forgiveness, not to mention the terrifying reality that if I don't forgive others, God will not forgive me. This is a great deal more serious and demanding than the simple perspective that having faith is merely feeling good. When our Lord says "have faith in God," He refers to a process by which we are transfigured into people who are actually *like* God. This means forgiveness is possible— we *can* let go of past hurts we have kept returning to over the course of our lives. We *can* cast that mountain of regret into the sea of God's forgetfulness. Rather than focusing on what we lack, we can concentrate on what we are becoming in Christ.

It all begins with having *real* faith in God, which consists of a relationship with Him in which success is measured by how closely we are able to follow Jesus Christ.

TODAY: Do you have faith in God? Let this be the year you abandon the childish idea that faith is a magic formula. Adopt the mature understanding that God wants you to be like Him, raking up the wise spiritual tools of our way of life.

Friday: Mark 11:27–33
Out with the Old, in with the New

Paradigm shift: a fundamental change in approach or underlying assumptions

PARADIGM SHIFTS OCCUR many times in history, in nations, and in persons. When they do, they are often disruptive, disturbing, and even unwelcome.

In 1962, American physicist Thomas Kuhn coined the phrase to explain how scientific advancement took place. He observed that scientific revolutions explode on the scene suddenly and with great effect. Think of the revolution in knowledge and literacy with the invention of the printing press. At one time, books were rare, expensive, and owned only by the elite. With the advent of the press, books gradually became available to everyone. And what about this startling statistic: Human knowledge now doubles every twelve months and is heading toward doubling every twelve *hours*. Imagine what we'll know tomorrow.

In our Gospel reading today, Jesus stands before the Jewish leaders as God in the flesh. St. Paul says that the Incarnation is "foolishness" to the Greeks and a "stumbling block" to the Jews (1 Cor. 1:23). The Old Testament was filled with hints and prophecies about the coming of the Messiah, calling Him "Wonderful, Counselor, Mighty God, / Everlasting Father, Prince of Peace" (Is. 9:6). Nonetheless, their human minds couldn't fathom the paradigm shift that was coming, now that the Uncreated had really stepped into His creation to be part of it.

Though Jewish theology and pagan Greek philosophy ruled Jesus' day, Christ came and changed (and continues to change) everything. And those who can't grasp the mystery are to be pitied, prayed for, and loved rather than hated.

The leaders of Christ's day, as is true today as well, simply couldn't process the paradigm shift created by the coming of Jesus. Their lack of understanding exposed their spiritual blindness, so this just made them hate Him all the more.

This often happens during a paradigm shift. The status quo fights to preserve that which is passing away; they can't conceive of a world outside the ordinary and predictable. They live in fear of change, concentrating their energies to engage in a rearguard action to keep things from slipping away from them.

Today, some are in a panic as they view the shift in demographics and what it means for religious observance in America, but we don't need to. Rather than scramble to preserve the former Judeo-Christian consensus we once enjoyed, we can ask how we can better serve this generation with the timeless message of Orthodox Christianity.

TODAY: As we part with the old year and greet the new one, let's not be gripped by fear and panic and worry. History is really HIS-story. Knowing that God loves our generation more than we can imagine, let's be diligent and faithful. Our generation needs the timeless medicine of Orthodoxy, and they will experience it through our loving service, creativity, and courage. In this New Year, join me in being Orthodox on Purpose, no matter what it costs.

To God Be the Glory

FAITH ENCOURAGED MINISTRIES[R] is the umbrella organization for all of Fr. Barnabas's media work. It all began with a belief that the timeless and beautiful message of the Orthodox Church is not only valuable, but also desired by the average person. Father Barnabas believes that using these media tools is one way we can reach out to the spiritually hungry people of modern life. They truly are seeking the Orthodox Faith, and we want to share this faith with anyone and everyone by using media outreach tools.

Father Barnabas believes this so strongly that he created a video series called *A Journey to Fullness* as an outreach tool to be used by parishes and groups to introduce the Orthodox Faith to seeking persons. You can find out more about this outreach tool at JourneytoFullness.com.

We also believe that our lifelong Orthodox people are hungry for ways to make their Faith present in their daily lives. Through our weekday devotionals, weekly homilies, and live call-in program, we are attempting to do our part in making the "faith which was once for all delivered to the saints" (Jude 1:3) available to all. We trust that this spiritual food of Orthodoxy is what will satisfy the deepest hunger of every human heart. That's why we believe in being Orthodox on Purpose.

You can discover more about the media outreach of Faith Encouraged Ministries at our website, FaithEncouraged.org. There you can sign up to have devotionals like the ones in this book delivered to your email inbox Monday through Friday. You can also watch or listen to weekly homilies and find out about upcoming live call-in programs heard on the second and fourth Sundays of the month on Ancient Faith Radio.

Faith Encouraged Ministries is a tax-deductible nonprofit ministry. You may contact Fr. Barnabas at frbarnabas@faithencouraged.org.

F R. BARNABAS (CHARLES) POWELL is a native of Atlanta, Georgia. Having been raised in a small Pentecostal church as a boy, Barnabas grew to love the church. He received a theology degree in 1988 and went on to establish a new church in the Atlanta area.

A reading program in Church History and Theology eventually led him to enter the Orthodox Church in November 2001. He studied at Holy Cross Greek Orthodox School of Theology in Brookline, Massachusetts, and was ordained to the Orthodox priesthood in 2010. He is now the senior pastor of Ss. Raphael, Nicholas, and Irene Greek Orthodox Church in Cumming, Georgia.

Fr. Barnabas founded Faith Encouraged Ministries in 2014 and is the host of *Faith Encouraged LIVE* on Ancient Faith Radio. He also produces the Monday-through-Friday devotional podcast, *Faith Encouraged Daily*. *A Journey to Fullness* is a video project he has released through the ministry to help parishes introduce the Faith to the average person.

Ancient Faith Publishing hopes you have enjoyed and benefited from this book. The proceeds from the sales of our books only partially cover the costs of operating our nonprofit ministry—which includes both the work of **Ancient Faith Publishing** and the work of **Ancient Faith Radio.** Your financial support makes it possible to continue this ministry both in print and online. Donations are tax-deductible and can be made at www.ancientfaith.com.

To view our other publications,
please visit our website: **store.ancientfaith.com**

ANCIENT FAITH RADIO

Bringing you Orthodox Christian music, readings,
prayers, teaching, and podcasts 24 hours a day since 2004 at
www.ancientfaith.com

Milton Keynes UK
Ingram Content Group UK Ltd.
UKHW011947210823
427215UK00004B/503

9 781944 967154